HOW NOT TO F★★★ THEM UP

The First Three Years

OLIVER JAMES

Vermilion
LONDON

7 9 10 8

First published in 2010 by Vermilion, an imprint of Ebury Publishing
This edition published by Vermilion in 2011

Ebury Publishing is a Random House Group company

The Random House Group Limited Reg. No. 954009

Addresses for companies within the Random House Group can be found at
www.randomhouse.co.uk

A CIP catalogue record for this book is available from the British Library

ISBN 9780091923938

Copies are available at special rates for bulk orders. Contact the sales development
team on 020 7840 8487 for more information.

To buy books by your favourite authors and register for offers, visit
www.randomhouse.co.uk

This book is a work of non-fiction. The names of people in the case studies have
been changed solely to protect the privacy of others.

The Random House Group Limited supports The Forest Stewardship
Council® (FSC®), the leading international forest-certification organisation.
Our books carrying the FSC label are printed on FSC®-certified paper.
FSC is the only forest-certification scheme supported by the leading
environmental organisations, including Greenpeace. Our
paper procurement policy can be found at
www.randomhouse.co.uk/environment

Printed and bound in Great Britain by Clays Ltd, St Ives plc

Praise for *How Not to F*** Them Up* from mothers:

'Thank you for making a difference in my daughter's life and for making me feel like there are other people like me … it has really helped me to feel more confident in my instincts for childcare … Thank you for giving me the confidence to say to the rest of my family "Thank you for your advice but I'm doing it my way."'

'Thank you for your recent book … I have found it so helpful and reassuring … There is so much pressure from society, and families, to get back to earning a lot and I have often felt looked down on because I am with a man who wants to spend time with his daughter, prioritising this over a huge mortgage or fancy cars. Your book has reassured me so much that we are doing the right thing.'

'By reading your book I have totally got all my confidence in my methods back and am so much happier to do my own thing, so thank you so much for this.'

'Thanks for writing a truly useful and inspiring books for parents. You inspired me to make my daughter my number one priority in my life and becoming a stay at home mum in spite of peer pressure.'

'Many thanks for writing a book which gives me validation and support that is so lacking in a society which is, as you point out, largely run by "Organisers" … We need more voices to speak out in the way you do. You have done a tremendous amount to counterbalance the macho un-child un-family friendly society we live in, for which I am grateful.'

'Not only did it give me a new found confidence in my parenting choices but it helped me cope with other peoples' differing parenting styles.'

'It confirmed that I feel I am doing the best for my children and very pleased I did not listen to certain members of my family on how to treat my baby.'

To Olive and Louis

This be the Verse

They fuck you up, your mum and dad.
They may not mean to, but they do.
They fill you with the faults they had
And add some extra, just for you.

But they were fucked up in their turn
By fools in old-style hats and coats,
Who half the time were soppy-stern
And half at one another's throats.

Man hands on misery to man.
It deepens like a coastal shelf.
Get out as early as you can,
And don't have any kids yourself.

Philip Larkin

This be Another Verse

They tuck you up, your mum and dad,
With heartfelt, steadfast, loving coos.
They fill you with the strengths they have,
And wipe the never-ending poos.

But they were tucked up in their turn
Spock flowing from permissive throats,
As mummies stuck it out at home
And daddies grafted hard for groats.

Woman hands on mental health to Man.
She puts her self upon the shelf
Or looks for someone else who can
Tune in to baby's needy self.

Oliver James

Contents

MOTHERING: THE EVIDENCE

Introduction

When I was three months old, in 1953, my mother regularly parked me in a pram at the end of the garden. Relatives tell me that I was sometimes left unattended there, crying for long periods. I can believe this is true because my mum was hard-pressed. I was the third of four children and by the time my younger sister was born, there were four of us under the age of five: a big burden for any mother.

Although I cannot directly remember much, I believe that things did not improve when I started toddling. While my mum was probably pleased to have a son – all my siblings being female – I doubt this enabled her to be very responsive. I suspect she was mildly depressed for most of the time and I am sure that she was both tired and irritable. She was an erratic provider of discipline, frequently resorting to clips around the ear-hole. While my dad was an exceptionally maternal parent for a man of that era, and while he did work from home, he can only have been much in evidence during the evenings and weekends.

My most vivid early impressions are of my mother's drawn face with down-turned mouth. She would slump at the kitchen table, exhausted, and her mood was one of resignation, with an undertow of anger. The main moments of emotional relief were provided by her packet of Gold Leaf cigarettes. From the first inhalation, she would become animated, as if this death-dealing habit had brought her to life (indeed, it is a little known fact that nicotine is a potent antidepressant*). For the duration of the cigarette, a light would be switched on, only to fade and die as the next set of burdens confronted her.

After a successful career as a psychiatric social worker, my mum qualified as a psychoanalyst. She was well thought of in that Woody Allen world, before she gave up work in her mid-thirties to care for her children. Her modern-day equivalent would probably have hired a nanny and continued with her career. So, I start with these reminiscences to raise two questions: how, if at all, did this early care affect what kind of person I became? Would I, as well as my mum, have been better off if she had returned to work?

In answer to the first question, I shall be brief, since I doubt you are seeking my autobiography.

I believe that my early infantile deprivation (the first six months) left me with a rather weak sense of self, meaning that I was unsure of what I really felt, liable to become disconnected and distanced, prone to second-hand living (like writing books about other people's psychology).

I also believe that my mother's unresponsiveness and irritability when I was a toddler made me emotionally insecure. Anyone who was there will tell you I was often surly, aggressive and what is technically known as 'avoidant'. Having felt rejected by my mum, I feared rejection in relationships, expecting others to be hostile or neglectful. As an avoidant boy, I would get my rejection in first, liable to hit other children or to give them the cold shoulder, making the assumption that they would do this to me if given a chance.

These observations about myself are strongly supported by buckets of evidence. Many studies of infants and toddlers, presented in Chapters 4 and 5 of my book *They F*** You Up*, show that if no one much tunes into you and is responsive when you are an infant, you build up less of a sense of self*. If the care you get aged six months to three years is erratic or unresponsive, you are prone to emotional insecurity in relationships*. As I also explain in *They F*** You Up* (Chapter 1), the evidence for the role of genes has been greatly exaggerated*. By contrast, the evidence that the quality of your early care hugely affects how you turn out is much more robust. The care sets your electro-chemical thermostat, the baseline of patterns of brainwaves and chemicals, the prism through which you experience your world*.

So the first point I want to make is that *it really does matter enormously how you care for under-threes*.

Writing this, I can picture the tsunami of apprehension sweeping over the reader. Perhaps you are pregnant with your first child. Perhaps you already have three. The danger is that your response to yet another person – a male 'expert' at that (I am a child clinical psychologist and father of two) – warning that the early years are so formative is a terrible sense of foreboding about becoming a mother, or anxiety that you have already screwed up your child, perhaps soon followed by a sense of outrage. Well, let me put your mind at rest, right away.

What I hope to do in this book is to explain that the actual practicalities of the meeting of the needs of under-threes are not the problem. By this I do not mean it is a piece of cake or that the work is anything other than back-breaking, repetitive and incredibly demanding, emotionally, intellectually and physically. What I mean is that, when you stop to think about it, most people can change a nappy, or pick up a crying baby, or warm up milk for a bottle. The physical steps entailed, in themselves, are easy. The difficult bit is knowing which steps to take, when, and how to execute them on a particular occasion.

A big part of reducing this difficulty is to get yourself into the right frame of mind. That means creating a life for yourself that makes you calm and emotionally open, so you can be 'good enough' at meeting those needs when with the child and make satisfactory substitute arrangements when absent. The challenge presented by mothering under-threes is how to arrange matters so that you are not in a permanent bate or feeling overwhelmed, like my mum was.

What an under-three needs above all is to have a responsive and tuned-in carer. But that person does not have to be the biological mother all of the time. Which brings me to my second question regarding my own early childhood: would it have been better for all concerned if my mum had gone back to work?

The short answer is that I do not know if actual paid employment would have really improved her mood, but I am certain that she needed someone to help out. This being 1953, she might have felt like a terrible failure if she had returned to work, because very few mothers did so at that time. She might also have felt disappointed that she was unable to express her intense desire to nurture us. Her own childhood had been awfully difficult and she felt passionately that she wanted to give us the experience she never had. In all sorts of ways, she succeeded in doing this, but not until later in life. Unlike her father or her favourite brother, she did not commit suicide. Unlike her mother, she was not a cold woman who showed minimal interest in her offspring and who finished her life in a mental hospital. Hats off to my mum for having been in many ways a tremendously stimulating, amusing, wise parent to me in later life. But in trying to care full-time for four children aged under five, she messed up. It was too much for a person like her. Arranging matters in such a way that she was irritable and depressed created a lose-lose situation for her and for us.

So, if the starting point for this book is that it is hugely important to meet the needs of under-threes and that this in itself, on a practical level, is not difficult, my main other point is that each mother (yes, and her partner too, I will come to that presently) must work incredibly hard to understand what is going to be best for her, for the sake of her child. That is what I hope to provide for you: *a way to understand yourself so that you can get it right for you and your children.*

This understanding starts with the approach you take (or in the case of pregnant mothers, will take) to nurturing your child, illustrated extensively through the stories of mothers of under-threes I have interviewed especially for this book. In my experience, mothers rarely find anything as helpful as talking with each other, such as with friends they have made in antenatal classes. I would ask you to think of the characters in this book as being like that.

Solid scientific research, mostly based on the theories and studies of a British psychoanalyst and psychologist called Joan Raphael-Leff*, reveals that mothers of small children tend to fall into three groups, in terms of their approach to mothering and the basic feeling they have about under-threes. The book is divided into three parts, each dealing with one of them.

1. The Organiser

She tends to see it as necessary for the baby to adapt to her and the needs of the family. She loves her baby as much as any other kind of mother but her attitude is that mother knows best. To her, the baby is a creature without a proper understanding of the human world, a bundle of hungry needs that require regulation to make them predictable. Insufficiently controlled, the baby can quickly become indulged, selfish and naughty. The Organiser sees it as her job to help the baby take control of its unruly passions and bodily processes. That is an important part of how she shows maternal love. Hence, she tends to see it as vital for the baby to acquire a feeding and sleeping routine, soonest. She is happy for others to care for the baby and regards a routine as very helpful for this. As quickly as she can after the birth, she wants to get back her 'normal', pre-pregnant life.

About a quarter of British mums have this approach*. They are the ones who are most likely to have a full-time paid job*.

2. The Hugger

The opposite of the Organiser, she places the needs of the baby ahead of everything. She is the sort of mum who may have the baby sleeping with her in the bed at night, who tends to feed on demand (when the baby indicates it is hungry rather than imposing a routine) and who regards herself as uniquely able to meet the baby's needs. She luxuriates in motherhood, happy to put her life on hold for at least three years per child. She adores being with her under-threes.

She is least likely of the three kinds to have a paid job, although some do work, even full-time. About one quarter of British mothers are Huggers.

3. The Fleximum

She combines both Hugging and Organising, cutting and pasting the pattern of care according to what the practical situation requires. She is aware of the needs of the baby and is led by them but, unlike the Hugger, she does not lose sight of her own needs. She may have the baby in the bed if it is ill, yet also seek to establish a sleep routine. She may try imposing a feeding regime, only to drop it if it is not working. Above all, she is concerned to create a 'win-win' situation, where both her own and her baby's needs are met.

About half of mothers are like this. Many have a part-time job, though some are at home or at work full-time.

You probably recognise yourself in one of these portraits, but it is vital you read all three parts of the book, in the order in which they unfold, rather than just jumping to the one which you think applies to you. About half of you will be Fleximums and since they are mostly a mixture of the other two kinds, you need to understand them. If you are an Organiser or Hugger, you can learn a lot about your approach by understanding the others.

As you will see, there are potential problems for mothers whatever their approach. Huggers can sometimes find it difficult to allow the child to become independent. Organisers may find the early months particularly trying. Fleximums can trick themselves into believing they have created 'win-win' arrangements (in which both their needs and the baby's are being met) where in reality, one or other is losing out.

My main objective is to help you define which approach suits you best and then how to make the most of it, minimising problems. Much depends on what kind of person you are and what your circumstances require, at a particular moment in time. While arranging things so that you are reasonably happy does not guarantee you will meet your child's needs, it certainly increases the likelihood thereof. Whatever your approach, there tends to be a constant trade-off between your need to stay buoyant and your baby's needs.

Mothers vary in how precisely they adopt an approach. Those who fit one of the three groups in most respects I describe as 'classic' or 'essential'. They would conform to many of the characteristics in the descriptions provided above.

A minority I characterise as 'extreme', meaning that they take the approach very seriously and push it to the limit. An extreme Hugger, for example, might breastfeed the child until it is three and still have it sleeping in the parental bed at that age. An extreme Organiser might use day care from when the baby is three months old and strictly adhere to 'controlled crying' (leaving the baby to soothe itself) from soon after birth. An extreme Fleximum might switch patterns several times, with several children.

A proportion of mothers change their overall approach. They may start out with one approach for a year, only to move to another when it does not seem to be working with that particular child. Or they may use one approach with their first child and adopt a different one with another. So even if you think of yourself as a confirmed Hugger or Organiser today, you may find yourself changing tack at some point in the future.

One of the hottest issues that both affects and reflects a mother's approach is her attitude to doing paid work during the early years. A conflict has broken out, dubbed the Mommy Wars by Americans. At its simplest, the warring parties divide into those doing paid work and those who stay at home. But a more nuanced division is between those who feel the care should be led by the child's needs, versus those who feel the child must adapt to the parent.

The evidence shows that, in general, all mothers are liable to feel that the wider society disapproves of their approach. Organisers who use routines are all too aware that lots of other mothers accuse them of being neglectful and cold-hearted. Huggers may feel socially deviant and accused of being over-indulgent, creating bad habits. A mother of either kind can feel torn between the verdict of her social world and what she believes is best.

My ambition is to declare a truce. With any luck, by the end of this book you will feel this is a bogus conflict which need not sap your limited supplies of emotional energy.

It is perfectly clear that mothers who stay at home when they long for the stimulation of work are at greater risk of depression. Likewise, a proportion of mothers find babies and toddlers, quite frankly, boring company, and can feel isolated and frustrated if they stay at home full-time. Many such mothers are Organisers and some are Fleximums. Since depression in mothers greatly reduces the chances of the needs of under-threes being met, it is imperative that such mothers do not feel trapped at home.

On the other hand, in general, it is a fact that offspring of working mothers do not do as well academically as those of non-working ones, and are more at risk of emotional problems*. A big part of the reason for this may be the inadequacy of the substitute care. Where the substitute is adequate, there is no reason why a working mother should increase problems for the child.

So from a scientific point of view, looked at in terms of the best interests of the under-three, there is no basis for saying it is better or worse for them to have a working mother. It all depends on what kind of woman she is and if she does work, what sort of substitute arrangements are made.

Whereas most parenting books offer strong injunctions about 'the best' and 'the right' specific childcare practices, that is not the primary purpose of this book. Instead, I explore how a number of varying aspects of your life can help and hinder you in the task of meeting the needs of your under-three. If staying at home and attempting to Hug would result in you becoming depressed, and you are someone who needs to work full-time, then I am in favour of you doing that. If you want to be at home and Hug, but money is tight and you are unsure what to do, you should find this book very helpful in working out the best solution. This is partly achieved by understanding three aspects of your past and present circumstances.

1. Your Own Particular Childhood

Your past hugely influences what approach you take, especially the way your own mother cared for you. About half of mothers do what their mothers did, the other half do something different*. You may be reacting against her strictness or her permissiveness, for example. Or, there is good evidence that if you had warm, sensitive and stimulating mothering when small, you are liable to provide the same to your children*. Mothers who were studied as children were followed up when they in turn became mothers. Sure enough, if they had been well loved, they were more liable to be loving. Studies of monkeys show the same*. The amount and kind of contact a monkey had with her mother precisely predicts the kind and amount she goes on to bestow. This is not caused by genes. The amount of contact with a particular daughter can be compared with the average for all her sisters. When they become mothers, the daughter's care precisely duplicates her particular dosage of love, compared to the average: it is the unique care she received that determines how she cares.

Whether you were emotionally deprived or had your needs very well met will greatly affect how you yourself mother. I hope by the end of the book you will see that understanding this can make a big difference. Instead of merely repeating the mistakes of the past or unthinkingly reacting against them, it can put you in a position of choice, behind the steering wheel on the journey of parenting your children.

In my own case, I believe that understanding my deprived early years enabled me to appreciate better what my children needed. It also helped me to appreciate the difficulties my mother faced and the possible solutions. It has not made me a perfect parent but, hopefully, I have done a better job than I might otherwise have managed.

2. The Mental Acrobatics by Which You Justify Your Decision to Do Paid Work or Stay at Home

New research shows that most modern mothers feel a tremendous conflict between two cornerstones of their identity*: mother and worker. There is a constant battle to rationalise their decisions about this conflict to themselves and others. I present examples of ways of doing this that lead to trouble and others that produce authentic win-win arrangements, in which the child's needs are met as well as the mother's.

3. Your Partner (If You Have One)

If you are a Hugger and your partner is an Organiser, sparks may fly. Equally, that can happen if you both have the same approach: the partner might want to give you advice on how to do it better. I provide a wide variety of examples of different kinds of set-ups, showing how they can sabotage or help in the ultimate goal of meeting the needs of the under-three. Practical implications for how to make the best of your particular relationship follow.

While this is not a prescriptive book, I certainly will use all the available scientific evidence to offer a great many practical ideas regarding how to look after children and organise your life, tailored to each type of mother. These are mostly spread throughout the text, but also condensed into a chapter at the end of each Part offering 'Practical Top Tips'. Primarily, I will be trying to help you to understand yourself better and then to apply that knowledge in deciding how best to meet the needs of your under-three. The interviews with mothers will hopefully help with this.

While the first chapter has no such stories, all but the Practical Top Tips chapters are largely composed of them, to illustrate my points.

Because the practical information is spread throughout the book, I have provided a Practical Top Tips Index at the end of this introduction (see page 14). Hence, if you wish immediately to find the section devoted to breastfeeding or to toddler temper tantrums, you know where to look.

Before you get stuck in, you need to be aware of one or two pieces of literary housekeeping which will help to make the book intelligible.

My Use of Language

I do not make a politically correct pretence that many readers of this book are male. Most of you, surely, are women and I will be addressing you as mothers. I am glad to say that an increasing number of men are taking on that role and good for them – there are plenty of men who can do the job very well, possibly as many men as women, at least after the first few months. So, men, please include yourselves when I write 'mother'; the role can be thought of as gender neutral. But if truth be told, only 3% of British three-month-olds are cared for primarily by men, rising to 7% at 12 months*, so the vast majority of what follows applies to women more than it does to men, especially where it concerns the enormous conflict and confusion that most women feel between their 'mother' and their 'worker' identities when they start having children. I only wish more men felt the same conflict. It would be a huge advance if all fathers felt the same degree of responsibility as mothers do for arranging and carrying out the care of under-threes.

Finally, regarding terminology, when I talk about working mothers, I am acutely aware that those with no paid employment do work. It is purely to avoid tiresome repetition and for succinctness that I will use the word 'work' to refer to paid work, not in any way to diminish the long hours worked by mothers who have no paid employment.

The Interviewees

Key details in all the stories have been altered, to confer anonymity. I contacted the mothers through various sources on the internet. I interviewed more than 50, selecting those which precisely illustrate key issues.

You may notice that none of the stories in this book concerns women in low-income households. The vast majority of my informants are middle-class, in terms of wealth. There are two reasons for this.

The first is pragmatic. An honest author of most parenting books should not pretend that it is likely to be read by many people who are living in poverty. Market research suggests that such women are unlikely to be spending scarce money on my thoughts or borrowing the book from a library. The second is that the whole point of the book is to explore how you can make the best choices for you and your child. If you have a low income, your choices are severely circumscribed. My concern here is to help mothers who are wrestling with the full range of alternatives, and that means those who are in a household with at least the national average income.

The Scientific Basis of the Book

For those unfamiliar with notes, it is worth explaining how I use them. Wherever I cite a statistic or a study, there is an asterisk in the text indicating that there is a note with the reference.

There is also a set of very brief summaries of scientific issues at the end of the book. Each one is numbered and a bracketed number appears in the main text letting you know when a particular issue has such a summary appended. For example, (R4) means Review 4, a summary of the Mommy Wars debate, with references to relevant texts and scientific papers. It appears in the section at the end of the book entitled Mothering: The Evidence.

With this house husbandry out of the way, off you go: I hope what you are about to read will make you better able to meet the needs of your under-three and, at the same time, your own.

Practical Top Tips Index

SUBSTITUTE CARE

THE MOTHERING ROLE

EMOTIONAL PROBLEMS AND HELP FOR THEM

CHAPTER 1

The Needs of Babies and Toddlers

The emotional needs of babies are simple and few. Those of toddlers are only slightly more complex. This chapter is, therefore, short: the real challenge of parenthood is you, not your child.

The hard bit is getting yourself into a state of mind where you can recognise and meet the needs of you both.

THE NEEDS OF BABIES*

Whether a baby is crying in a paddy field, a swanky New York penthouse or an overcrowded inner-city tower block, there are just a handful of possible reasons why. Once physical illness has been ruled out, there are always only five basic needs (forming the acronym WHEPT):

⟨ Wind: except in cases of colic, a massage and a burp usually does the trick

⟨ Hunger: feeding ends the tears

⟨ Emotional distress, like fear or anger, which may happen for many reasons: responsive love sorts it through cuddling, rocking, singing and so on

⟨ Physical discomfort, including a dirty nappy or lying uncomfortably: corrected, the crying stops (unless there is a physical problem, like colic)

⟨ Tiredness: a sleep solves the problem

Greedy teenagers and adults are everywhere but there are no spoilt babies. They cannot be spoilt, they are satiable.

In most cases, they are born perfect, with total potential. They know exactly what it takes to be a baby and if we follow their cues, they will eventually show us what they need and how to supply it. Their needs and wants are indivisible, their understanding unclouded by the shades of grey that language creates. They really know how to live in the moment.

The peace that descends when a baby has its needs met is a joy to behold. The body relaxes, the facial expression becomes serene. Alert eyes survey its surroundings with total absorption. It offers uncomplicated, unconditional love to its mother.

For her, the experience of being able to confer complete gratification is deeply rewarding. Not since her own infancy may she have experienced such a sense of released tension and of being at one with the world. If things go well, the experience can be repeated hundreds of times a day, making the first year a gilded memory.

Of course, this is not the norm. For most mothers, it is sometimes like that, and at other times very tough. The best any of us can hope for is to be 'good enough'. Even the most responsive mother in the world sometimes misreads the baby or is too tired to give it what it wants, so all babies inevitably endure a considerable degree of frustration and powerlessness.

After our first child was born, despite (or should that be 'because of'?) the four university degrees my wife and I had between us, there were plenty of occasions when we simply could not work out what was wrong. If you are totally exhausted and disorientated by lack of sleep, and by an unfamiliar role, you can practically forget your own name, let alone what the letters in WHEPT stand for, or the acronym itself.

Not being able to meet the infant's needs can be as nightmarish as meeting them can be dreamy. Few souls can feel more tortured than those desperate to soothe an intransigent baby. Far from seeming satiable, at such times the baby seems like a bottomless pit of neediness, like a heroin addict or shopaholic or gambler in need of their fix. Babies' cries are delivered at a pitch and volume to signal to mothers that they need something, now. The urgency of the need is hard to ignore. Their complete powerlessness, unable even to sit up, let alone to walk and talk, is overwhelming. Small wonder that more than half of mothers report that at some point they have felt like throwing the baby out of a window or picking up a pillow to do something, anything, to restore silence*. Just as a mutually fulfilling pattern results from a mother repeatedly finding herself able to identify the WHEPT need, a vicious circle can develop from not doing so. It can reach the stage at which the slightest whimper is enough to bring tears to your eyes or a stream of swear words – or a strong impulse to open a bottle of wine.

That is if you have a calm, straightforward baby. About 15% of newborns* are made difficult by the pregnancy or birth: irritable or floppy or fussy*. Around four out of every five babies that are born pre-term with low birth weights, for example, are difficult at five months: irritable, hard to pacify, irregular in their rhythms, slow to adapt to change and easily distracted*. During the second month, as many as one fifth develop colic, often lasting several months*. Undoubtedly, this increases the risk of the mother becoming depressed, depending on her vulnerability*. The needs remain the same but they are harder to meet, placing a large additional strain on mothers, who, if anyway vulnerable, have a still greater risk of depression as a result.

But even in these cases, so long as the mother is able to hang on in there and keep meeting the needs, it turns out all right in the end, with happy, secure babies and toddlers*. These are anyway, thankfully, the exception.

Whether born difficult or not, once a baby's WHEPT need is met, it disappears. Babies know what is enough. If their tummy is full of milk, if they have had a good sleep, if their fear has been cuddled, they will not demand more milk, will not crave more sleep, will not go on crying to be held.

This results from sensitive responsiveness, in which mother tunes into baby and gets the message*. Such care has been said to be as vital to a baby's emotional health as vitamins for its physical survival*.

THE NEEDS OF TODDLERS
(One- and Two-Year-Olds)

Having responsive care is equally vital for toddlers*.

On the one hand, they must begin the long march from seeing themselves as the centre of the universe – magically feeling able to alter the world just by wishing it so – to an acceptance that both objects and people have their own separate existence, and that being separate from mummy is enjoyable*.

On the other hand, this independence is only possible in the presence of a familiar adult who can meet their idiosyncratic need for love and attention, often expressed through particular foods, games and special words only known to the two of them, as well as cuddles. It does not matter at all whether this person is the mother, so long as they can provide this care, but toddlers are still highly dependent beings.

Three widely held myths exist about one- and two-year-olds' dependent needs:

Myth One

There is no truth whatsoever in the idea that they 'need' other children to play with at this age*. It seems like commonsense that they would do so. But if you think how emotionally immature toddlers are, it's obvious why they do not get much out of each other's company. Other toddlers are mostly a menace, taking their toys, grabbing at their food, pushing and shoving, making upsetting or loud noises. Watch closely: they play in parallel, not together, almost all the time. Whether charging about on scooters or in pedal cars, pushing trains on rails, giving dolls a bath or putting teddy to bed, they simply do not have the emotional and intellectual kit to cooperate much. Yes, the closer they get to age three, the more brief periods are jointly focused on interesting toys. But there is hardly any actual shared play. Left to their own devices together, play will nearly always break down quickly, usually ending in tears when one wants something the other has got. Even with supervision, the shared element does not endure for more than two or three minutes.

Myth Two*

Many parents make the commonsensical assumption that the sooner toddlers (or even babies) learn to look after themselves, the better. For their own good, it is assumed, the earlier they realise the importance of basic social skills, like turn-taking and self-reliance, the better they will be able to cope with what the world will throw at them in later life. Alas, the opposite is true. Leaving toddlers with strangers, or with unresponsive or only vaguely familiar adults makes them much less able to rub along with other humans and be independent. It makes them insecure, either clingy or stroppy, and if done too much too young, creates an enduring fear of dependence on others and tendency towards stormy or empty relationships with friends or intimates. While it is tempting to imagine that 'they've got to learn', you are actually creating a rod for your own back which may still be chastising you as they enter adulthood.

Myth Three*

For the vast majority of children it is not true that their mental abilities – language, reading, number skills – will be helped by early education. An understandable desire for children to do well at school deceives us into accelerating development from birth onwards, but it actually handicaps performance to start education too young. Toddlers need companions who can quickly turn into mother-figures, as required. They do not need teachers.

The dependent babyishness of the toddler addressed, we come to the gradually increasing need for independence, sometimes audible in the legendary tantrums of The Terrible Twos.

To a large degree, initially, independence follows physical growth. Once babies can sit up and their hands can manipulate objects, the potential is there for them to pick up a carelessly dropped sharp object or poisonous substance (like a bottle of pills with a loose top). Once they can crawl, you are into those 'oh my God' moments as you just catch them reaching towards the red-hot electric fire or about to put an electric cable into their mouth. From there it is only a few steps to having to break into a sprint as the newly toddling explorer heads towards the busy main road. At its most basic, therefore, you have their ever-increasing physical capacity to explore up against your ever-greater terror of disaster.

On a more sophisticated plane, their expanding vocabulary combines with a growing capacity for fantasy play to create the potential for social atrocities. They start causing havoc in the supermarket, pulling down sweet boxes or loudly demanding what they want. They get into fights with other children who thwart them or do not enact the desired role in their imaginary world. They cannot always have things their way. You are constantly banging up against the fact that they find it hard to see things from your point of view or that of other children. As far as they are concerned, if they want a toy or sweet, why should they not have it, right now?

Understandably enough, the response of some parents to this new problem is to create lots of rules, accompanied by punishments. Countless books offer regimes for taming the toddler, using star charts, naughty steps and time out. If the alternative is to frequently lose your temper, with increasing resort to violence, these regimes are far preferable. But it is worth asking yourself just how much of a conformist you want your child to be and what motives for conformity you want them to have.

It is certainly possible to train your child, like a dog in a laboratory. There is a level at which we are animals and just as Pavlov, the famous Russian psychologist, managed to coach dogs to salivate on seeing certain cues which had become associated in their minds with being fed, so with toddlers. However, many parents would prefer a child who is freely choosing the safe and desirable course, rather than acting out of reflex. You might wish to consider how much you want your child to grow into someone who will be capable of questioning the *status quo* and deciding for itself what it prefers, having considered the alternatives.

Most important in having a well-adjusted, contented, emotionally alive child, is not your choice of values but whether the child voluntarily adopts the ideas, so that they feel they own them. All the evidence suggests that children who have chosen their values are much happier and better functioning in every way than those who have been coerced through fear*.

I shall elaborate on these points as the book proceeds but that is all you need to know for now about babies' and toddlers' needs. There are no lab-tested formulae for meeting them. The real challenge concerns you: working out what is going to enable you to stay sane and then creating arrangements which will ensure the needs get met. Read on, and you will find your particular solution.

Part One

THE ORGANISER

CHAPTER 2

Meet the Essential Organiser

Many Huggers and some Fleximums will be enraged by aspects of this part of the book. Nonetheless, my advice is for you to read it closely. While it may serve only to confirm many of your ideas about working mothers or those who believe in routines, it may also lead some of you to rethink your approach. If nothing else, you will get a clearer definition of precisely how you differ from other kinds of mother. But it is also possible that you will see that elements of organisation and routine can be helpful, sometimes.

THE ESSENTIAL ORGANISER*

There are two fundamental differences between you and the Hugger in your underlying responses to the baby.

⟨ Whereas Huggers adapt to the baby, you expect the baby to adapt to you.

⟨ If the Hugger has a feeling about the baby that she cannot face, it is hate. The Organiser's greatest fear, deep down, is of falling in love with the baby.

During the pregnancy the Organiser tends to want to keep the interference with their normal life to a minimum. Evidence that there is a baby inside you is not necessarily welcome – the morning sickness, the growing bump, the kicking and the reduced mobility. You do not spend much time wondering what the baby may be like, do not feel it is a person yet. While you may be delighted that you are to become a mother, you may be quite humorous about the difficulties and shortcomings of being pregnant.

Most likely you do not care whether the birth is natural, you just want to get it over with. You may even dread it. If the doctors can find ways to make it as painless and civilised as possible, that's good news. Pain relief or even an elective Caesarean may seem like a welcome idea, although they tend to make you a bit groggy in the hours afterwards. Immediately after the birth, if the baby is put somewhere that does not interrupt your need for sleep and recovery, so much the better.

When first introduced to you the baby may seem like a stranger. You may feel wary and nervous about holding it. A sensitive midwife may gradually encourage cuddling and eye-contact, but this must not be rushed or done with too much interference from them. You may be someone who is used to being in control and who needs time to compose yourself. Getting used to having a round-the-clock dependant takes time. You react very badly to any hectoring from staff or relatives – you will decide what to do, in your own time.

You do love your baby as much as any other kind of mother but your attitude is that mother knows best. You regard your baby as a creature without a proper understanding of the human world, in some respects a bit like a new pet that needs training. It is a bundle of hungry needs that require regulation to make them predictable and more easily met. Insufficiently controlled, the baby can become unmanageable, overtired, underweight or antisocial, so it is your job to coach it to take control of its unruly passions and bodily processes.

That is an important part of how you show love. Unlike the Hugger, therefore, from early on you distinguish between 'real' cries and ones that can safely be ignored, like niggling or fussiness, these are just noise. The real ones require action as part of a systematic routine.

Back home, if the hospital has not already established a regime, this becomes the main goal. You are all too aware that breakfast can run into lunch, hours passing without any apparent achievement: nothing is getting done. This is an indeterminate situation, one that can quickly descend into a chaos governed by the potentially imperial baby's poorly socialised demands. Instead, you feel you must create regularity so that you have time and space in which to do things like clearing up and phone calls, through to personal hygiene, doing exercises to bring back your figure and other activities which will restore you to something approaching your pre-baby state, rather than letting yourself go.

For you may see your primary task in the early weeks as to make as rapid progress as possible in regaining your adult life, despite having a baby to look after. This, you may reason, will give you a good chance of not getting depressed, still being able to earn enough to keep the boat afloat and keep your relationship with your partner alive, or allow you to give enough attention to older children. A routine is a critical component of the plan because it will enable the care to be shared with other adults, freeing you to take those vital steps to getting your life back. You may feel frightened of losing your identity altogether. Nothing in your upbringing or education has prepared you for these early days and months of motherhood.

You prioritise the long-term good of the family as a whole, things like your own mental health, paying off the mortgage, looking to save enough for a house near a good school. Therefore, you plan to return to work and have probably already arranged alternative care. If wealthy enough, you will have employed a maternity nurse. An au pair or nanny is already in place in three-quarters of cases of Organisers who can afford it*. If you cannot afford this, you already have mothers, mothers-in-law, neighbours or friends on standby. As an Organiser, you believe small babies can hardly tell carers apart. So long as the baby's physical needs are being met, once a routine is established all you have to do is explain the details to the substitute and if they are competent, all should be well.

You may be rather easily made to feel guilty that the baby is not being looked after 'properly', so sharing the care is a relief, diluting blame if things are going badly. You would be doing the baby no favours to hand it over without a routine, as the substitute carer needs to be told what is required. How else would they know what to do? Because you do not think of the baby as having much sophistication, substitutes are hardly going to discover what care it requires from scanning its face or listening to its cries. Since the carer has no idea what is best, or what will stop it crying, it is your duty to let it know and to pass that information on to substitutes. As Joan Raphael-Leff puts it*, the way the Organiser may think about her situation, more or less secretly, is as follows: 'I have this deep wish for set order. I want each day to be the same and to know just what the baby needs. When she won't have her nap I feel such a failure. I should be able to control things. Other people's babies sleep on time. That's why having a nanny is great – she can really get things straightened out and I'm not the only one responsible.' Just like the Hugger, you are very much at risk of feeling guilty but the reasoning is completely different. Whereas the Hugger feels she should be able to find the answers in the baby, being led by it, and blames herself for failing to read the baby correctly, the Organiser blames herself for not having been sufficiently rigorous or efficient in establishing or implementing a routine.

Even holding the baby can seem alarming to Organisers at first. It is so fragile and breakable, with its over-large, lolling head and its little stick-like arms and legs. When its weeny hand grips yours it may feel like it is clutching at your heart. Yet the nestling sweetness must be resisted to some extent, for if you become too devoted, you could be sucked into an excessive involvement that will make it harder to hand it over to others. You would end up being landed with it all the time, which is not the plan.

In some cases, you may feel that every startled or jerky over-reaction from the baby is an accusation that you cannot cope and are liable to drop it. An unhappy cycle can develop. If you are tense and rigid when holding it, the baby stiffens. You may notice that the baby seems much more relaxed in the arms of others, which makes you feel rejected. You are hypersensitive to its refusal to relax in your embrace, becoming still more tentative. Studies show that mothers who felt rejected by their own mothers are more likely to have this kind of response to babies. Feeling rejected, you make the baby feel rejected and it, in turn, becomes unresponsive, confirming your feeling*. In such cases, the mother is particularly keen on rockers or mats, or on encouraging others to hold the baby. Unlike the Hugger, spending hours on end with the baby in your arms is not your idea of heaven.

Nor is breastfeeding. You are acutely aware of the need to move to a bottle so that other carers will be able to discharge this vital role as well as you. Some Organisers feel the sucking on the breast has a cannibalistic quality, as if they are being eaten up. As well as being devoured, it may feel as if you are being sucked dry, your vitality draining out of you. As the baby searches to catch your eye during the feed, it can seem accusing – that you are holding the milk back, or that the milk is bad in some way, perhaps insufficiently rich. The baby has no idea that you are exhausted and need your sleep, it is insatiable, screaming and raging if the breast is not made available in the middle of the night, guzzling away without a thought for the poor woman on the end of it. While breastfeeding you can't take aspirin for headaches, you cannot have a glass of wine, not even one of your favourite curries or some garlic with your chicken.

A bottle seems so civilised by contrast. What a relief to get shot of those ghastly nursing bras, the leakages, the lopsidedness of the breasts, the expressing for night-time feeds. Perhaps breastfeeding was painful or difficult, or upsetting, keeping you stuck in one place for hours. Formula creates a sense of precision and purpose, washing out a lustily emptied bottle seems so much cleaner in every way. You can get a real sense of control from knowing exactly how much milk has been consumed. Without confidence in your instinct about the baby's needs, you are reliant on measuring what goes on from growth charts and health visitors' opinions. With the breast you have to worry about timing how long has been spent on each side and keep weighing the baby to check if it's getting enough. No wonder you aim for a feed only every four hours during the day, and eliminate night feeds as soon as possible.

Burping is important to you, much more so than for the Hugger. This may be done between breasts as a simple stroking or back-patting. But it's important to make sure the milk has gone down, so it can become quite extensive, with rhythmic pummelling. If it seems as if the milk is proving indigestible or in some way bad, the winding procedure may become a way for both of you to relieve tension.

Whereas Huggers often take pleasure in the plentiful poos of their babies, Organisers are more likely to feel repulsed by the sight and smell of the faeces which results from breast milk. The more 'normal' stuff that comes into the nappy once bottle feeding is established is reassuringly familiar, of a similar consistency to adults'. If there is constipation or diarrhoea, that can be remedied by adjusting the intake and there is no question of your breast milk being to blame.

The baby certainly does not sleep in your bed. It's in a cot from the start, usually in its own room. You stick to your rule with all the rigour you can muster, however tired or stressed you may feel – you owe that to the baby in the longer term. The reward is that many Organisers report the baby is sleeping right through the night by seven weeks. You may joke that, being so tired, you have learned to sleep through the night even if the baby has not – you cannot hear it. You feel, anyway, that it has to learn to soothe itself, that babies must be trained to do so. Better sleeping is one of the reasons you race as fast as possible from milk to solids. Get them eating 'properly' and they will grow faster, making it easier for them to develop the independence which you see it as your job to help them acquire.

Given all this, it's hardly surprising that most Organisers say they do not much like having to look after babies in the early months and that they greatly prefer offspring when they are older. Only 37% of Organisers report enjoying the mothering of newborns, whereas this rises to 60% once the baby is older*. Indeed, there is good evidence that Organisers are much more likely than other types of mothers to be depressed when their baby reaches two months of age – 30% are, compared with 14% of Huggers and 11% of Fleximums*. Let's face it, as far as you are concerned, once the child starts talking and becomes manageable, it seems much more interesting. While you love your baby every bit as much as Huggers, they find babies endlessly exciting. You may comment that babies are not the most stimulating of company, and in fact will confide that, if truth be told, looking after them can be pretty boring and frustrating.

Like Huggers, deep down, Organisers may be reacting to difficult early childhood experiences of their own. But Huggers cope with the unhappy memories that a tiny baby stirs up in them by trying to supply the mothering they never had. Distressed Organisers have a different, and in some ways more logical, reaction. They hated feeling weak and vulnerable in infancy, so they naturally recoil from being reminded of it. If so, they may find a boy easier to tune into. A girl may remind them of their former selves, something they would prefer to forget.

Whatever the motives, the Organiser's usual aim is to return to the much more familiar, less chaotic, altogether less stressful life of their workplace. If they do not, it can be disastrous. Few categories of mother are more at risk of depression than the Organiser who is unemployed, looking for a paid job and unable to find one*. Better by far that they return to the workforce and entrust the baby during the early years to the care of someone who enjoys that stage. They still make a huge contribution to its life but they do so with a cheerful mood, rather than feeling desperate and unvalued.

If their partner is an Organiser, he shares all these reactions. He is definitely not known for his militant support of legislation to increase paternity leave! Indeed, he may use any such leave as a chance to embark on that much-cherished walking expedition or if not taking the leave and in a management position, find himself urgently required to go on a foreign business trip soon after the birth. Seeing his home turned into a giant nursery, with nappy-sterilising buckets clogging up the bathroom and toys and rockers liable to trip him up in his sitting room, he heads off at the first opportunity to places which he regards as familiar and reassuringly masculine, like the pub and the golf course. If trapped at home, while he may do his best to maintain a patina of civility, he buries himself in the newspaper or the sports channel on the TV. He may stretch to the odd bit of bath-running or cooking, but daddy Organiser tends to draw the line at nappy-changing. Attempts to get him to hold the baby tend to fail, or if forced to do so, he is scared that his roughness or incompetence will destroy the vulnerable little bundle of newness. He is 100% in favour of introducing routines and of signing up as much substitute care as possible. He wants his life and his wife back. With time, some male Organisers get more involved in their babies, especially with a first-born male*, offering themselves as a 'solid rock' upon which the mother can rely. She may look to the man to provide approval and encouragement, and will be especially pleased if he displays admiration of a supposedly feminine stoicism or skill.

If the man is a Hugger, it can work fine. The Organiser mother is relieved that someone else is enjoying the baby so much and that she is not in so much danger of being blamed if things go badly. However, there is obviously a potential for clashes over basic issues of nurture. He may want the baby in the bed, or feel they should rush to feed it if it cries. He may spend so much time cuddling it that the mother feels left out, or implicitly criticised. If he resists or sabotages her attempts to establish a routine, there can be more than tears before bedtime.

Tracy, a Classic Organiser: Employed Full-Time, Baby Adapts to Mother

Tracy is a breezy, cheerful, 43-year-old woman, amused by life but well aware of its dangers. You should never take money or health for granted, and just as adult life can seem perilous, so babies are fragile little things.

She finds her job as a graphic designer in Newcastle fulfilling but she also loves her son, Seamus, nearly three, and her one-year-old daughter Sandra. To her 'having children is the most important thing you will do in your life' – but equally 'your former life doesn't have to come to an abrupt end just because you have had a baby'.

Approaching her 40th birthday, she was grateful to have conceived Seamus so easily while on honeymoon with her husband, Tim. Her approach to the pregnancy was unsentimental. 'I just kept working and I didn't want to indulge it too much, because I was newlywed. I didn't want my first year of married life to be me sat on the sofa wailing and groaning.' She had neither the time nor inclination for musings about the nature and destiny of her foetus, except in one regard. 'Naturally you worry that the baby could have died and you wouldn't know – it's not as if you can listen to the heartbeat yourself. The scan is a bit of a lifeline.'

Tracy describes herself as 'quite controlling'. As a woman who had determined her life for two decades at work and play, the limitations and lack of control of pregnancy were a challenge. 'You really have to let go and let nature take its course. I was pretty slim and sometimes there would be an overnight growth spurt and you would wake up with your stomach noticeably bigger – comedic. You can't control that and you have to just give in to it.'

When it came to the birth, in true Organiser fashion she wanted to put herself in the hands of the professionals and get it over with, as safely and quickly as possible. For some Huggers it's akin to a sacred ritual but not for an Organiser like Tracy. 'I wanted to be in hospital with the professionals. I didn't have a clue what would happen, I wanted their guidance and reassurance.' However, she had also tried to take possession of the experience by doing an excellent yoga ante-natal class. She was clear that she didn't want drugs if possible because 'I wanted to be in control of my senses, with a clear head'. Thankfully, things went according to plan, bringing an enormous sense of achievement. 'Obviously it's very nice having the baby there but (a) you're just so glad it's over and (b) you're feeling quite self-congratulatory: "my work is done".' The relief is so great for Organisers because the loss of control is so terrifying. 'The next day I remember referring to the birth as "like surviving a car crash" – it's that big a deal. I probably handed Seamus to Tim immediately after-wards, I was just so relieved to be through it without problems.' For the Organiser, survival is all and their delight in the baby is based on the fact that it is alive rather than feeling the Hugger's sense of an almost mystical link to it.

Unfortunately, due to a minor infection, they had to stay in hospi-tal for a week. She did not like it there: 'just the baby and the wall to look at'. Around the third day the baby blues kicked in and it was a relief when she finally got home.

Mothers feel at their most vulnerable in the hours and days after the birth. Possibly because of hormones, between half and three-quarters have at least a few days of baby blues*. But it is also true that the manifest dependence of the baby triggers primitive feelings of what it was like to be in that vulnerable position oneself. For Organisers, the solution is to focus on the practicalities, rather than intimacy with the baby.

A book saved the day when Tracy ran into a fellow mother from her antenatal class. 'She gave me her copy of Gina Ford's *The Contented Little Baby Book* because she hated it so much. But that's the only book to give you firm outlines, what to do during the day – which I know a lot of people don't like – but that's what I needed at that point. I just wanted someone to tell me when I should be feeding, for how long, because babies haven't got our feeding patterns. Essentially you are completely retraining yourself, learning how to be a mother, nothing's prepared you for it and it's so high-risk. They're tiny and so dependent, they could die. That was very helpful, it gave me a rubric to work to.' Such books can seem like manna from heaven to Organisers because they are not expecting to get their lead for what to do from the baby, not tuning into its every burp or smile or cry. So where is the plan for how to get organised to come from? They need an answer urgently since they are all too aware of the baby's extreme vulnerability to physical danger (rather than emotional neglect). They want to regain control of a seemingly chaotic, potentially hopeless situation. In the absence of an approach based on the assumption that the baby can tell them what they need, clear instructions from a book are the perfect solution.

From then on, Tracy gradually reasserted herself. To start with, Seamus slept for about four hours at a stretch. At night, he was in a Moses basket by her bed and she would feed and then settle him every four hours, getting used to interrupted sleep. Then, at around six or eight weeks, she changed the arrangement. 'His crying was really loud, like having a farmyard animal next to the bed. I started putting him in his own room in the cot.' Her mother thought the move was too early but luckily she did not live nearby. 'I wanted to get to the end of this initial period. You desperately want the dust to settle so you bring these things forward to get things a bit more under control.' In the back of Tracy's mind was the fact that she was scheduled to return to work when Seamus was seven months old. It was vital to have him eating and sleeping in a predictable fashion for that plan to work.

From the moment she had become pregnant she had known she would return to her work. Like many Organisers, she finds it hard to understand why any professional woman would not do so. Indeed, she feels strongly that they should. 'I get quite angry when trained barristers or doctors say, "I'm not going to go back to my job, I'm just going to hang around making cakes all day, or work in the village shop." You think "what about that life you've had, training and doing exams and revising, years and years and years of learning theory and applying it, competing with men and trying to outperform them, going for all those job interviews, working, working, working, trying to get some pissy little promotion, worrying about your finances, buying the house, working your way up and then just eradicating all that because you have had a baby?" I think women who don't go back to work probably had a rubbish job or weren't fulfilled, are looking for a way out. Caring for a baby is the most convenient excuse and nobody can really argue with it.'

That is about as lucid and frank an account as you are likely to get of the position of the classic Organiser in the Mommy Wars (R4). Just as the Hugger lampoons the Organiser as a cold, neglectful woman lacking in emotional intelligence, the Organiser depicts the Hugger as a slacker swanning around 'making cakes all day', someone who is ultimately letting down her sex by failing to compete with men in the workplace. Interestingly, I was once at a meeting where I heard Harriet Harman, the Labour Minister, say almost exactly that: 'I suppose we have to give mothers a choice. If they want to hang about at home all day doing nothing, well, it's up to them.'

Tracy is right in believing that Huggers specifically, as opposed to mothers who are at-homers in general (not all of whom are Huggers), do not place nearly as high a value on their work lives as Organisers. This is partly because their identity is less vested in their career achievements – which, nonetheless, can be considerable – and for some, because they actually found their work dull, or disliked being in an office*. However, there is also good evidence that only one quarter of mothers with small children give disenchantment with work as the reason they are at home full-time (R5). Rather, they argue it is absolutely essential for their child's well-being*.

Tracy's reasons for returning illustrate the sharp differences between the two sorts of women, and also make clear that neither are better people, or necessarily better parents, than the other. Her first point is that 'it's quite important to reclaim some normality after something so extreme'. As with the birth, she also likened the early months with Seamus to 'a traumatic car crash'. That is how distressing caring for babies often seems to an Organiser, just as, it should be noted, it can be that distressing for the Hugger when confronted by the growing independence of their baby. If Organisers can find the intense, relentless dependence of the small baby deranging, Huggers can be every bit as deranged by the opposite.

Like about 60% of working mothers of under-threes* Tracy did not cite money as the reason for returning to work. Perhaps surprisingly, size of salary is irrelevant to women when they return to work. Those with a large one (over £65,000) are no more or less likely to see it as important than poorer ones*, earning much less (under £20,000): plenty of high earners say earning money is essential and just as many who are poorly paid say it's irrelevant.

In Tracy's case, her husband earned enough for her not to work. 'He earns double what I do. He said it was my decision but I think he knew I would go back.' She suspects he would not want a companion who could only talk about her 'uninteresting' day of walking the baby and so on. Nor did she feel comfortable solely being defined as a mother. 'On the rare times when I went out socially when Seamus was small, if I was asked what I did I would talk about my job, not being a mother, though I would add I was on maternity leave. If I'd only been looking after my son with no plan to go back to work I would have felt the need to justify it further, maybe say "I'm developing this or that project". Mothering certainly is a full-time job, but saying "I'm a mum" would not have been enough. Anyone can be a mum, but not as many can be professors or doctors.' So the lack of status attached to the mothering role did affect her, coupled with the feeling that she did not want to throw away the decades of hard work that had gone into building her career.

But with great honesty, Tracy explained that a third reason was she did not believe she would be able to provide as good care for Seamus as a substitute. This goes to the very core of the difference between Hugger and Organiser. 'I was getting a bit bored, it was becoming difficult filling our day. He needed quite a lot of stimulation – still does. I thought "I'm probably boring him and hindering his development". Good nurseries do all sorts of activities, and crafts. They can play, go outside and they make friends. When he was seven months or so, I thought "he's going to get more out of his day if he's in a fun environment like that, where they're doing little games and he's got somebody looking after him who's completely energised and wants to play peek-a-boo for the eighteenth time that day".'

Since the baby did not seem very interesting company, her day stretched ahead in a menacingly dull fashion. 'The problems were repetition, lack of intellectual stimulation and lack of direction. I'd be going out of the door on a Monday morning and I would have only one thing in the diary, meeting up with my NCT class on Thursday. I'd think, "I've got Monday, Tuesday, Wednesday to fill". It's like being on the dole. You've got no direction or structure. I'd think, "hum, well let's go to the park, let's go swimming", but of course it's a huge ordeal leaving the house (buggy, nappies, wipes etc), much easier not to, but you do it because what else are you going to do? I thought "If I was him *I'd* be bored".'

This articulate account of how Organisers often feel about caring for babies contains some intriguing ambiguities. Tracy was bored. It's less clear whether she is right in believing that Seamus was, as well. The scientific evidence shows this age group needs tuned-in responsiveness, subtly different from stimulation*. In fact, it is older children and adults who become bored if unstimulated, not seven-month-olds. Politicians and psychologists alike use the word 'stimulation' on the grounds that it will supposedly advance educational and cognitive achievement. That is true later on, but not at such a young age*. What counts with under-threes is responsiveness from a familiar adult who understands needs that cannot yet be conveyed by words (R3). But like most Organisers, Tracy has quite an adult model of the baby (R5), operating best on the adult rather than the non-verbal, baby wavelength. So baby and Organiser mum can be like two walkie-talkies tuned to different channels. This has nothing to do with being 'cold' or 'unloving', it's simply that Organisers struggle to be on the same wavelength as a baby*. They expect little or no communication, so less happens. Eventually, that becomes very dull and potentially depressing for the mother.

Tracy acknowledged this point implicitly. 'If I'd continued I would have become more and more introverted, possibly quite down, because playing peek-a-boo wasn't me. It was better if we had quality time together, so that I would come back home from work and be very upbeat and pleased to see him. And once I was working we had these fantastic weekends completely dedicated to our new family unit, so it was best all round. That's what's right for us, anyway.' This gets close to the key reason she went back to work: while she was doubtless finding it pretty boring caring for Seamus, since she was not seeing him as an entity with much to offer, the problem was that her boredom, combined with the lack of status and stimulation from work, created the risk of depression for her.

Seamus's 'boredom' was not the real issue, it was that Tracy rightly realised that it would be bad for him to be cared for by a depressed mother and, at some level, intuited that she was not attuned to him, and that that was not good for him either. She is equally right that it was far better for him to be cared for by someone who enjoyed children of that age and could tune in (though as we shall see, it was not that Tracy was incapable of it; she was not lacking some crucial bit of brain or lacking some mothering gene). What was more, as she so enthusiastically described, so long as she got the emotional benefits of working, she was a much better mother when she was with Seamus.

These observations also help us understand the Mommy Wars (R4). While Organisers are not cold, uncaring, selfish mothers, they frequently find it hard to tune in to babies, to be responsive in the way needed. In such cases, it is best for all concerned if they do go back to work. Equally, while Huggers are not work-shy slackers, they are often as unexcited by the workplace as Organisers are by babies. These are two groups of women whose bells are rung by different things. In reality, there is nothing for them to fight about. The grounds for their 'War' are as flimsy as a squabble about whether it is 'better' to have tennis as a hobby rather than line dancing. These are just different activities, not better or worse.

The venom arises because each feels the other's approach to mothering (adapt to baby or baby adapt to mother) and lifestyle choice (to work or not to work) is an all too visible reproach. The Organiser feels the Hugger spoils their baby, the Hugger feels the Organiser deprives it by returning to work. In fact, both are doing the right thing for their particular personality which, in turn, is right for their baby (so long as the Organiser finds truly responsive one-to-one substitute care that remains the same person for their baby, and so long as the Hugger is able to tolerate the baby's growing independence). Deep down, in some cases, each may partly envy the other: some Huggers secretly might like to have an exciting career, some Organisers secretly might wish they were Earth Mothers. Where envy is involved, the venom is at its most plentiful and poisonous* – the other's desired attributes must be destroyed to avoid feeling they are missing out.

In terms of rationales for mothering, although most Organisers and full-time working mothers say nurture is important (especially for academic and social development), they see genes as playing an even greater role in explaining what we are like (R5, R7). Tracy believed her own history illustrates the point. Born the third of five children with a manual labourer father, she feels all the children had very similar care from both parents, and yet some are very different from the others. While she and two of her siblings went to university and have had successful careers, one sister has had long-standing depression and one brother has been 'loafing around doing not very much in Spain' for much of his adulthood. She is convinced this is evidence for the key role of genes. 'Basically, it's genes. If you look around at my cousins you can see bits of all our genes all over the place, nothing to do with upbringing.' Of course, this is highly debatable. Closer inspection of what went on in her family might reveal that, in fact, her siblings had very different care from both parents.

In believing genes are so important, Tracy is typical of full-time working mothers. It helps to explain her comfort about her choice of substitute care for Seamus: day care.

As a whole, only a small minority of working mothers (10%) either use day care or say that, given the choice, they prefer it for an under-three (R2). But if you share Tracy's picture of what a small child needs and her confidence that nature is so much more important than nurture, it makes perfect sense. Safety was a big factor in her decision. 'I like the way nurseries are inspected. If there are a few people in the room, a bad apple would get noticed eventually. The last thing you would want is some psychopathic childminder in charge of your child. Nurseries have got managers, all the staff have been rigorously checked. They're qualified, they love children, that's why they are doing this job. I couldn't see what they would get from a nanny that was better.' According to Tracy's logic, a nursery would be better. 'At a nursery they've got children of their own age, planned activity, little trips, there's always stuff going on for them to look at. I can't provide that, and if it was a nanny, she might as well be me because she can't provide it either. Worse still, if it was some random nanny from Bratislava you just know they would be sitting watching telly quite a lot of the time and I don't want to pay for that, thank you. A small child needs plenty of stimulation, variety and interesting things going on.'

An intriguing twist to Tracy's story is that she was much less of an Organiser in the early months with her second child, Sandra. It shows the extent to which almost any mother can shift her approach from child to child.

Tracy assumed her second child was going to be another boy and was delighted to hear it would be a girl because she felt it would be a 'gentler' baby. This time she got home from the hospital the next day and felt much more relaxed. Seamus played about in the room and – very unlike an Organiser – Tracy 'lurked about in the bedroom, having cups of tea and meals, not getting dressed for about a week'. This time she decided to ignore all advice on breastfeeding. 'I just stuck her on and saw what happened, which seemed to work. I was doing it all the time in the first few days, which I think you've got to do. Every time she woke up or if she seemed remotely hungry I would give it a go.' This sounds more like a Hugger.

Second time around, Tracy felt much less socially isolated. With Seamus, having recently moved house, she had lacked many close intimates in her immediate vicinity – terribly important for all mothers. With Sandra, Tracy knew many more mothers with babies and rather to her surprise quite enjoyed the days. She had the basic structure of taking Seamus to the nursery, then she and Sandra might have a little play, then meet up with friends, then a nap, then a visit to the shops or a café. It was all much more relaxed.

Sandra was calmer than Seamus. 'She'd be happy on my knee in a café, fiddling with a teaspoon or just looking around. Seamus would be grabbing the salt or pepper, or need to be bounced or want to get down, more restless. With him you could never relax and have a proper conversation with a friend.' Naturally, Tracy puts the difference down to inborn temperament and her expectation that a girl would be gentler (also presumed to be genetic). Indeed, Sandra may have been born calmer but it is also possible that she was the same as Seamus when he was born. The real difference could have been that Tracy was more able to tune into Sandra, be relaxed enough to hang about in her pyjamas for a week and enjoy the breastfeeding. Tracy had assumed Sandra would be more gentle, which may have been a self-fulfilling prophecy since the attributes mothers project on to a baby often affect its future behaviour* (how negative a mother feels about her newborn has been shown to predict how secure an adult that baby becomes in middle age). That Tracy was also able, for whatever reason, to put off her previously urgent need to get her adult life back may also have made a big difference to Sandra's calmness.

The period of Hugger-like tendencies gradually ended as Tracy began to introduce routines, although this time based more on what suited Sandra, not her. But the Organiser was still very much there. As Tracy put it, 'I enjoyed it but only because I knew exactly when it would end. In the same way that you can be really pleased to get home after a good holiday, I was pleased to get back to work. Even while I was with Sandra I did have some quite strong work ideas, which I passed on to the office, even spending a couple of very satisfying days doing designs while she was asleep and sending them off.'

Nonetheless, she did not go back to work until nine months this time and arranged for a four-day week, so that she very much enjoys her one day with Sandra. Although not quite a Fleximum, she has shifted in that direction. So a key message of Tracy's story is that mothering approaches are not set in stone.

A critical element of the Organiser approach is that, in the vast majority of cases, it entails others looking after the child. Those Organisers who stress the importance of stimulation and social development are the ones most likely to favour nursery care. When Tracy settled Sandra into her nursery at nine months she was worried it might be a bit late because by then, she felt (correctly), children are more likely to feel upset at being separated from their mother. Having spent time in nurseries with her children, she has seen plenty going through the process of settling in and believes that, after a few minutes of tearfulness following the mother's departure, they will start playing. 'Once they've got their head around it they adjust. Presumably initially they think "what the hell's going on?" when their mother disappears. Sandra still cries occasionally when I drop her off. But they get the hang of it.'

That is one way of looking at how a toddler or baby copes with the mother's absence. However, as is explained in Chapter 6 and Review 3, there are strong grounds for believing that there is no advantage for a middle-class child to being in day care and, unfortunately, that there are well-proven risks. It may be that many parents sense this. The vast majority of under-threes with working parents do not have day care and nor do their parents favour it (R2).

Unlike Tracy, many Organisers put responsiveness and affection from a single person in the early years ahead of learning and sociability. For them, a relative, neighbour, minder, au pair or nanny are the main options. It can be difficult finding and keeping the right person, a recurring issue throughout succeeding chapters.

CHAPTER 3

The High-Achieving Organiser

Just as many high-achieving men would never be able to much enjoy mothering, it is also true that some high-achieving women find early mothering completely at variance with the very adult skills and strong motivation which enable them to succeed in the workplace. Rarely are these kinds of people the sort who find it congenial to have one person completely dependent on them, emotionally and physically, for 24 hours a day for years on end. The truth is that the personality traits of being strongly driven and that of responsive mothering rarely coexist in one person. The trouble is, we still live in a sexist society. Most people would assume that highly competitive and ambitious men such as Rupert Murdoch, Mick Jagger or Simon Cowell would be ill-suited to the full-time care of infants and toddlers. Because they are men, if they become parents, it almost never crosses anyone's mind that they should give any consideration to the possibility of mothering their offspring – alas, we rarely imagine that role will be taken up by fathers. But when Madonna or Cherie Blair give birth, completely different rules apply. It is time we stopped stigmatising high-achieving women for not being motherly; we should cut them the same slack as we do their male equivalents.

For fairly obvious reasons, the sorts of people who run the country are probably Organisers. If you are used to organising a large corporation or a government department, you think in logical ways and make the assumption that people are rational, and can be motivated by rewards and punishments. The irrational, emotional, blurred world of the infant is unlikely to seem familiar. Understandably enough, you might look to bring some order to such chaos, whatever your gender.

Julie, 46, is just such a person. Although not a public figure herself, she is a senior member of our ruling elite. She has worked mind-bogglingly hard to get where she is today, a powerful role which affects all of us.

After a judicious and sensible initial scepticism about my motives, she revealed herself to be a decent, passionate and troubled person, unsparingly honest, constantly challenging herself, on a quest to discover what is best for her children, Leo, aged three, and two-year-old Sarah. She was also perceptive and displayed the intelligence you might expect, but do not always find, in such a high achiever.

Like so many Organisers, she is plagued by the fear that she has not adopted the right regimes for her children and she has gone through an agonising struggle about whether to continue with her career rather than care for them. She is still unsure which of these roles is the real her but because her relationship with her mother is difficult and that with her partner effectively over; for much of the time she is having to soldier on alone, emotionally, albeit with a good deal of paid help.

She met her ex-partner, Terry, 37, through their shared love of surfing on the beaches of Devon and Cornwall. As well as being younger, he is not university educated and does casual jobs with little earning power. They decided to have children but since she was already in her forties, she did not expect to fall pregnant easily.

The period during which they were trying to conceive coincided with Julie working under a notoriously brutal and exacting boss. She remembers vividly getting a text one Sunday which announced his departure and the arrival of a much more benign replacement. She was incredibly relieved and believes it is no coincidence that she conceived Leo that night.

Unfortunately, within a short time she began to have serious doubts about Terry, as their relationship became rocky. Although now working for a less savage boss, she still had huge pressures at work, with big decisions and horrendous office politics stacking up like planes over Heathrow. On top of that, she had grave doubts about her obstetrician and, being a highly capable, well-read woman, questioned his decisions. As if that were not enough, she had the Organiser's usual unawareness of her pregnant state – 'I mainly noticed how enormous I was, I didn't much think about the foetus' – and she was also full of worries about would happen after the birth. 'I did have a problem visualising my child, seeing forward. I didn't have much confidence I would know how to care for him, so I booked a maternity nurse. I also worried a lot that although this was something I wanted very much, "what if I get it wrong?" What if I didn't want children at all, that it was just a big fantasy?'

Much to her relief, she adored him from the beginning. However, as with almost everything in her life, it was not straightforward. 'The maternity nurse was brilliant on the practical front but a bit of a witch. She really caused big trouble between me and my mother, and with my partner.' Alas, the kind of office politics which dog her life at work strayed into the home, with a complicated 'who said what to whom' series of falling outs. As is so often the case, having children brought Julie's relationship with her mother into sharp focus. 'She so wants to be in my life. But my having children has made our relationship a hundred times worse. I can see the over-controlling parent she was with me through the way she relates to my children. It drives me bonkers.' Although she felt a tremendous gush of love towards her son, he was also the occasion for a crisis. 'I'd always been a bit of a rebel, liked to see myself as cool, and I had not stopped feeling like that even though I was a 40-something. I was still a freewheeling Bridget Jones in my mind. As such, I found the routine hard. That was the hardest thing: for a child to have a routine, you've got to have one. I'd never had one before.'

That Julie had never been organised in her personal life might seem odd, given what a high achiever she is, but until this point, she had been something of a divided person. On the one hand, there was the good girl at school who became the star at university and in her career. She was completely clear why. 'I've always felt my mother's pressure and pushiness. She's always said she was one step behind me and I joke, "Yeah, pushing my back". I had my mother's ambitions poured into me. She did not go to university, she wanted me to fulfil her hopes. If I got 98% in maths it was "what about the other 2%?". If I got a 2:1 in my initial university exam it was "never mind, you can get a first next year". I had been colonised by her. A lot of my success was her in me.'

While Julie did get a kick out of her achievements, they also left her drained and resentful, rebellious. So on the other hand, there was another Julie crying out for something that was for her, not for her over-controlling mother (see pages 68–71 of *They F*** You Up* and pages 267–74 of *Affluenza*, for detailed accounts of this pattern between mothers and daughters, resulting in pathological perfectionism). Up until now, that something for her had been her non-career life, including the relationship with the younger and not very solvent father of her child. This Rebel Julie had a plan. 'In my head I had a picture that when I had children I would give up my career. I somehow thought children would give me the power to leave it all behind, a new direction.' Children were going to be the spark for a revolution against her (internalised) tyrant of a mother. However, Rebel Julie was not a very grown-up person.

Like, surprisingly, many of the hundred or so high achievers I have interviewed over the years, she was still wrestling with unresolved issues from her childhood and teens, placed on the backburner by the need to surge ahead and be prematurely adult. In particular, women who were hijacked by such mothers are frequently very undomesticated: the deal was the daughter saying 'I'll pass the exams and get to the top, you do the cooking and tidying up'. For such women, ordinary domestic challenges can create an enormous rage because unconsciously, they feel they have kept their part of the bargain by working themselves to death, so how come the mother is no longer cleaning up after them in their flat, and doing the cooking and shopping?

In a report of burnout in eight cases of young (29–38-year-old) female corporate lawyers, the New York psychoanalyst Brenda Berger provides a deep insight into what life is like for many high-achieving women[*]. She presents the case of Meg, in her twenties, who was working 60 hours a week and at the end of her brutal day, would 'zone out' in front of the telly. She had rejected less prestigious alternatives, choosing her firm because she felt more 'at home' there. Meg came from a home in which her mother was a fragile, self-centred woman whose love Meg could only attract by acting in accord with her mother's perfectionist demands, which were based on feeling thwarted in her own ambitions and lived out through Meg. Her father was no better, taking any signs of independence as a personal affront. Berger describes how Meg had developed a self-damaging need to repeat this scenario in her work life, agreeing to conceal her misery from her employers (parents) in exchange for status and money. In her appearance and conduct of her life, Meg was utterly chaotic, all domestic work having been taken care of by her mother when Meg was small. Indeed, other than when executing her tasks at the firm, she was helpless, angry and incapable of thinking for herself. Similar patterns were found in Berger's other cases and in summarising her conclusions, she points out that the pathological need to please and to join cruel working environments is viciously exploited by such corporations.

In Rebel Julie's case, accustomed to a pretty chaotic personal life, suddenly she was having to work out how to look after a baby when, in many ways, she was still in need of being looked after herself. As part of her rebellious side, she had shacked up with a man who was never going to be the breadwinner, something she had overlooked. So the plan that she could jettison Good Girl Julie and use motherhood as a route to authenticity was banging against practicalities, like who was going to earn the money and who was going to change the nappies.

An identity crisis ensued. 'I probably did have baby blues. Looking back, my moods and emotions were probably all over the place. My mental body chemistry has always been pretty weird, difficult to manage. I get terrible PMS and I'm currently having Cognitive Behavioural Therapy' (CBT). This account reflects a very common view of human psychology among the current ruling elite of both genders. Body chemistry is portrayed as the problem: the mental is physical, often assumed to be primarily dictated by genes. However, there is good research evidence regarding what really makes many high achievers tick.

Many of them have what is known as a Type A Personality. Although it is unfashionable to cite this body of evidence and the theory has been modified*, it is still regarded as having some validity. Type As are defined as people who are 'aggressively involved in a chronic, incessant struggle to achieve more and more in less and less time, and if required to do so, against the opposing efforts of other things or other persons'*. Constantly driven to achieve and frequently feeling herself to be frustrated at work and home by others, Julie probably fits this category (though she does not have the cynical hostility which Type As often exhibit, nor does she have the rampant, 'me, me, me' narcissism proven to be common in many senior managers or leaders*). Such people (more are men than women*) tend to come from higher social classes, work longer hours and feel less supported by and more critical of co-workers than non-Type As*. Female Type As work even longer hours than male Type As*. They are less likely to place a high value on family life* and tend to report having felt unloved as children*. Indeed, they tend to have had parents who set high standards* and who dealt with their own feelings of failure by attributing them to their offspring*. Whether employed or not, when female Type As have children, they are at greater risk of depression than other women*. As mothers*, they tend to be controlling and to put pressure on the child to be a high achiever, resulting in the child being impatient and aggressive. When Type A mothers are asked to play with their children doing a task requiring careful, slow, enduring application, they are more controlling*. They mention the importance of speed and time if the task has a time limit, and are more liable to give instructions and make copious judgements about the child's performance, both positive and negative.

Given all this, it is sad that Julie is getting a form of therapy that will not address any of the causes of her problems. She realises her mother hijacked her but CBT explicitly rejects any investigation of the childhood origins of problems, forcing the topic back to present thought patterns. She would also greatly benefit from feeling supported and emotionally held, something she would not get from textbook CBT and would get from what is called psychodynamic therapy*.

CBT offers mental tricks to play on oneself instead of a real solution to the fundamental causes*. Julie would do better to explore the childhood history of Good versus Rebel. It is hardly surprising that she felt identity confusion on giving birth since, again like so many successful modern women, she received a very mixed message in her childhood. Her mother was a full-time housewife without a degree whose message was 'do as I say (don't be a housewife, be a high-flyer) not as I do (housewifery)'. But as a small child, Julie identified in part with a housewife, and an over-controlling one at that. This led to a particularly vicious resolution to her crisis.

Completely at sea, faced with the challenge of how to be a mother, Julie automatically replicated the approach of her own mother. Of course, it can work the opposite way, as we shall see when we come to the Huggers. Some women like Julie very consciously decide to do the opposite of what was done to them and become Huggers. But in her state of uncertainty and fear, it was the Good Julie, her mother in her, who took charge when it came to the childcare, demanding that it be Organised. Instead of Rebel Julie taking over (which might have led to Hugging), Good Julie insisted on high standards of routine and organisation, making her terrified of failure in the classic Organiser pattern.

It started with the 'witch' maternity nurse. 'She had got Leo into a routine, which you have to do or else you don't ever stop. It was a pretty upsetting time but I am a pretty tough person. The nurse had taught us how to tap and swaddle him to sleep, rather than cuddle – I could see that if you start that, where does it end? You find yourself driving the baby around in cars late at night, that's where! I could see the logic of that, I would be doing it all night unless limits were established. It wasn't going to help him for me not to get a routine going.' Here is the Organiser's greatest terror: if you 'give in' and 'indulge' the baby, it will completely take over your life.

Being a diligent, practical, effective person, Good Julie started reading up on what to do. Rebel Julie occasionally kicked back so that 'I read that book everyone reads about how to make them contented and I hated it, so I threw it into the bin. You can never keep to that kind of routine, I ended up feeling like a failure the whole time.' Even so, Good Julie was determined to bring an end to the chaos. 'I wrote in my diary when Leo was three months that it made me cry to hear him crying. I suppose I had been trying to do controlled crying [gradually leaving the baby for longer periods to soothe itself] but there were some difficulties. The more I went in, the more he'd wake up. I remember shutting the door and thinking "OK, I'm going to leave him". I could hear him cry and I sat on the stairs writing in my diary, because I thought "this is right for him, he must learn to go to sleep by himself". Otherwise he would have gone on and on. It was fascinating, apart from anything else.'

Eventually the crying was stilled. 'I sang a lot, used my voice, talked to him and patted away. We really got it quite licked – oh dear, I know that sounds quite awful! But then I remember another mother who was doing it completely differently came round, and Leo was in his recliner and she said, "Aren't you going to cuddle him?" She was really shocked, and it made me doubt and question myself. Because you do question yourself, well, I do, you ask "am I doing it properly?".'

This issue of doing it by the book endures into toddlerdom for many Organisers. 'Throughout, the great question I always asked myself was, "if you continue this behaviour what will be the logical outcome of it?" Only today he was misbehaving and I put him on the naughty step, which I haven't for a long time. You've got to ask "If I let this go on, where will it ever stop?".'

Controlled crying and naughty steps so appeal to the Organiser because they perceive the child as a dangerous, potentially bottomless pit of needs. They do not understand that, in the case of babies, if you identify the need and meet it, they are satiable (unlike many adults). With toddlers, they regard discipline as the necessary imposition of rules that have to be learnt – how else will the child know what is right and wrong? They do not understand that a toddler can gradually develop its own desire to behave in a civil fashion, that a single barbarian act left unchecked is not inevitably the first step in a slide towards anarchy and animalistic selfishness (toddler discipline is fully explained in Chapter 11, page 179). Above all, they do not realise that both babies and toddlers only want to feel loved and that if they do not, they feel insecure. These insecurities get expressed in aggression, sullen self-absorption, attention deficits and problems of regulation, like in eating or sleeping. They are very quickly corrected by love.

Overall, if insecure in early life, there is a much greater risk of being an insecure adult. One study measured how much mothers responded to their babies and tuned into their needs at one, eight and 24 months*. The degree of responsiveness at those ages independently predicted how insecure the person was 18 years later, over and above the many other factors which might have influenced this in the inter-vening years. In about two-thirds of cases, people have the same pattern in adulthood as in early childhood*. About 40% of adults are inse-cure*. While being insecure is not in itself a mental illness, studies of 10,500 adults show that the insecure are much more likely to suffer the commonest problems, like depression*. In short, early care creates insecurity that often lasts into adult life, and such people are at greater risk of mental illness.

Interestingly, though, Rebel Julie intuitively knew all this and sometimes overrode Good Julie. I mentioned the idea of Love Bombing; the idea that if an over-three-year-old child has felt emotion-ally deprived in the early years, thereby making them insecure, you can repair the damage by allowing them to behave like a baby or toddler for brief periods, bombarding them with love. Julie told me she had already done a version of this with Leo. When he was 18 months she noticed a subtle way in which he was indicating that he had been upset by the attention his sister was getting – she had arrived when he was aged one. 'I got this sense that he was self-soothing too much, just getting by on his own. I remember one occasion when I got back from work and he carried on with what he was doing, made no fuss that I had arrived. Not long after I had to go out again for an evening work event and he suddenly got really, really upset, having ignored me. I thought "gosh", his apparent contentment was not what it seemed.' She had a think about it and then found a helpful book. 'I read *Raising Boys* by Steve Biddulph, explaining how boys develop more slowly than girls. Love Bombing is a good phrase for what I did, just giving him lots of extra hugs and kisses. I had a visual image that I was having to reach in and get him. So he's a little sweetheart now.' It may be seen that Julie has all the capacities needed to meet her children's needs but that she is completely torn.

Her partner Terry turned out to be a willing and able mother during Leo's first year and for six months after the birth of their daughter, Sarah. 'He was absolutely brilliant with them, great, in a way the best sort of mother, full of energy and very good with them.' However, the relationship finally broke up after this 18-month period and Julie found a nanny. The first was 'useless' and departed after two months; her replacement was 'OK' but she felt the children were suffering. 'I used to come home and they would be crying all the time.' Thankfully, it was third time lucky and they have had the same very satisfactory nanny ever since. 'She's got a lovely way with them. She's incredibly firm, actually, enforces boundaries, but she never raises her voice, is very gentle and very, very playful. They really love her and she handles me very well, makes me feel like the mum. To be honest, I think she makes a better mother than I might have done. She gives them her absolutely undivided attention which I might not have been able to.'

In saying this, she did not sound mournful but I detected elements of the Good Girl Julie at work. I suspect that the Rebel Julie believes she could be as good as the nanny. 'When I got back to work full-time I had this sickening pain and I couldn't work out what it was. One day it came to me: it was like losing a boyfriend, a break-up. I realised, "I'm broken-hearted at being parted from them". Once I recognised that, it made it a bit easier and I learnt to live with it'. Now a mournful note was sounded, sad to hear. 'I was torn in two trying to keep the job going but all the time all I wanted was to go home and see them. I hated the fact that I wasn't really performing at work but the children were my priority. I just lived with the balance that I had, organising things so I could be with them for a few hours in the morning by moving to a house near the office.'

Before returning to work she had decided that this was a part of her 'journey' which she had not anticipated but which was for her, after all. Her idea that the great revolution would come when she junked her career for children had been an illusion. 'I had always been ambivalent about my career but when I returned to work I thought perhaps that incredible drive to get to the top was me after all, not just my mother.' Now she is not so sure. 'I don't know if it was really for me, going back to work, looking at it again. Maybe I do have a lot of my own drive but then I would ask why my confidence levels are so low that I need the constant approval I get from achieving things daily in my career. That's possibly why I have a permanent gut ache, gastric pain, and why I need to have CBT.'

At the end of the interview, Rebel Julie was still fighting the good fight. 'Work is so full-on that I'm not sure I can do it any more. It satisfies me that my role helps so many people but it's the awful office politics, all that shit, which drives me nuts. My guts are hurting, it's a real gut feeling that says "you know what, I just can't take much more of this". It's a tremendous emotional conflict. I am only really happy when at home with the children, they are just so lovely. You can barely catch hold of the years as they slip by and it's going to happen ever faster. I'm still thinking "you do have options, choices, maybe you should step away from work for a bit".' That sounds like someone thinking of giving up work altogether but you would be forgetting just how much drive Julie has. Her final thought was 'I can foresee a time when I would work three days a week, that would be a very nice balance.'

Perhaps we should be grateful for the sacrifice this woman is making in pursuing her career, which greatly benefits us all. Aside from pleasing her mother, she is genuinely motivated to do good for British people. The tragedy is that her real needs, her authentic self, get left out of the plan.

Many modern mothers feel a less dramatic version of this problem, whether they work or not.

Some are like Julie, regarding their work as relatively false and empty compared to being with their children. When they say they want 'something for myself', they mean being at home with the kids. Yet there are a whole lot of other mothers without jobs who say they also need something for themselves. They will tell you that 'something' entails stimulation, status, earning money and suchlike, rather than changing nappies.

It begins to seem like 'heads you lose, tails you lose' until you realise a critical point: each mother needs to understand how her childhood history got her to where she is today and where her true self lies. In the end, the most important conflict for a mother is neither 'work versus not work' nor 'baby routine versus demand-led'. It's 'true self versus false self'.

CHAPTER 4

An Organiser on the Brink of Hugging

Approaches to mothering are not set in stone and mothers of all kinds should do their best to avoid stereotyping themselves. As we shall see, it can be best all round if some Huggers go back to work. By the same token, some Organisers can be amazed to find themselves developing Hugger leanings. However, their deepest motivations can be remarkably similar: having felt neglected as babies. So it is not as odd as it first seems that Organisers can swing across to the opposite approach, without pausing at the halfway house of Fleximum.

Florence (Flo) is an Organiser who developed some Hugger characteristics and who may well, if she has a second child, go the whole Hugger hog. Aged 34, she was raised in a small town in north-east Scotland. She lives in a maisonette in Edinburgh with her seven-month-old son Sammy and husband Tom. She has worked extremely hard to attain her position as the director of audio-visual services in a large media company, while her husband earns a steady income in an insurance company. She chooses her words carefully, sometimes speaking of her life as if it were cinematic, a drama that is happening to someone else. Slender and alert, she is intense, with restless hands and eyes.

Like many Organisers, she did her best to ignore the fact that she was pregnant. Partly, she puts this down to the fact that she was relatively new to her job, with staff to hire and fire, and important decisions to make about updating editing equipment. However, as she repeatedly pointed out to me during the interview, she also realises that she has a tendency to ignore anything tricky in her life. 'I wouldn't say I had a relationship with the foetus as such. It wasn't denial like "I don't want this to happen" but as in all other aspects of my life, I will only deal with things when they are there. The baby was months away. I'm not a "dweller", don't sit around musing. If I'm going on holiday I only read the travel book when I get to the destination.'

Although they had hoped for a natural birth, a Caesarean was required. Flo loathed hospitals. 'I hate any sort of gore at all. Throughout the pregnancy, every time the word hospital came up I stopped listening. When the surgeon started explaining what he was about to do I made it very clear I did not want to know. From the moment they said it was going to be surgery I closed my eyes and kept them closed until Tom brought Sammy to meet me. During the actual C-section Tom distracted me by describing a business meeting he had had that day, in minute detail.'

One might suppose that this level of denial would be inauspicious but what happened when they got home came as a big surprise to Flo. 'Our NCT teacher had given us a really good piece of advice: deny visitors access for a week. For the first couple of weeks we had a very together-as-a-family time. Looking back, it was really lovely. We lived in a beautiful bubble.' She was beginning to sound like a Hugger. 'I was completely and totally astonished that it could be like that. Everything I expected was blown away. Sammy turned out to be the most important thing in the world without question.' The Organiser tendency did try to reassert itself during this special time. 'We're quite "DO-ey" people. On day two of being at home I decided we were going to Mothercare because we hadn't bought anything. I only made it to the post box at the end of the road. Tom and Sammy went without me and I took to the sofa. But about a week after that we went for some proper shopping in Princes Street. I bumped into somebody from my home town and he asked "what are you doing here?" It felt like we were in our own little bubble, just the three of us in the whole world.'

Flo was able to embrace motherhood because she felt supported, reducing her sense that only she was responsible for what was happening. 'Tom has far surpassed my expectations, although I admit I've been good at letting it be "us" doing it. He's quite surprised how bowled over he's been and from really, really early on he's been very involved.' Only three weeks after the birth, Flo went for a hen weekend, something a Hugger would never do – but then there was more than adequate substitute care. 'I went away for two days and a night; he was still feeding every two hours and I'd saved up milk for about two weeks. But it was no problem because Sammy had Tom. There was another time when I had to go away again during the post-pregnancy period. But it was not horrendously traumatic.' Not only was Tom happy to muck in on all the baby care, he is also something of a Domestic God. 'I know other people who have had "house meltdown shambles" scenarios, and I kept waiting for it to happen. But I think the combination of our two personalities evaded it. He's a brilliant cook, totally domesticated. I'm a pile maker and he's not fond of piles, likes things clean and clear.' This combination of Organiser mother and Hugger father can work very well.

On top of Tom's help, his mother provided regular substitute care. Although having Sammy 'had blown my world apart, in a good way', this was fortunate because Flo did not feel her personality was well suited to early mothering. 'I'm not brilliant at chilling, and contemplative lying about. So if Sammy wakes at six I'm fine about getting up and maybe going for a family coffee before daddy has to go to work. I've got one friend who will lie in bed and wait until the baby is ready to go back to sleep, then they'll do that together. I'm terrible at sleeping during the day, I've never done that. I know you're meant to sleep when they do but I tried it once, unsuccessfully, so I've definitely been short of sleep.'

At the point when we met, Flo had only been back at work for a week. For the time being, her boss is happy for her to work a three-day week, and with her mother-in-law and Tom doing the childcare, it's an ideal arrangement. However, she knows that her boss is expecting her to go back to full-time when she is ready, since hers is an important role within the company that in the long term cannot be managed part-time. She is feeling tremendously torn about what to do when the pressure rises to go full-time. Given how rewarding and revolutionary she has found motherhood, I wondered, why does she not wait a few years before returning to work?

Money is not the reason. Although they would need to watch the pennies, they could afford to live on Tom's salary. Like so many of the women I interviewed (and doubtless it would be true of many of their partners too), she is not fascinated or thrilled by her work, as such. 'I don't love my job, I'm certainly not defined by it, definitely a reluctant manager, and I care about it even less now.' But on a practical level, she does worry that if she drops out of her senior position she will not get back in at that level. She has worked hard to get to where she is today and does not want to throw that away, although she would really prefer to be making films, not managing the editing of them. Nor would she much relish telling strangers that she is a housewife – the low status mildly bugs her. But interestingly, so bowled over has she been by motherhood that she feels she could tolerate these dissatisfactions if she stayed at home.

A more profound reason for not doing so is that she does not want to repeat her mother's experience. 'Neither of my parents went to university, though they were smart. They had other interests, a bit hippyish. They divorced when I was eight; my father was a bit flighty. My mum lived for us, still does. I don't want Sammy to be my life because I think that's a hell of a pressure to put on your child.' She feels her successful career was partly the result of having so many hopes vested in her (a very common trend in her generation of women – having a bright mother who was a housewife and did not go to university, wanting her daughter to achieve her unfulfilled ambitions). However, for all this, Flo went on to say that 'I wouldn't say "the mum element" is primary. That is me being a stubborn bugger, wanting it all and wanting it with bells on.' It emerged that what she meant by this was that she is still terrified of two dangers were she to commit wholly to mothering.

The first is that she is already scared of Sammy not needing her. 'At the moment he needs me and it's been completely sustaining me in an entirely compelling use of my time. But deep down I know that he will need me less and less all the time.' This sounds similar to a Hugger and indeed, as noted, Organiser and Hugger psychology can often have the same wellspring: both may have felt very vulnerable and deprived as infants; one (the Hugger) reacts by trying to give the baby the experience she never had, the other (the Organiser) tries to keep the memories of deprivation at bay by reducing its dependence on her as quickly as possible. As we know, Huggers can find the emerging independence of the baby distressing. But an Organiser like Flo goes one further. She forestalls feeling rejected or abandoned by not allowing herself to depend on the baby, or the baby to depend on her, too much in the first place. Flo is much more enchanted by her baby than the average Organiser but has that type of mother's fear of getting to enjoy his company and of settling into the role of full-time mother. As she said of returning to work, 'If I left it too long I'd find it difficult to ever go back.' Sammy is potentially as dangerous as heroin to an addict. Hence, the second great danger of full commitment to motherhood is that it will destroy her.

That was not her first reaction. Initially, she felt a strong desire to stay close to him. 'I'd originally said I would be back to work at four months but when it approached I went into meltdown because I wasn't ready to leave my baby.' Instead, to her astonishment, she preferred to bask in domesticity. 'Until two weeks before returning to work I was in a lovely little bubble, most days going to meet my friends and eat cake and drink coffee, really enjoying it.' But that was only part of the story. 'All the time I was really conscious that it was a bubble that I would need to come out of at some point. *It was only safe so long as I knew it would end.*' This could be the utterance of someone who felt insecure as a child and who is terrified of being let down or rejected as a result. Security with her baby came from knowing she had an escape raft and that it would be her, not the erratic mother of her early childhood, who would determine when it was used. 'Even if it wasn't for two years that I go back to work, I would need to feel that there's going to be something for me. I find it ridiculously satisfying to get up and purée some carrots, get Sammy to eat them and go for a walk. But it's almost felt as if there's a bit of a time bomb – knowing the sort of person that I am – that that won't sustain me in my soul for very long. Also, knowing that it wasn't forever has meant that I can enjoy it. God, that sounds really selfish.' Ostensibly she is right, but at a deeper level I think not. Although a great one for suppressing uncomfortable thoughts and feelings, somewhere she knows there is a real danger for her son, as well as her, if she stays at home without a career option.

The way she puts it is: 'I have an ongoing need for contact with the world, to see and read and do. I hate missing out on things. I have quite an intense need to be engaged.' A Hugger would be getting that from her baby but an Organiser does not see babies as a source of this kind of stimulation. 'I need to engage my brain, not to feel ... almost depressed, I suppose. I think it's because my head goes like this and it implodes' (she gestured with her hands, fingers splayed, moving up and away from her head, meaning her head is exploding with ideas and feelings). Depression was lurking in the shadows. 'I don't think I was sitting still long enough to let the baby blues bite me. There's nothing to stop me giving up work apart from my own belief that I would go mad if all I did was stay at home.'

Logically enough, Flo assumes that Sammy is like her, that he will also 'go mad' if stuck at home for too long. 'At some point he'll want more sociability, in fact, he already does. Just being here at home with one adult is not enough [remember, this is a seven-month-old she is talking about]. He's already incredibly interested in the world, mostly much happier outside seeing stuff than he is with his toys. At the moment, when he's with another child a bit older than him, he looks rather than wants to interact. But soon it might be worth him going somewhere like a nursery, with a few more other children. He might already benefit from less time without other people.' This reveals the difficulty she has in understanding the extent to which babies and small toddlers are largely interested in the company of one responsive adult and get little from other children. It seems clear from her next statement that she is seeing herself in him. 'He's ever so inquisitive, he's not somebody who can be left with one toy for a long time, he gets bored. He needs engagement.' That she used the word 'engagement', one she repeatedly applied to herself, strongly suggests she is experiencing him as the slightly restless person she is herself.

Of course, in theory, he could have simply inherited her personality through genes and in recognising this reality, she is doing him the favour of realising what he needs. As suggested in Chapter 1, I doubt this. Much more probable is that if he is as she describes – and there is always the possibility that he is not – then it is because of the way she relates to him and, in particular, that having attributed to him a need for engagement, she relates to him as if he has this attribute. Crucially, what he needs is not external stimulation (which is what she means by engagement) but responsiveness and love. Supplied with that, if he is as restless as she suggests, there is abundant good scientific evidence that he would quickly calm down*.

But here is the rather wonderful conclusion to this story. Despite everything, at some level it may be that Flo does grasp what Sammy needs and has organised matters so that his needs are met. She has allowed Huggerish Tom to be responsive to him and for all her worries about Sammy needing greater stimulation and a varied social life, she has happily handed Sammy over to Tom's mother to be looked after at home by her during the working week. Tom's mother is the responsive carer Flo cannot quite be and the probable reason why Tom is himself able to be responsive.

Furthermore, while Flo cannot yet quite cope with being at home, if she has a second child she may be an example of an Organiser who switches to Hugger. She is already in two minds. 'I won't let full-time work take up such a large part of my life. I want to be with Sammy during some days in the working week. I'll be a happier, better person if I do. If my boss won't let me do that I'll just have to do something else. I'd never have believed it could be like that but I'm simply not prepared to give as much of myself to my job as I used to.' Regarding the future, she said 'having put it into words speaking to you today, I would now say for sure that if I have another child I have no expectation of going back to work for some years afterwards'.

CHAPTER 5

How Organisers' Childhoods Can Help and Hinder Meeting Their Children's Needs

Among all kinds of mothers, half adopt a similar approach to that of their own mother, and the other half react against it*. This is as true of Organisers as of other types.

In general, if you ask an Organiser why they are like they are, they will either say they do not have a clue, or that genes played a big part. In some cases they will also say they learnt from their parents – like other kinds of mother, they will usually have some views about whether they reacted against, or modelled themselves upon, their own mother. But whereas many Huggers see themselves as rejecting their mothers' strictness by embracing hugs, Organisers hardly ever offer the reverse idea: that they had overly permissive mothers and that their impulse to organise is fuelled by wanting to avoid that with their child (in some interesting respects, the author of *The Contented Little Baby Book*, Gina Ford, is an interesting exception to this rule – see my interview with her: guardian.co.uk/lifeandstyle/2003/jan/29/familyandrelationships. healthandwellbeing).

Commonest among Organisers is that they recall mothering which, if not strict, certainly was firm. There were clear lines and their parents let them know if they crossed them. Insofar as they have thought about it at all, they will tend to report a happy childhood in which everyone knew their place. In Organising, they may see themselves as simply implementing the 'sensible', 'structured' practices which they believe armed them to cope with the world.

As a result, Organisers often have a stoical, no-nonsense, unsentimental approach that can be a strength. One component of being a mother that too few men appreciate is the sheer physicality and organisation demanded. A baby requires someone fit and active, able to cart it around the house, from house to car, from car to pushchair. Keeping house is no holiday either, whether that be washing, cleaning, shopping or cooking. The boundaries and realism that Organisers' parents often provided protect them from fanciful idealism and can make them able to see what is front of their noses – a nappy that needs binning before the house stinks, a baby rash that needs ointment, a system for storing the Infacol or Calpol that needs sticking to so you know where it is the next time you need it. Being so close to the practicalities can also enable blunt truthfulness about their own parenting.

If they do not much enjoy hanging out with babies, for example, it's a great advantage that they may have no compunction in saying they find this boring and that they would rather do something else. There is a refreshing directness about Tracy, in Chapter 2, when she says that she suspects substitute carers will do a better job than her because playing peek-a-boo simply does not ring her bell. She is equally straightforward in spelling out that too much of it could depress her. That she showed little or no sign of guilt about being a working mother makes the whole arrangement much more likely to work for her and her husband, far better than self-deception or paper-thin rationalisation.

Huggers may dismiss a well-stocked larder and efficiently run Organiser household by saying that tidiness or cleanliness are not as important as love when it comes to babies. But at other times they may curse the mess in their own homes, occasionally going so far as to wonder if they have made a bit of a mistake not taking more trouble with these practicalities. Perhaps their partner would be a bit better-tempered. Indeed, it's all very well not bothering with their own appearance (as many Huggers feel is acceptable in the early months) but might it not be quite nice to have got their figure back as much as that Organiser they see looking trim and put-together at the NCT group?

If Organisers' own childhoods hinder them in any way, it may have reduced their capacity to recognise the importance to under-threes of playfulness, of a single responsive adult always being there and of cuddly, unconditional love. If so, they may not appreciate the critical significance of these things in the early years, as outlined in Chapter 1. That can prevent them from realising what kind of substitute is needed when they go back to work. It shows up in the tendency of Organisers to stress the need for six-month-olds to have educative stimulation and playmates, when what they need much more is responsive love and the undivided attentions of a familiar adult tuned into their unique habits.

Although no research has been done into the matter, it is possible that fewer Organisers had Huggers or Fleximums as mothers than other kinds. This may explain the anxiety that babies can prompt in them and the urgency with which they seek to get back their normal adult life. Not responded to as babies themselves, they may find the fragile powerlessness of their baby stirs up that feeling and makes tuning in more difficult – the 'walkie-talkies on different channels' problem. But this apart, there are three particular childhood experiences which can create difficulties for the Organiser: over-controlling mothers; parental divorce; and having had a mother who was a housewife and whose consequent passivity or depression they are desperate to avoid reproducing.

ORGANISERS WHO HAD OVER-CONTROLLING MOTHERS

As we saw in Chapter 3, an over-controlling mother caused Julie to become divided into Good Girl and Rebel. When it came to caring for her children, it was Good Julie who won out, the Organiser. But there are other variants of this pattern.

One is the Organiser who is rendered pathologically perfectionist and overly self-critical by an over-controlling mother*, placing her at particularly high risk of depression or of extreme compensatory activity to keep it at bay. The self-criticism is crucial, easily turning into the refrain of 'I'm fat, I'm stupid, I'm lazy' of the depressive, or equally, into that boss who is prone to temper tantrums at work when you do a job less than perfectly. For example, Joan, aged 35, would have risen considerably higher than her post as store manager in a supermarket chain if she had been less prone to losing her temper. 'I don't know what happens but I am afraid I just see the red mist, and you're never going to make it to head office like that. It just drives me potty when the organic cheeses start getting muddled up with the non-organic ones in the dairy section towards the end of the day. Is it so much to ask that the person responsible for rearranging that section just makes sure it is regularly checked? I know I get too worried about it but I don't see why they can't make a bit more of an effort to get it right.'

When Joan had her first child she became deeply depressed within a month of the birth. 'I just could not stand the level of inefficiency I was displaying. One time, can you believe it, I ran out of formula? What kind of mother starves her baby? There I was trying to get him into a routine and I didn't have anything for him to eat.' Blaming herself as failing, she was saved by her partner. She began raging against him and in doing so, the depression rapidly lifted. Luckily, he was very understanding and although her aggression towards him sometimes reached the physical, they weathered the storm. Back at work when her son was three months old, she is incredibly relieved that period is over. 'No way would I have another kid, not a chance. I love him to bits but thank the lord we survived those early months and I can get back to what I do best.'

Perfectionists can be healthy*. In such cases, they derive very real pleasure from their strivings, which are for the highest standard, but about which they are prepared to be flexible, depending on the situation – they realise that pursuing perfection may carry costs (like excessive worry or workaholia) which are not worth incurring. They may have such high standards in order to gain others' approval to some extent, but this is neither their primary goal nor motive, which is the enjoyment of executing a task exactly as they wished. Above all, so long as they feel they have done their best, that is good enough. If they encounter a limit to their capacities after giving their all, they do not repine.

Unhealthy perfectionists are insatiable and compulsive – they feel as if they have no choice about their standards. For them, 98% is failure, because it is imperfect: what went wrong with the 2%? There is always something that could have been better about their performance. They are usually strongly driven by a fear of parental criticism and many studies show that they are liable to have come from punitive, authoritarian or over-controlling families*. Sometimes these families seem outwardly relaxed and very often the children will say that their parents have never pushed them. The truth is that they were hijacked by impossibly high standards from the early years, a time they cannot remember.

Unhealthy perfectionism is commonest where it is accompanied by severe self-criticism, itself most likely to be provoked by over-control. If a mother is just authoritarian or harshly punitive, the daughter is at greater risk than normal of pathological perfectionism, but it is even more likely if over-control has created hyper self-criticism. The unsavoury phrase 'Helicopter Mothers' is sometimes used to describe over-control. In practice what it means is constant monitoring and analysis of the child's every utterance and action (like a helicopter, hovering over one spot).

In Joan's case, she was an only child. Her mother was highly intelligent and channelled all of her abilities into making Joan perfect. 'When I tell you that my mother had high standards, I really mean it. On the rare occasions I was allowed out to play with other children, I could feel her eyes burning into the back of my head. She would watch me like a hawk. If something went wrong and I grazed a knee, she would say "you cannot jump off walls, you're not athletic. I've warned you about that before, why don't you listen?" ' Joan did her best but her mother always found fault. She grew up so filled with self-critical thoughts that she never did as well as she believes she could have at school. 'Exams were my worst nightmare. I just couldn't get going. If there was an essay I would sit there for 20 minutes planning the answer and then have only 10 to write it. Even then, I would be liable to get stuck on the first line, constantly rewriting it.'

Another offshoot of over-control is Obsessive Compulsive Disorder. Although desperate to have a baby, one mother also dreaded becoming pregnant because she knew she would have to overcome her ritual of tapping every light switch in the house before going out. To her surprise, the baby ended that ritual but instead, she became obsessed with its routines. When it did not eat or sleep according to her wall chart, she would frequently burst into tears.

A final example is where having been over-controlled makes it hard for the Organiser to settle on a substitute carer and stick to her. One mother I interviewed found herself spying on the minder she had left her six-month-old with and horrified to catch her texting her boyfriend when her son was crying. It led to no fewer than five changes in carer before his second birthday, a sequence which is disastrous for an under-three's sense of security. Constantly changing carers, even if they are less than perfect, makes babies and toddlers into an unhappy mixture of angry, scared and detached (R3).

ORGANISERS WHO ARE REACTING TO THEIR PARENTS' DIVORCE

In general, divorce is particularly upsetting to daughters in the long term (boys show greater distress at the time)*. Even more than sons, it makes them vulnerable to depression, educational underperformance and to unstable adult romantic relationships. However, there are many variations in how it takes a girl, depending on where she comes in the family, her particular relationship with each parent and her age at the break-up*.

Diane, an Organiser, is in her late thirties and has three children. Her father went off when she was 12. He was constantly travelling for his work, prone to infidelity. After the divorce, Diane felt she had to keep the family show on the road. As the eldest, even at the tender age of 12 she was very aware that no one else was going to help them 'to fulfil their potential'. She would keep an eye on their school performance and in later life, has continued to see herself as their motivator. She is particularly scathing about her youngest sister, who she feels was over-indulged by her mother, making her into 'a lazy, dozy girl who could be achieving so much more than working as a receptionist in the local arts centre'.

When it came to her own children, she was determined that she would protect them from the impact of divorce and maintains that an Organiser approach is vital for this. She believes it is crucial to get her children into a routine so they do not impact too much on her relationship with her husband. Regarding him, 'I made sure my brain ruled my heart in looking for love', a man hand-picked for his reliability. Having found him, she was determined to hang on to him. 'You have got to help the baby to learn when to eat and sleep. If you let it do whatever it wants from the start, you can easily end up with the sort of shambles we had in my childhood. I want my husband to come home at night to a calm, welcoming home. Frankly, we enjoy our sex life and we enjoy our time together in the evenings. It's best for the children if they are in bed and we keep our relationship alive; in the long term that is the essential core of the family.'

While there are plenty of exceptions, and whether from divorced parents or not, Organisers are more likely to see things this way than Huggers, who often put their relationship with their partner second.

There is no right or wrong about this, in terms of whose relationship will last longest. If it's a Hugger couple who both feel passionately that the needs of the child should come first, that ultimately nourishes their relationship and they would be rowing if one was putting the relationship first. Likewise, disagreement between Organisers: if one was saying they should be putting the baby first and the other prioritising a romantic night at the movies, sooner or later there would be tears before bedtime, not just from the baby. The most important factor is to have a partner who fits with you, usually with the same approach (page 328, R8), although it's not always as simple as having one who is like-minded. It can work very well where a husband is a Hugger, ensuring their child gets support from him that the mother is happy for him to provide. Likewise, not all Hugger mothers end up at daggers drawn with an Organiser husband. So long as he is not too aggressive about it, she may find his desire for order helpful, especially if he channels it into shopping, cooking and washing up.

ORGANISERS WHOSE MAIN GOAL IS NOT TO BECOME A HOUSEWIFE LIKE THEIR MOTHER

Diane's mother did not have a career and Diane vowed never to leave herself as vulnerable as that, making sure to establish herself in a safe occupation which would mean she could always earn a living in the event of her husband leaving. However, there are also plenty of Organisers who have other reasons for not wanting to repeat their mother's housewifery. Some believe their mother's lack of career left her unfulfilled and depressed. Others report a contented housewife mother but stress that they are different creatures, often because they have identified with a more careerist father, to whom they were close, or because their mother used them as a vehicle for unfulfilled aspirations. Whether reacting against desperate housewifery or expressing a parent's aspirations, these women see being Organised as a crucial sign to themselves that they are not turning into their mother.

For example, Rita, 34, came from a tight-knit family. 'Dad was a postal worker with a lot of shift work, and mum eventually did part-time secretarial jobs, once we were at school. I was determined not to end up like her so I applied myself to exams, got a career that brings in steady money.' Her mother was someone whose horizons were limited. 'It frustrates me even now that she does not have more personal ambition. She lived for us, devoted herself to being a mother. I am sure that is why she was depressed for most of our childhood.' While Rita is grateful that her parents were so stable, 'I would feel very claustrophobic living that kind of life and above all, I do not want to be depressed.'

When Rita became a mum she strongly associated Hugger-like patterns of nurture with her mother. Being an Organiser suited her better on a practical level, since she was determined to keep her career going, but she also would begin to feel strangled by even the idea of having the baby in the bed or feeding it on demand. She and her mother had some major falling outs over Rita's approach. 'In one way it was horrible because I love my mum, but in another it sort of made me think that I was doing the right thing. If my mum disapproved of how I was doing it, I could be sure that I wasn't turning into her!' Organising and avoiding her mother's depression became almost indistinguishable. 'I stuck closely to the books that help you work out a routine. That way I could be sure my babies would be ready for nursery when the time came and that way I could be sure they would not have to deal with a depressed me.'

Overall, difficulties with responsive tuning in are the commonest legacy of Organisers' childhoods. Instead, they can be overly concerned with stimulation and the idea that their little ones need friends. This is especially problematic if the Organiser exaggerates the importance of genes in how their child turns out. If they are convinced genes are crucial, the Organiser can persuade themselves it only really matters that the child is fed and clothed, the kind of care provided is not that important (page 314, R7).

But whatever theories they subscribe to, most Organisers do realise that love and responsiveness are important. Some provide it themselves all day long, but most find a substitute. So long as that substitute is right, it works just fine, for everyone concerned.

CHAPTER 6

Practical Organiser Top Tips

RELAX AND ENJOY ORGANISED MOTHERHOOD

Organisers can be 'get up and go' sort of people and if so, rarely find the slowness and inactivity of the rhythms of the early months simpatico. An Organiser may be used to a fast-moving day at the office, on and off the phone, in and out of meetings, firing off emails, trying to keep ahead of the game. Suddenly you find yourself spending hours on end doing nothing but breastfeed your baby or listen to it making incoherent goo-goo, ga-ga noises. While you feel love for it, you may also feel somewhat mystified by how anyone can find a baby enthralling company. You may not have felt inclined to try some basic games with it, like seeing if you can catch its eye, then looking away, then looking back, or imitating its noises back with the same pitch and rhythm. Or you may have done that and bought the T-shirt (and wiped the sick off it), but feel it's time for something else. Either way, when you meet other mothers who gush about how wonderful it is being with their babies, it's easy to feel there must be something wrong with you or your baby, or equally, to have some fairly venomous thoughts about those mothers ('wallowing in babyishness is about all their infantilised minds can cope with', 'flaunting their Earth Mother pretensions to escape having to go back to work', that kind of thing). Preferable to these reactions would be to feel that there is nothing wrong with your set-up, nor is there any need to trash others to make yourself feel better. But how do you get to be cool, chilled, comfortable in your skin, proud to be an Organiser?

One important skill is in dealing with media information that makes you feel bad (R4). Newspaper articles and TV documentaries seem to assail you from all sides suggesting you are wrecking your baby's life by wanting to return to work. Ironically, the Hugger feels just as under siege, except in her case she feels unsupported by the government and attacked by 'having it all' newspaper columnists for wanting to stay at home. It's only the Fleximum who feels relatively unscathed by public commentary*.

The way out is for you to be completely honest with yourself about what you are feeling and then to decide what is best for you and your baby, preferably with your partner's support. So long as you are confident you understand what is going to work for you, you can regard all the commentary with interest and sometimes wry amusement. At the heart of your Organiser approach must be four considerations:

⟨ The needs of under-threes are the same everywhere, as described in Chapter 1. You are going to ensure they are met, but in your own way and not necessarily by you, 24/7

⟨ Responding to babies and tuning into them may be something you actually find very difficult or largely impossible, or else, it may be something you can do but find deathly dull. If so, it is much better from the baby's standpoint to find someone else to be the main carer during the working week, and to return to your paid job. Hopefully you have found the examples provided in preceding chapters helpful – many are women who have been remarkably honest about their feelings about caring for under-threes. If you have figured this out and come to similar conclusions, you know you are doing the right thing and it does not matter what other people write in newspapers or say on radio programmes or on TV: you are the person who knows best about your particular situation

⟨ It is not a con or a self-deception for you to conclude that your baby will get a lot more out of you if you are in a good mood, vitalised by your paid job. Put the other way around, it would be potentially very harmful for your baby if you were caring for it full-time and became depressed (page 326, R8). It is more important that you have well-being, for the baby as well as for you. As several mothers described to me in the preceding chapters, they knew they would be depressed by feeling under-stimulated by the company of a baby. However, in some cases, I suggest, they do make an important error in assuming that it is the baby who needs stimulation: babies need tuned-in responsiveness, not the kind of stimulation which adults need. It's important to grasp that what you need and what they need are very different. Not getting depressed yourself is one thing, ensuring that your under-three is getting its needs met is another

⟨ Most parents want to maximise the long-term social and academic success of their child. But take on board the idea that, perversely, from the baby and toddler's standpoint, living in the moment and putting everything else on hold might achieve that more than trying to speed up its development at this stage*

Of course, you may be like Flo in Chapter 4. She believes she will turn into a Hugger if another child comes along, or at least, that she will want to be a full-time mother (perhaps compromising as a Fleximum). That is fine, it does not mean you are flaky or going to be giving one child a better deal than the other. So long as you organise for the needs of your under-three to be met, it will be tickety-boo. So a critical issue for the Organiser is how to find good substitute care. I will come to that in a few pages' time, but first, some important prior points ...

BEWARE OF BELIEVING 'IT'S IN THE GENES' (SEE PAGE 314, R7)

As an Organiser, you are more likely than other kinds of mother to assume that genes play quite a big part in how your child ultimately turns out. As you probably know, this is a highly contested matter (see *They F*** You Up* for my account of the evidence, and Robert Plomin's *Nature and Nurture During Infancy and Early Childhood* for a scientific account of the opposite view). Actually, the scientific whys and wherefores need not concern us here. Much more important is the evidence that mothers who believe genes are critical are at greater risk of not meeting their children's needs and of reducing the likelihood of the child fulfilling its potential.

This applies even in those few cases where biology or genetics have been established beyond much doubt to play a crucial role, such as in pre-term babies or cases of autism*, but even in these latter, nurture can help a lot. If genes have altered the limits of what you can expect of your child, it is still enormously helpful to the child if you believe you can help them, resulting in more positive care that is also proven to result in better outcomes (within the parameters of the disability)*.

To start with, as described in Chapter 1, it is now accepted by almost all authorities (including geneticists) that differences in the way babies behave in the early months are unaffected by genes, except in a tiny minority of extreme cases, like autism. Exigencies of the pregnancy and birth explain why babies are more or less irritable, floppy, fussy and so on, and whether these differences disappear or not depends on the care the baby receives. Hence, even if it is true (which it may not be) that genes become increasingly influential as the first three years progress, in most cases, what is crucial early on is the way you, or whoever cares for the baby, relates to it. While putting how it turns out down to genes may take the pressure off you, it really is not the best way to think about the situation. In order to meet your baby's needs it's important to grasp that responsiveness and tuning in are going to make a big difference. It's no good just making sure the baby has enough milk, nappies and clothes, and for the rest of it saying to yourself 'Genes play such a big part, it's born with its personality.' How you relate to it early on has a huge impact on what sort of toddler, and ultimately adult, it becomes.

BEWARE OF IMAGINING YOUR UNDER-THREE IS 'A LITTLE DEVIL' (SEE PAGE 314, R7)

It's understandable to attribute intentions to your under-three that they do not possess. You can easily feel they are winding you up by crying just as you are getting comfortable with a cup of tea. You may feel you can see it in their eyes, even as babies. When a little girl baby coos at her father, many are the times that the mother will only half-joke that she is flirting with him, although the baby has no idea what that even is. When an 18-month-old chucks the food on the ground for the tenth time, a lot of parents feel it is doing so to annoy them, rather than a standard response of that age group to that situation – nothing personal, just a developmental stage.

Of critical importance is not to start believing that your baby or toddler is in control, that you are somehow at its mercy, a victim. Parents with what is called a 'low perception of control' are more likely to blame their under-threes for negative interactions or behaviour. That imputation makes them more liable to react harshly and less sensitively – the mother thinks the 'little swine' is deliberately, wilfully, intentionally playing up, which naturally makes her angry and leads to her punishing the child to teach it not to be so naughty. If the baby is born a bit difficult – fussy, floppy, irritable – parents who were already expecting from before the birth not to be able to cope are at even greater risk of feeling they have no control. Such mothers are at greater risk of becoming depressed.

You must never lose sight of the fact that babies are tiny little things who cannot even feed themselves, let alone walk and talk, and that you are the one in control, however much it might not seem that way at 3am as you stagger towards the cot for the fourth time since you first put your head down. This is equally true when your two-and-a-half-year-old throws a wobbler in the supermarket because you refuse to buy the sweeties. It cannot control itself at that moment, but hopefully, you can.

Once you realise who is boss, it does not mean you necessarily need to turn into a tyrant. As an Organiser, of course your inclination is to get the child organised. But do not let that deceive you about what is really appropriate for such an undeveloped being. While it is possible to train them to eat and sleep to order – though not at all easy and a great many who follow routines give up – it's always best if you can take your lead from them in the early months and first year. If a routine is important to you, build it as much as possible around what suits the baby, starting very early. If it seems to like a sleep after its first feed, go with that and work forwards from there. When it wakes up, it won't be expecting any more kip for a bit, so no need to try until it looks as if it's getting sleepy again. Rather than applying an inflexible rule, such as 'now it must not sleep for another four hours', try to read the baby's cues.

Although you are tuning into its needs and using them to establish the shape of the 24-hour cycle, you are still in charge. Unlike you, the baby has no choice in the matter. Despite appearances, you are the one with all the power.

KNOW THYSELF 1: YOUR CHILDHOOD

As an Organiser, you may not be a great one for dwelling on the past, but it's surprising how helpful you may find even a basic grasp of the origins of your ideas about mothering.

For example, your Organiser approach is very likely, to some extent, to be either a reaction against the way your mother cared for you ('too permissive', 'chaotic', 'no boundaries' you may say) or a duplication of it ('it worked for my mother, it works for me'). Fine, if you are completely happy with all aspects of the approach, it may not matter where it came from. But hardly anyone is like that. You are almost bound to regret some of your reactions as a mother, like the things that make you lose your temper or the things you worry you do not do well enough.

A top tip for dealing with these is to ask yourself if you feel absolutely compelled to do them. If so, you will often find that this is because you are either reacting against or mindlessly duplicating what was done to you. Just realising this can be a liberation, in matters tiny or huge. One mother felt compelled to iron all the Babygros. A very busy woman, she knew it was a crazy waste of her valuable time but she just could not bear to see them piled in the cupboard unless they were pristine and unrumpled. As soon as I asked her what attitude her mother might have had to such matters she was released from serving time at the ironing board. It was as simple as that, just realising she was pointlessly paying homage to a futile ritual invented by her mother.

On a much larger scale, another mother found herself getting hypercritical of the minder. Asked in detail, she agreed that the minder was doing a great job with her 19-month-old, providing clear boundaries but also buckets of love. However, she could not get away from the feeling that the minder was too disorganised and a poor timekeeper, even though, when pressed for examples, she could see they were not very convincing or, at least, that they were not really important in the grand scheme of things. It was only when she began to describe the chaos that her own mother had created that she understood her problem. She was so anxious to avoid re-creating the untidy kitchen, mountains of unwashed clothes and erratic rules that had been her own childhood that she could not help feeling that the minder was guilty of these, even though she knew this was not true.

At a deeper level, as we saw in the examples in earlier chapters, Organisers can be adversely affected if their mothers were over-controlling, harsh, authoritarian or perfectionist. These are the exception: by no means are all Organisers 'control freaks'. But if you are one, it's best to get help. I give more detail about what kind of help in the section below entitled 'What do I do if mothering is driving me bonkers because I had an over-controlling mother who deprived me of love?'.

KNOW THYSELF 2: RECONCILING YOUR WORKER AND MOTHER IDENTITIES (R5, R6)

The risk for the Hugger is not just that she has no confidence when it's time to go back to work, having lost track of her worker identity. It's also that her whole self gets left on the shelf and she feels seriously bewildered, lost and depressed: her needs have been over-subordinated to those of her under-three.

The Organiser runs a different risk: ricocheting between mummy and worker identities.

Half of mothers who work full-time report feeling a constant and severe sense that they are being torn in half. While a few try to bind themselves together again by working from home and even fewer try taking the child to work (especially if there is a crèche provided), it rarely reduces the terrible tension. As we saw in several of the cases described in this part, the anguish can be heart-rending. No wonder that mothers of under-threes who work full-time are the most at risk of depression (at-homers come next, then part-timers – see page 326, R8).

One way of coping is to put your different lives in different boxes. As we saw in Chapter 2, Tracy felt this worked for her. For a long time she had no pictures of the children in her office and deliberately excluded thoughts about them when there, resisting the temptation to make any calls to check how they were getting on. Likewise, when at home, she did her best to seal herself off from work. If some had to be done, it was dealt with only when the children were out of the way, asleep.

That Tracy has made this work for her is evident, but only 17% of full-timers use it as a strategy (page 310, R6). Most find they cannot be as disciplined as Tracy or are too emotionally torn to stick to it, so that worries about one domain keep crashing into the other. While Tracy finds it possible not to have to retire to the loo for a sob, a lot of others do so. Instead of using different boxes, they end up using 'blending', in which they try to feel they can be both mummy and worker, as required, whether at work or home. But alas, alack, this rarely works either. Without the strict walls erected by a Tracy, one world has a way of bleeding into the other (email and BlackBerries do not help, in this regard).

So what's the answer? I believe it follows from the issues raised in the previous section regarding your fundamental motivations and level of self-knowledge. What you are looking to be is an Organiser who is *comfortable in her skin*. I appreciate how hard this is. As I have tried to explain in some previous books (*Britain on the Couch*, *Affluenza* and *The Selfish Capitalist*) there is a host of very powerful forces at work in the modern world which explicitly seek to achieve the opposite, to make you wish you were someone else. Some are obvious, like the declared intention of advertisers to do their best to make you dissatisfied not only with your possessions but with your very self, in order to get you to buy new products and services. Some are more complex, like the rise in individualism since the 1950s, which can make us feel that we cannot keep up with the Joneses. These pressures apply to all kinds of mother but for the Organiser, the specific difficulty is that her upbringing and society pressurise her to develop the skin of a chameleon, constantly changing according to context, rather than encouraging her to stick to one colour.

More than any other kind of mother, therefore, the earlier that an Organiser can see that is what she is like, the better. Having correctly defined yourself as not a Hugger or Fleximum, at least with regard to this under-three, you can do your best to relax about that. Yes, there will be endless stuff in the media trying to unsettle you but so long as you really understand who you are and what your trajectory is, personally and professionally, hopefully you can just shrug this stuff off if it upsets or annoys you, and yet still remain open and calm, able to learn from what is useful.

I admit that this is a tall order. Alas, in my experience, very few people of either gender or any age are truly very comfortable in their skin. A veritable wardrobe of costumes is available, from smug certainty, defensive pedagogy and moralising, to bland but insincere 'live and let live' relativism. Your chances of feeling OK about your life will be greatest if you can just acknowledge that you feel a certain way about caring for under-threes, satisfied that, having made successful arrangements regarding substitute care, this is genuinely all right for you and for your children, and yes, you do want to feed your worker identity as well as your baby. This 'reframing' as it is known (page 312, R6), will help you to avoid constantly comparing your decisions with those of other mothers and so long as you can get your partner with this programme, you can enjoy your life without excessive guilt (never forgetting that a measure of guilt is actually healthy if we are to properly consider the feelings and needs of others – only psychopaths feel no guilt at all).

With these thoughts in mind, let us briefly consider how the normal hurdles of mothering under-threes impact on Organisers.

PREGNANCY DENIAL

If you are one of those Organisers who largely tries or tried to pretend the pregnancy was not happening, there is one important body of evidence that you need to take on board*. This measured how mothers felt in pregnancy and then examined whether this was connected with how the child turned out. It revealed a strong independent impact of high levels of stress in the last three months of the pregnancy (known as the third trimester), including measurement of cortisol, the fight-flight stress hormone. Even when the children had reached the age of 10, there was still an effect if the mother had been stressed in the third trimester. The high levels of cortisol are passed through the placenta to the foetus and when it is born, it is already liable to have abnormal cortisol levels. This is still the case at the age of 10, expressed in such problems as anxiety, attention deficits, hyperactivity and behavioural problems. The levels in the third trimester continue to predict these troubles even after you take into account the other known causes of them, like whether the mother got depressed after the birth or whether the child had been put into low-quality day care at an early age.

The implication of this evidence for an Organiser is to cut out stressful experiences as much as possible during the third trimester, but that does not necessarily mean you need to go and sit on a beach and do nothing. You probably like to keep busy and it may be that nothing is more annoying to you than the endless exhortations of your partner or mother to take it easier. Indeed, there are probably some Organisers who find it least stressful if their work is full on, even though most other people would feel that was incredibly wearing.

So you need to carefully evaluate yourself during this time. If keeping busy is what keeps you calm, then fine. Less satisfactory is if you have got addicted to a high-cortisol, high-pressure life and simply cannot let up – you will probably be passing high cortisol to the foetus. If that is the case you are going to need to learn to relax, something that you may have been thinking for years but have been unable to do.

Apart from all the clichés, there is only one measure I can unequivocally guarantee: some kind of daily practice in which you switch off has been shown in many studies to reduce stress. I am not advocating alternative therapy quackery; these methods really do work*. Some people find meditation is best, others that it is yoga, others massage, others still jogging. It really does not matter which. In my case, for the last 20 years I have done 10 minutes of very simple yoga, morning and evening, without which, I can honestly say, I would soon go bonkers. Admittedly, I have never been pregnant.

As part of knowing thyself, therefore, you need to take the trouble to work out what is really going to work for you during the third trimester. Keeping busy may be fine but if you do one new thing that you have never done before, my advice is to take up a daily practice which gets you out of the normal stressful zone of everyday life.

BIRTH HORROR

It's easy for a man to say, but I believe there is good reason to suspect that the degree of focus by modern women on the manner of birth is sometimes a displacement of anxiety about what will happen once it is over. I am not trying to pretend giving birth is like shelling peas. I can never know exactly how painful and scary it is, and it is a fact that it can be a dangerous, even occasionally fatal, process. But the really scary bit for a great many women, and especially for Organisers, often begins around two weeks after the birth, when the visitors and flowers stop coming and in our miserably atomistic society, the mother suddenly finds herself left holding the proverbial.

Rather than focusing on the birth, it is far more important for the Organiser to start getting herself plugged into a social network that will support her. The research shows that Organisers are especially at risk of depression if they do not feel they have friends or family to rely on, or their partner is not pulling his weight*.

Rich Organisers tend to start looking for maternity nurses, doulas and nannies, while the less affluent majority turn to neighbours, friends and family*. But whether rich or poor, what you need to challenge is any reluctance to hook up with other pregnant mums and, after the birth, other new mums. Shy or standoffish Organisers really need to override those tendencies at this point in their life. If necessary, get therapy during the pregnancy if this is really going to be a problem (see below for advice on what sort – Cognitive Analytic Therapy is probably best if you are shy).

Be sure to join an antenatal class during your first pregnancy, as it's a vital mother and baby dating agency. You might find some of the information interesting but by far the most important thing when you have your first child is to have other mothers nearby who are in exactly the same boat as you. Social isolation is the greatest threat to any mother's sanity in the early months. However much you may find it hard to enjoy sitting around nattering about breastfeeding and the mechanics of nappies, this contact is really important for keeping you sane. You also learn a lot about how to care for your baby. Modern mothers increasingly rely on their peers, rather than their own mothers, for tips and reassurance about how to do the job. Do not allow your horror of being hijacked by the baby's needs and of turning into a brain-dead milk machine lead you to reject hooking up with other mothers. Beware of feeling that everyone else seems to be getting on with their baby brilliantly except you – be sure that many other mothers will be feeling just the same, even if it is not obvious. Organisers are tremendously prone to believing there is a 'right' way to be doing it, and to imagining that they are failing to read the right books or put the techniques into practice. Resist these feelings with all your force: there is no such thing as the 'right' way and always remember that your best is good enough, that no parenting is ever perfect and that the kind of mothering you are aiming for only needs to be good enough. This phrase was invented by Donald Winnicott, a famous psychoanalyst, and he meant that no baby's needs can ever be completely met. Let yourself off the hook: perfection is impossible in this domain. The baby will be absolutely fine and dandy so long as someone is tuning in and responding for a reasonable amount of time.

It's unfamiliar to be at home all day with a baby, but do not panic, there is almost certainly another woman out there within walking distance who you can bond with and who will want to share the difficulties, as well as the joys. You are best off finding that woman before the birth, but for that to happen, you do need to recognise that you are pregnant! Pretending nothing is going on during the pregnancy or obsessing about what kind of birth you want distracts you from the real challenge: responding to and tuning into your newborn.

WHAT IF I AM ACTUALLY NOT RESPONDING OR TUNING IN?!

1: Where the Cause is Depression (R8)

Not being able to feel love for a baby is some mothers' greatest fear. It can take hours or days or even weeks to really feel it. Yes, there is a tiny number of mothers who never feel it.

In some cases, the lovelessness is the result of depression, in which case you obviously need help: get past the depression and you will nearly always find the love is there.

Nearly four in five mothers suffer some sort of baby blues in the first month after giving birth, but 13% develop a full-blown depression. If this hits you, it has massive implications for the whole family as well as yourself.

Geneticists have now mapped the human genome. Until very recently, it looked as if a particular gene might be a significant cause of depression, along with early childhood experience. However, it has now been shown that this gene is very probably not a cause of depression and it is looking quite possible that genes do not play a big part in causing it*. Hormonal fluctuations very probably do play a part in causing baby blues, at least in some cases to some degree. But the key factors are your own childhood experience, alongside what sort of society you live in, and what class within it (page 323, R8). So you really do have very good reason to seek out a therapist who can help you to grasp the childhood causes of your problem and who accepts that genes are not likely to be of great significance.

Assuming you have a choice, which treatment should you opt for? The main alternatives are antidepressants, Cognitive Behavioural Therapy (CBT) and psychodynamic psychotherapy.

In the great majority of cases, even when antidepressant pills do have an effect it is a placebo – people given chalk pills but told they are antidepressants are almost as likely to claim to feel better as people given the real thing*. While they may be of temporary assistance, they are not a cure. People who find them helpful tend to get depressed again when they stop taking the pills.

Regarding the talking cures*, in one study, depressed new mothers were randomly assigned to eight sessions of CBT, or to counselling, or to psychodynamic psychotherapy. Four and a half months later, the ones given dynamic therapy were most likely to have recovered (71%, versus 57% for CBT, 54% counselling). If CBT is all that is available, then it is certainly better than nothing. Hold out for a therapist who is warm and prepared to deviate from strict CBT manuals – willing to provide more than a handful of sessions and to talk about childhood causes of problems. I realise this is tough if you are depressed with a newborn. That makes it vital that partners take a big interest in what kind of care is being offered and don't just go along with the tendency of GPs to dole out pills or CBT. If you can pursue the alternative, I would strongly advocate doing so.

For many years psychoanalysis was written off as unscientific because untestable as a theory, but studies done in the last 15 years have largely confirmed Freud's basic ideas*. Dreams have been proven to contain meaning – they are not just a mental rubbish bin. Early childhood experience has been shown to be a major determinant of adult character and of what sort of parent you are. And it is now accepted by almost all psychologists that we do have an unconscious and that it can contain material which has been repressed because unacceptable to the conscious mind.

The treatment Freud's theory gave rise to entailed patients attending 50-minute sessions up to five times a week, lying on a couch and speaking whatever entered their mind. Childhood relations with parents were used to interpret dreams and their relationship to the analyst.

Although slow to be tested, the clinical technique has now been demonstrated to work. The strongest evidence for its long-term superiority over cognitive, short-term treatments was published in 2008*. Initially, eight to 20 sessions of short-term CBT-like therapy reduced depression and anxiety, more so than going two or three times a week for psychoanalytic therapy. However, after three years, those receiving the long-term psychoanalytic treatment were dramatically better off: less likely to be depressed and four times more likely to have recovered from anxiety. A recent survey of 23 other studies had similar findings*.

Many studies show that the sort of person a therapist is – especially whether they are warm – is more important than their orientation*. There are undoubtedly some very good CBT therapists (despite, rather than because of, their training) and some appallingly bad psychoanalysts.

Since hardcore CBT explicitly rejects scrutiny of parental care in the early years and close attention to the therapist–client relationship, it will never be of enduring, profound value to distressed people. If it's all that's on offer, look for one who will deviate from the manuals and offer more sessions.

If you can afford it and if you are still only pregnant, a crash course in understanding your childhood is provided by the highly imaginative

Hoffman Process (see hoffmaninstitute.uk). This residential eight-day roller coaster might not sound like the sort of thing to do during pregnancy but I can vouch for its success in several cases of women who have done it then.

Otherwise, to find a psychoanalytic therapist, go to the British Psycho-analytic Council website at www.psychoanalytic-council.org/main/. What you are looking for is someone who answers 'yes' to these questions:

'Are you aware that the latest evidence shows that depression does not appear to be much caused by genes and that the care a person received early in life is proven to be highly significant?'

'Are you familiar with Attachment Theory, and is it help with my attachments that you will provide?'

'Will you focus primarily on the way my childhood is causing my depression?'

In asking these questions, do not let the therapist get away with evasions – repeat the question, firmly insisting on a proper answer. For example, if they reply to the first question by saying 'I think both genes and early care are important factors in what a baby is like' maybe you could say 'I'm sorry, it sounds to me like you are sitting on the fence. Please give me a specific example of something you believe was largely or partly caused by genes.' If you still have doubts about the therapist you can email me with your query via www.selfishcapitalist.com.

2: Where It's Not Because of Depression

Plenty of mothers feel cack-handed, at sixes and sevens, or just that the baby seems like an incommunicative blob. If so, you will hugely benefit from mother–infant psychotherapy, although a parenting course may suffice.

The trouble with parenting courses is that they are sometimes prone to teach parenting as if it is a matter of training a pet, rather than a human. They may encourage you to impose inflexible routines or to employ unhelpful naughty chairs.

Where they are at their best, parents meet in groups and help each other to talk about what is bothering them and jointly discover solutions. So long as the therapist/convenor encourages parents to talk about their own childhoods, and so long as they do not offer simplistic behavioural solutions, this can be tremendously helpful. You can find a parenting course via www.parentinguk.org and following the links to search for a course near you. However, if you are really not responding or tuning in, you probably need something more specialised.

Parent–infant psychotherapy* entails helping you to understand the feelings that your baby is evoking in you, or the lack thereof, by exploring what happened in your own childhood. It usually takes at least six sessions. Sometimes it is helpful to video yourself with your baby, or they will video you together, and by watching the way you react, you get a feel for what is going on. You are helped to see what your baby is trying to communicate to you, its needs. One of these is for face-to-face interactions; above all, eye-to-eye contact, smiling and gesturing. Gradually you may come to find the baby an entertaining companion, be able to play.

Provision of such help is patchy around the country. This would not be so if the government during the last 13 years had devoted the money it spent on setting up day care centres to a massive expansion of parent–infant psychotherapy.

In London, you can find The Bowlby Centre, The Anna Freud Centre and The Tavistock Centre, which have world experts in this field. In Oxford there is OXPIP, the Oxford Parent Infant Project. For other regions, you can go to www.aimh.org.uk, the website of the Association of Infant Mental Health (UK), and email them asking where your nearest parent–infant psychotherapy provision might be.

I realise you probably have rarely felt less like searching for a therapy, especially one that you may not have much stomach for. It might be that you could ask your partner or another intimate to look into it for you. But I strongly recommend that you pursue this, if you possibly can. Your lack of responsiveness or tuning in are nearly always completely curable and it will come as a huge relief for you to overcome the obstructions to your doing so, quite apart from being of great help to your baby.

WHAT DO I DO IF MOTHERING IS DRIVING ME BONKERS BECAUSE I HAD AN OVER-CONTROLLING MOTHER WHO DEPRIVED ME OF LOVE?

Just as there is a small minority of Huggers who become really quite disturbed because they cannot let go as their baby develops an increasing need for independence, so there are a small number of Organisers who find themselves cracking up. However, whereas the trigger for Hugger crack-ups happens later, rarely before four months, for Organisers the trigger is the very infantilism of the baby, its extreme dependence, in the early months.

Some of these Organisers may be driven high-achievers with the Type A Personality described in Chapter 3. Others might not be so outwardly successful but have rigid, inflexible personalities, finding the chaos and disruption to normal adult life intolerable.

The cause of the problem often lies in their early infancy, coupled with harsh, authoritarian, punitive subsequent care. High-achievers, like Julie in Chapter 3, they may have been hijacked at an early age as vehicles for the fulfilment of their mother's ambitions.

If this is what you are like, you need psychoanalytic psychotherapy. A fascinating book which explains why it will help is, oddly enough, a biography of a famous psychoanalyst called Masud Khan. Entitled

False Self, by Linda Hopkins (who is a psychoanalyst), it explains how early infantile deprivation and subsequent harsh treatment result in a carapace which acts as a barrier between the person and their true feelings, as well as falsehood in their relationship to others. The best treatment is to find a therapist who can be completely trusted and with whom there is what is known as 'regression to dependence' – your babyish, dependent, vulnerable feelings can be allowed and, in experiencing them, you may be freed from the need to be so false.

Finding such a therapist is not easy, always assuming you can afford the time and money it entails. However, there are provisions made by some organisations for free or low-cost sessions. In finding such a psychodynamic therapist you would follow the advice in the section before last, asking the same questions, with this additional one:

> 'I believe my difficulties may stretch back to early infancy. Do you have experience of the Middle Group method known as "regression to dependence"? Would you expect that to form a significant part of our work together?'

COPING WITH DIFFICULT BABIES

Few if any mothers find it easy if their baby is born irritable, fussy, floppy or easily upset. But some Organisers find it particularly difficult.

The commonest problem is to feel that these traits are a rejection, to take them personally. If you are that kind of person, you will be liable to deal with rejection by rejecting*. It is easy to find yourself trying to tame the little devil, perceiving it as bad and malevolent. You may then punish it by leaving it to cry or ignoring it, a natural response if you feel it is getting at you.

Of course, there is nothing personal about its difficultness. It's the result of the exigencies of the pregnancy or birth (or in a tiny minority of cases, may have to do with genes). Whoever was trying to look after it would have the same problem. But if you start cold-shouldering it, a vicious cycle develops: baby rejects you, you reject it back, it gets even more difficult, you become even more distant or angry.

The other big problem is if you experience the baby's difficultness as evidence either that you have failed to find the right mothering methods, or that it suggests you are not applying the method correctly. This leads quickly to guilt and more or less self-attacking thoughts and depressive mood. Again, you need to take a deep breath and realise that the difficultness is not your fault, nothing personal.

The solution in both cases is to remind yourself that you are only looking to achieve good enough mothering and, above all, to remember that if you hang on in there, even though it is going to take a matter of months, the baby will cease being difficult. You have to feel empathy for it but you also have to give yourself a break, try to relax and ride it out.

ORGANISER BREASTFEEDING

Some Organisers who know they will be returning to work at six months understandably have mixed feelings about breastfeeding. If you get the little lovely addicted to breastfeeding , how easy is it going to be, literally, to wean it off?

Fear not, there is no reason why this should be a problem. Three months of breastfeeding is going to supply well-established medical advantages to your baby's immune system. There is also the fact that the process of feeding can help you to bond. Weaning to a bottle is normally not a problem.

Regarding how to do it, unfortunately, and rather shockingly, training of health visitors in the best methods for helping mothers is patchy. (For excellent advice, go to www.bestbeginnings.info; it's worth watching their DVD, given out to many mothers by NHS health visitors. Go to 'resources for you', find 'i'm a parent' and scroll down to the DVD.) If you are lucky, you will get a midwife who is skilled in the technique identified by Chloe Fisher and Sally Inch, the World Health Organization's experts. This is described in a book, *Bestfeeding* (2004, Celestial Arts) by Mary Renfrew et al. Interestingly, they have done studies showing that colic is twice as common in mothers who do not always drain one breast at a time.

When my wife had difficulties with our son we visited Chloe at her clinic in Oxford (now – disgracefully – closed). In a *Guardian* article I described her advice as follows (for the full article go to www.guardian.co.uk/lifeandstyle/2005/mar/30/familyandrelationships.healthandwellbeing):

Chloe enunciated two principles: 'First, Don't assume the breast is like a bottle. The milk is in the breast, not in the nipple whereas with a bottle, the milk is in the teat. To feed effectively from the breast the baby must scoop in a deep mouthful of breast whereas with a bottle, it can just suck on the end of the teat. Secondly, people wrongly assume the middle of the baby's mouth is halfway between the top and bottom lip. In fact, the middle is between the upper surface of the tongue and the upper palate. For the baby to draw sufficient breast tissue into its mouth, it must be able to get its tongue well away from the base of the nipple and that won't happen unless the breast is presented between the tongue and the upper palate.' If the baby does not attach properly, it will not drain the breast properly and would continuously compress the nipple between the tongue and hard palate turning it into something resembling minced lamb.

Putting this into practice proved surprisingly difficult but after a bit my wife got the hang of it. Next came the other important point: 'Only switch breasts when the well-attached baby comes off the breast spontaneously and seems completely satisfied. In offering the second breast, let the baby decide whether he wants it. When coming to the next feed, if the mother starts on alternate breasts (regardless of whether the baby has had one or two at a feed) the breasts will get roughly even use. The important thing is to allow the baby to "finish the first breast first".' Failing to do this was the main cause of colic.

Chloe explained that the initial milk is low in fat and calories. If you switch breasts before the high-fat milk has been drunk the baby will take more from the second breast than he would otherwise have done. Despite the relatively huge volume of liquid in its tum, the baby will then be wanting another feed before long, because low-fat feeds are processed quickly, leading to a pattern of very frequent feeding. This is mental illness-inducingly sleep-depriving but worst of all, it will cause colic.

Both poor attachment and breast switching result in the baby taking frequent, large-volume, low-fat feeds which in turn lead to rapid emptying of the stomach into the large intestine. If too much gets there too fast, there is not enough of the enzyme lactase to break the sugar in the milk (lactose) down. The gut turns into a malfunctioning brewery, with fermentation of the sugar in the excess milk creating gas and explosive poohs. The crying, arched back, rigid tummy and irritability of colic follow.

You may find it oppressive to be reminded of the benefits of breast-feeding if you are an Organiser who is intending to return to work and have mixed feelings about breastfeeding, or indeed, are a mother who has found it hard. However, it is worth mentioning that if you can get it going and sustain it, the benefits go beyond a strengthened immune system and other biological ones. It is proven to help mothers to bond with their babies*. While it is difficult for studies to prove an independent effect of breastfeeding on the well-being of infants, there is good evidence that breastfed babies sleep better than bottle-fed ones*. There is also reason to suppose they are more secure*. These kinds of advantages may partly be simply because the sort of mother who breastfeeds also tends to be the kind who is responsive. But breastfeeding helps most mothers to feel close to their baby, a valuable link in a virtuous circle.

ESTABLISHING BABY ROUTINES

The equation here is all about weighing up your mental health and chances of being able to get your life back to normal, against the mental health of your baby. From its point of view, the more that sleeping and eating routines are based around its needs and natural rhythms, the better. From your point of view, this will also be best because the baby will sleep and eat better if you do it that way.

On the other hand, you may be feeling this little monster is liable to take over your life and wreck it if you 'give in'. You may be desperate for a decent night's sleep, feeling you simply cannot stand such a level of disruption. There are many mothers who start out intending to impose a routine, come what may, and who grit their teeth and block their ears as they battle with controlled crying or not feeding in between 'mealtimes'. However, interestingly, quite a few find that this simply does not work. While a measure of routine based on the infant can help to promote sanity for all concerned, they find that trying to force something which does not fit the baby is unsuccessful: the baby is permanently starving or ends up not sleeping well.

Another problem some mothers encounter is that the routine impedes socialising. You are so anxious to stick to the plan that you fear that meeting up with other mothers will stop you being able to ensure the baby has its feed or sleeps at the right time. Routine may seem important, but it's also important that you do not feel isolated.

The great thing to remember is that babies are satiable, that once they are fed, or get some sleep, or are given a hug, the need is met. They are not like many adults in this regard. There is a great deal of evidence that very strict routines do not lead to so-called contented babies*. It is true that, on the whole, babies whose mothers go to them when they cry in the night or who co-sleep are less likely to sleep through the night. However, there is also good evidence that strict sleep routines do lead to more insecure, and to more irritable and fussy, babies. While you may be scared that 'indulging' them will be just the first step towards a clingy, greedy, needy, selfish toddler and to a child who cannot obey rules at school, the very opposite is the case. It is the babies whose needs have been met who become the secure, calm, satisfied children and productive schoolchildren*, and adults – the ones you might say were spoilt and indulged as babies.

TODDLER DISCIPLINE

There is also a mountain of evidence that harsh, authoritarian, punitive patterns of punishment are harmful*. It is equally true that erratic patterns are just as bad, where what was rewarded last time is punished this one.

Huggers may find it hard to allow their toddler to be independent, and if they have a fault, be too permissive. Organisers more often veer the other way. If you are too strict, the risk is of getting a compliant toddler who has an undercurrent of snarling resentment, or just a flat, empty soul that has given up trying to express itself. This is particularly liable to happen if you use day care nurseries from a young age (see below).

As I describe in Chapter 11, it really should not be necessary ever to hit your child. If you learn how to use reasoning and love, in the right mixture, the child will end up obeying rules because it has chosen to. The idea that they need to be sent to their room or put in naughty chairs appeals to television producers (it makes good telly!) and authors of manuals purporting to offer 'tough love' in place of supposedly indulgent parenting. But it simply is not true that it is best for children.

I provide a more detailed account of the best ways to manage toddler discipline in Chapter 11 (page 179).

SUBSTITUTE CARE: DADDY VS GRANNY VS NANNY VS MINDER VS DAY CARE (R3)

We come to the critical question for many Organisers: what substitute care is best?

In this highly controversial matter, there are a number of competing issues if the best interests of under-threes are taken into account.

For example, half of under-threes who are at home full-time with a depressed mother are insecure*. If the mother is a drug abuser, violent, or severely neglectful, that rises to 85%. So it is hardly good news for an under-three to be at home all the time with a desperate mother. On the other hand, if the child is put into inadequate substitute care, there is also a risk of insecurity. Of the under-threes who are in day care for 20 hours or more a week, 43% are insecure, which is markedly greater than the 26% with stay-at-home mothers. Overall, the most secure under-threes are cared for at home, but that is only if the mother is happy.

It is also important to consider the impact of different kinds of substitute care. One problem is accepted by all scientific authorities: some kinds of non-maternal care (particularly day care) considerably increase the risk of the child becoming aggressive and disobedient. In the most widely accepted study of the subject, the longer a child was cared for by substitutes, the greater the risk*. Just 6% of children who had less than nine hours a week cared for away from home were aggressive and disobedient, compared with 15% for those spending 10–29 hours away. It was 16% for 30–45 hours, and 25% for more than 45 hours, four times more than the ones mainly at home.

Closely allied to these figures is the evidence regarding the impact of substitute care (but especially day care) on levels of cortisol. This is the hormone secreted when a person feels under threat. Abnormal levels have been repeatedly found in insecure children, and in children who are aggressive and disobedient: these raised levels are a sign of trouble.

There is strong evidence that when children are first placed in day care, this raises their levels. A study of 70 15-month-olds showed that during the first hour after being left in day care for the first time, the levels doubled compared with those found at home before they had ever been to day care. This increase continued to be found on the fifth and ninth days after starting. In part, this could be put down to a child having to learn to adapt to a new situation, except that when the levels were measured at five months, they were still significantly higher than the original ones at home*.

When cared for at home by their mothers, the cortisol levels of under-threes fall during the day, between mid-morning and teatime. However, in nine different studies of under-threes in day care*, their levels rise rather than fall between these two times, probably because the child is feeling stressed. The rise may not be a temporary change. The definitive study showed that when children are aged 15, their cortisol levels are still affected by how much time they spent in day care when under-three*.

The studies strongly suggest that it is the quality of care being provided in day care which causes the dysregulated cortisol, especially the extent to which the need for responsive, tuned-in care is not met. Overall, for children in day care, the higher the quality of the provision, the smaller the danger of cortisol problems, although even children in the best-quality day care are at greater risk than ones with no day care*. Two studies show that it is possible to normalise levels through better care*: when relatively insensitive mothers are given special training and become more sensitive as a result, their children's cortisol levels are more likely to be normal.

As I have explained in detail in my review of the evidence (R3), there does not seem to be much of a case for any middle-class parent to place their child in day care. There is overwhelming evidence* that cost is not the main consideration for most parents: the great majority are far more concerned about quality of care. It is as if they intuitively understand the problems which the evidence exposes.

For one thing, the vast majority of day care is either low- or middle-quality (in the case of America, only 9% is high-quality): it's not easy to find a place that is good. If it is not high-quality, the risk of problems has been repeatedly demonstrated to be greater. But even more decisive, the studies nearly always show day care to be the most problematic kind. It is much better to use a minder or relative or friend.

I have put the alternatives in the order in the title of this section because this list is the league table of types of care most likely to meet the needs of your under-three: Daddy is better than Granny is better than Nanny is better than Minder is better than Day Care. The definitive study proved that the closer the substitute care is to a one-to-one ratio, the better*. Substitute care at home (whether nanny or granny) is far superior to out-of-home care, because it is usually one-to-one. For example, there are studies showing that children who are cared for by a substitute at home, one-to-one, are as likely to be as secure as those cared for at home by their mother*.

The proportions of use of these different kinds of care is interesting in that most mothers seem to realise that day care is least desirable. One of the best sources (although not a nationally representative sample) is a study of 1,000 English mothers. For those children aged one, 53% had a mother with no paid job. Among the remaining 47%, the proportions of the one-year-olds with substitute care when their mother was out doing a paid job were as follows:

7% were cared for by their fathers. Twice that proportion – 14% – were cared for by a grandparent or other relative, 11% went to a minder, 4% had a nanny, au pair or sitter, and 10% were in day care*.

Before considering the pros and cons of each in turn, a basic problem must be confronted.

As an Organiser, you have a clear notion of what is the right approach. You may also be someone who is used to arguing forcefully for your case at work and to getting your way. But if you are going to use a substitute you must allow them to do it their way and that can be difficult to tolerate. If they are being Huggers, that could be particularly uncomfortable, especially if you are working full-time and the baby starts reaching for the substitute rather than you when you are both present. Hugging would also tend to conflict with your desire to introduce sleeping and feeding regimes.

The answer has got to be that once you have settled on a substitute, and so long as they are responsively tuned into the baby, you must grit your teeth and stick to it. Nothing is worse for under-threes than a constantly changing cast of carers. Obviously, as happened to Julie in Chapter 3, if you pick a substitute who is not sensitive then you will have to make a change. But much better, also obviously, is to put the time (and alas, money) in at the outset to make sure you have the right person. That means you need to hang out jointly with the substitute for as long as practically possible before handing over the baby (there is good evidence that children do better if the mother takes longer over settling a child into substitute care*). Ideally, you would spend a full week sharing the care before you are satisfied. For babies, you are looking for someone who you can see with your own eyes is tuning in and who is clearly making your child happy. Under six months, the baby will get used to your absence quicker, but after that age you need to make the transition even more gradual, preferably over a month. Start with all three of you together for several half-days. Then try leaving the baby alone with the substitute for half an hour while you are on hand in another room. Emphasise that if the child is distressed you want to be called in. Only when this is working without problems should you start nipping out to do the shopping for a couple of hours.

This will minimise problems in making the transition for the baby and it will also give you plenty of chance to see if the substitute is the biz. If they are not, you have to politely and diplomatically get rid of them and start again. Much better to go through all this grief at the start and establish a stable set-up that you can feel completely confident about, than to have to unplug after two or three months. By then, almost however bad the substitute, the child will have adapted to them and will feel the wrench when they leave.

Daddy Substitutes

If Daddy really is the kind who can tune in responsively, as several of the stories so far have illustrated (and there are more to come in the remaining parts), then he may well be the best substitute. So long as he does not feel emasculated or isolated by the role, it is plain commonsense that he will be highly motivated to go the extra mile that babies demand. While blood is not always thicker than water, and there are plenty of both mothers and fathers who find themselves not hugely drawn towards full-time care of their babies, on the whole, progenitors tend to be the ones who care most what happens to offspring.

An obvious potential problem here is if your partner wants to follow Hugger principles. Again, teeth-gritting is required. If you are working full-time, he is effectively the mother and you have to go with it. You may be able to help him to see that some measure of routine is going to be useful, allowing the baby to show what suits it best. But in the early months, and especially with the firstborn, the potential for screaming rows between sleep-deprived, anxious parents is huge (and, by the way, normal; do not kid yourself that everyone else is getting on hunky-dory; as surveys show*, this situation puts massive strain on the best of relationships, if nothing else, because of lack of sleep but also because both adults are liable to feel they have no 'me time', so everyone starts feeling like a deprived baby at times).

Granny Substitutes

The blood relationship also explains why grannies (and sometimes, grandads) come next. However, it must be said that a decreasing number of grannies may feel inclined to take on the job. Improved health and longevity make them more mobile and vigorous as a generation, more liable to want to get on with the things they did not have time for before retirement. At the same time, they tend to be much older by the time they have grandchildren. Their children become parents at considerably older ages than even 20 years ago, meaning that grannies are also older when they have grandchildren. Once in their late sixties or seventies, despite their generally better health, it's asking a lot of someone to have the energy and dedication required to look after a baby full-time.

But the greatest potential landmine of the granny is when you (or your partner) do not agree with their approach. Few situations are more explosive than a mother who has burning resentments towards her mother, then watching all the same mistakes being made with an offspring. Of course, there are some wonderful mother–daughter relationships in which collaboration works a treat. Indeed, there is strong evidence that a mother is more likely to involve the granny in care if she was cared for by her and feels it will be good for the child to be with its gran*. Nor is there anything odd about that. During a four-week spell researching in Shanghai, I met only one person who had been cared for in the early years by their biological mother; almost everyone had been looked after by their granny. Not that these granny–mum relationships were always conflict-free sweetness and light, and, quite possibly, considerable tensions in the UK are liable to be the norm, too.

On the one hand, there are Organiser mothers who have read modern childcare books advocating routines and naughty steps and are appalled at the granny's Hugger approach; on the other, some Organisers hope the granny will provide the Hugging that they feel either unable or too unstimulated to provide themselves, but then are horrified to see the gran adopt a strict, routinised approach (sometimes justified as 'the old-fashioned discipline not enough parents use today') which is doubly distressing to witness if it was the regime used to care for the mother.

Nanny Substitutes

Organisers are more likely than other kinds of mothers to make the mistake of imagining that their babies and toddlers are gagging for the company of their peers. Organisers often are, but not their under-threes. Because of this misconception, some Organisers (like Tracy in Chapter 2) worry that a nanny is going to be insufficient stimulation for their under-three, just as they feel they themselves are ('if I bore the child, why should a nanny be less boring?' they reason, quite logically). However, in terms of the needs of under-threes described in Chapter 1, babies like nothing better than the undivided attention of a single adult. For this reason, so long as they are responsively tuned in, daddy, granny (or other relative) and nanny (or au pair) are preferable as substitutes to any group care setting all the way up to the third birthday.

The greatest problem for most families about a nanny is the expense. In terms of the national average wage, a woman who goes back to work full-time and employs a nanny will be out of pocket on the deal. I would not let that stop you employing one, if you are an Organiser who needs to get back to work, if you can afford it – do not stint on the expense if you want the needs of your under-three to be met. This is a very important point. At least 60% of mothers do not return to work for the money*. It is important that they are allowed to admit this and not pretend that it is financially necessary to their partner or anyone else. Let money be no object when it comes to finding a substitute, if you can. If you are like several of the women described in the preceding chapters and you know that returning to work is best for you and your child, do not let the fact that it might actually be costing you more than you earn get in the way of your providing the best possible substitute care.

Another major problem is finding a nanny who is going to see your child through to its third birthday. Many nannies tend to be women of reproductive age who become impregnated and go off and have children themselves. They are also often women from foreign countries who can decide at any time that now is the moment to return to the bosom of their family. So the likelihood of a potential nanny staying the course is a major consideration when picking. But of course the biggest issue is finding one who is going to be responsively tuned in.

As described above, ideally take a month to check her out. Although Tracy in Chapter 2 worried about the dangers of leaving her children alone with one person at home, this is not a serious issue (the odds of a woman being an abuser or an agent of a paedophile network are too tiny to consider; alas, anyway, a couple of peculiarly grisly recent cases have shown that day care centres can be the basis for paedophile rings too). The real, rather than phantom, difficulty is in knowing how to interpret your reactions to the nanny when choosing her.

After the initial introductions, you meet. She seems all right, but how can you really tell? Perhaps she has references and you speak to her previous employer, but how reliable is that information? The only truly reliable evidence is going to be spending time with her and your child, observing how they rub along over a reasonable number of occasions (two is the bare minimum). Where you have to be particularly insightful is that, just because she does not dress or have the personality or even the smell that you would like, it does not mean she is wrong. Perhaps you have a strong bias against young women who favour a loosely Goth style, perhaps you do not like overly pressed floral skirts: whatever your superficial prejudices, you need to get beyond them and form an impression of whether this woman can provide l-o-v-e. So long as she can, she is probably right, unless she has some outlandishly weird nurturing ideas, like insisting that a baby must never be within six feet of any electrical apparatus or that toddlers should only ever eat carrots. Assuming you are satisfied she is not going to be disappearing before your child reaches age three and happy to commit to a long-term relationship, l-o-v-e is what matters.

Minder Substitutes

While minding is preferable to day care and attractive because of the lower cost than a nanny, there are disadvantages. Alas, partly because the government for the last 12 years has been fixated on day care as a policy*, minding has become increasingly difficult to practise as a profession. Cumbersome regulations make it harder to be qualified to provide minding and the funding system privileges day care places. Nonetheless, despite these obstructions, it continues to be used more commonly by mothers than day care and if it is the only option, you need to understand how to make the most of it.

The main disadvantage of a minder is that they are usually looking after more than one child (that they are doing so in an unfamiliar home is also an initial problem, although the child gets used to it). If only caring for one child, then they are effectively a nanny working from their own home, in which case the observations in the previous section apply, but this is rare.

Minding is particularly disadvantageous if the other child or children are the same age as yours, or even younger. You only have to look at the strain that caring for twins places on a mother to see how hard it is to care properly for two babies or toddlers of the same age, simultaneously. Another problem is if the minder is feeling stressed by a particularly difficult other child, of whatever age. A further potential problem is if the minder has her (nearly all minders are female) own children. Inevitably, the risk exists that they will receive preferential care.

These negative observations should not obscure the fact that there are plenty of minders who know all there is to know about providing l-o-v-e. So long as she is only caring for two children, and so long as one is much older than the other (the closer to three or older, the better), then she may be able to meet the needs of your under-three. Such minders are often plugged into good social networks of others caring for small children, creating a cosy, supportive environment that stops the minder feeling lonely or depressed. If so, she can be a cheery soul who knows just how to ring a baby or a toddler's bell.

In choosing a minder, you have the option of discussing her with the mother of any other child she cares for. As already described, it's best to take a good deal of time before leaving your child alone with the minder. Hanging out at her home should give you a pretty good feel for what it is going to be like for the child. Of course, if the minder is hostile to the idea of your hanging out there, it's a strong signal that she is not right.

Day Care Substitute Care (see R3 for details)

I realise that there will be some readers who have already sent their child to day care and who will find what I have to say about it painful or objectionable. I do not want to exaggerate the 'evils'. For one thing, the best day care – alas, only about 10% of facilities – is almost certainly better for a child than being with a depressed carer all day. Where affordability dictates that day care is the only alternative and where the mother would be depressed if at home rather than working, then it can work. There is abundant evidence (see page 275, R3) that for children with depressed or heavily overstretched (perhaps because young and single) mothers, it provides real cognitive benefits. This is especially so if the mother is helped to provide sensitive care, if the day care is only part of a wider intervention. If so, such schemes can actually reduce a child's vulnerability to depression in early adulthood.

However, for middle-class mothers who have a choice, there is just no good reason to favour day care over the alternatives, and indeed, the vast majority of parents realise this. They put day care at the bottom of their list of substitutes, given the choice, and in practice, as already noted, only 10% of under-ones are in day care. Having discussed day care extensively with several New Labour luminaries, they defend their advocacy of it by arguing it provides an educational, stimulating alternative for mothers with low incomes. By getting back to work, the mothers (especially the young, single ones) are able to escape poverty and to build their self-esteem, in turn becoming better mothers when with their children. There are many objections to these arguments. The most important is that, instead of providing day care the money could have been used to support those mothers who wanted to care for their babies themselves to do so. This could have included mother–infant psychotherapy for those who had trouble relating, a hugely helpful intervention that can make all the difference to the mental health of all concerned. Indeed, the famous Highscope project in America which is so often cited as justification for New Labour's day care scheme (called Sure Start) aimed to help mothers to care for their children rather than offering substitute care.

For those mothers who really do want to go back to work and for whom this is best, day care should have been at the bottom of the government's list, as it is for the vast majority of mothers. I believe the money could have been spent much better on supporting relatives to be paid to do it, and failing that, minders or even a subsidy towards the cost of nannies. Instead of hugely expensive shiny new children's centres, instead of bricks and mortar, the money should have been spent on maximising the chances of under-threes receiving l-o-v-e from a single adult, with one carer per child.

This is all rather academic. More simply, albeit below the belt, if day care is so wonderful, how come no New Labour luminaries use it themselves? Funny how Tony Blair's son Leo did not spend any time in day care …

If you are a mother who can afford options, I would urge you to question why you are using day care. Of course it is true that, while aggressiveness, disobedience, hyperactivity and insecurity may be a higher risk from day care, all of these can and do occur in children raised exclusively by their parents. My key point is that day care is based on the misconception that under-threes enjoy the company of their peers and the failure to grasp just how important is the undivided attention of a responsive, tuned-in adult. Day care may dilute creativity, the spark of liveliness which is so striking in children raised at home by responsive carers (and speaking anecdotally, so conspicuous in those who have been home-educated, as well).

For mothers who can organise and afford alternatives, I would go so far as to risk your ire by pointing out that it is never too late to change. A good minder would always be preferable to 'good' day care (which, arguably, is not possible), and as I have done my best to explain, the other alternatives are even better.

One of the saddest findings from the best evidence on day care is that children whose mothers are relatively unresponsive are much more likely to have problems if placed in day care, to become insecure. Alas, it is exactly these kinds of mothers who are the most likely to favour day care over other kinds of substitute (page 292, R3). These mothers said they believed it was actually beneficial for their child if they worked, yet offspring of mothers with that view were more likely to be insecure. Such mothers strongly agreed with the statement 'children whose mothers work are more independent and able to do things for themselves'. Mothers with these views were less sensitive or responsive when observed with their child. Not only that, but these relatively unresponsive mothers are also the ones most likely to use low-quality facilities: ones where the ratio of child to carer is bad (it should be no more than one carer for every three children, under-three); where there is high staff turnover; and where the emphasis is on cognition and social development, not the nurture that is required. To top it all, such mothers are also more likely to switch their arrangements, moving the child between different nurseries or carers, and they also leave the child for the longest hours in substitute care. This is tragic: the very children – those with relatively unresponsive mothers – who particularly need responsive, one-to-one substitute care are the very ones who are most likely not to get it, because placed in bad day care.

ENCOURAGE YOUR CHILD TO SEE ITSELF AS MALLEABLE, NOT FIXED (PAGE 317, R7)

As your baby becomes a toddler, be very wary of labelling. Organisers can be a bit more prone to assuming that genes are limiting what their child is like, thinking of their traits as categorical and fixed. But there is powerful evidence that encouraging children to see themselves as malleable improves their performance.

Overall, children with a malleable view of their potential perform better. If those who have a fixed model are taught to see themselves as malleable, their performance improves. In one study, young teenagers were given just four lessons teaching them about how people can greatly alter themselves and their performance. Compared with other teenagers not given this lesson, those given it had greatly improved their performance in maths when followed up a year later. The greatest improvement was found in the children who had started out with a fixed view of themselves.

Parents inevitably develop perceptions of offspring's personalities and aptitudes. We have to be very wary of these turning into labels. To some degree they will be based on our own childhood experiences and natural prejudices. If a mother was raised with lots of brothers and no sisters, she might have a picture of boys as being bumptious and difficult. Or perhaps you were the youngest and have strong ideas about how that affects people. These kinds of ideas may be more or less anchored in reality but we have to be careful not to slap them on our children. It's complex, because to quite an extent the attributions we make to each different child are part of our expression of love towards them, especially the positive attributions. But the negative ones can sometimes be our way of dumping unwanted aspects of ourselves.

The simplest tip is to keep a close eye on your negative ideas about them. Maybe your baby or toddler really is a bit more tetchy or impatient than usual, but fight tooth and nail to resist the temptation to assume that is an inevitable destiny. All too often, when we look in the mirror, we may find that the child is reminding us of ourselves. Just because you have these tendencies does not mean your child will. The great danger is that we get ratty or tricky when the child is like that, bringing it to pass, a self-fulfilling prophecy which could have been avoided.

If You Think You or Your Child are Going Bonkers, Do Not Assume That Genes are the Reason (page 319, R7)

Leave aside the evidence about whether mental illness is caused by nature or nurture. Even with very extreme problems, like schizophrenia, the outcome is much better if the patient, or the patient's parents or any professionals treating the patient, do not assume the problem is caused by genes.

If schizophrenics are sent back from hospital to a family who assume that genes are the cause, that person is more likely to relapse. They are less likely to take steps to help themselves and more likely to take to the bottle or become depressed. They become more passive about their treatment and leave it to the professionals to decide what happens, which predicts they will fare worse. Professionals who believe mental illness is down to genes are more likely to perceive patients as disturbed and less likely to involve the patient in plans to help them.

As an Organiser, you are at greater risk of depression than Fleximums and Huggers. This is especially so if you are a Type A personality, or if you have a partner with whom you disagree about the best way to mother, or if you feel unsupported, or if you wish you could be working or not working and are doing the one that does not suit you (R8). If you feel yourself succumbing to depression, whatever you do, do not assume your genes are the reason. That is almost certainly not the case and there is a lot of help you can get, as explained above.

FINAL TIP: DON'T ASSUME YOU WILL BE AN ORGANISER IF YOU HAVE ANOTHER BABY

Mothers can vary enormously in how they nurture their different offspring. As we shall see, Huggers can shift to being Organisers and the reverse can happen – remember Flo, the Organiser in Chapter 4, who believes that if she has a second child, she will become a Hugger.

Mothers can also shift from one kind of care to another at different stages in the same child's life. Most of us tend to have age groups which appeal to us more, others that appeal less. The sort of person who adores babies may not feel the same about toddlers – that is true of some Huggers. They may be very child-centred in infancy but become stricter and more like Organisers with their toddler. In the same way, some Organisers prefer over-threes who can talk, walk and then read and write, to under-threes. These Organisers may be requiring the under-three to adapt to them but when it gets older, become more like a Hugger.

Especially with Huggers and Organisers, these approaches can be a way of defending against anxieties thrown up by the vulnerability of the under-three, reminding them of their own infancy. If so, mothers may radically shift the form their defence takes. Just as Huggers can occasionally take the fast train to Organising without stopping off at the Flexi station, so with Organisers.

CONCLUSION: POTENTIAL PITFALLS OF ORGANISING

⟨ *Pregnancy and Birth Horror*: you are liable to be the sort of person who does not especially revel in either pregnancy or birth. The more you can acknowledge pregnancy, the easier the birth and first few weeks will be

⟨ *Bored by Babies*: if you feel the baby is dull and unstimulating, you have got the 'walkie-talkies on different channels' problem. The more you can overcome this, the better: a few sessions with a parent–infant therapist could work wonders. Do not feel your lack of interest in goo-goo, ga-ga makes you a bad person, there are plenty like you – it's different, not worse

⟨ *Too Eager to Tame the Beast in the Nursery*: because you do not feel the baby can communicate its needs to you much, you may get too hung up on trying to impose routines. As much as possible, allow the baby's natural patterns to emerge during the early weeks, and build routines around them. If you are finding this hard, reach out to intimates and tell them all about it

⟨ *Believing Much of What Under-Threes are Like is Inborn*: because you may find them so unstimulating – because you happen to be the sort of person who is not tuned to under-three wavelengths – you are more prone to attributing inborn traits. That quickly leads to a disciplinary mentality and to ever less pleasure from being with them, a vicious circle. Once you grasp that they are tremendously responsive to care and that their personalities and abilities emerge from relationships with carers, not at all from genes at this age, you may also see they are not as boring as they first seemed

⟨ *Thinking that Under-Threes Need Stimulation, Education and Friends*: they actually need nurture and l-o-v-e more than anything else. Beware of confusing your own boredom and feeling of being unstimulated with what they are feeling. They just want to hang out with you and for you to recognise their needs, and to be talked to and with. They do not need constant entertainment, they do not need friends, they do not need IQ-building games

⟨ *Attraction to the Wrong Sort of Substitute Care*: they want nurturant companions, not nurses or teachers, and they want one-to-one care. That rules out day care if you can possibly avoid it. If picking nannies, minders or other substitutes, look for someone who is loving and not hyperactive, above all things. Lovingness is more important than cleanliness or efficiency at this age

⟨ *Too Many Naughty Chairs and Punishments for Toddlers*: they need clear boundaries about what is allowed at this age, but pick your battles carefully and keep them to a minimum before age three. As much as possible, help them to do the right thing because they want to, not because it suits you. Try to avoid imposition and coercion, to avoid nagging and overcontrolling

⟨ *Depression from Workaholia and Too Many Balls in the Air*: the more you can solve the walkie-talkie problem, the less risk of depression. Find some other mothers you can have a good moan with, preferably via an antenatal class. If you are a Type A personality, find a psychoanalytic therapist, avoid CBT

Part Two

THE HUGGER

POLLY FILLER'S ESSENTIAL GUIDE TO WHAT TO DO WITH THE KIDS OVER SUMMER

IT'S that ghastly time of year again. Eight weeks of Holiday Hell stretching into the distance with nothing to relieve the misery. How can you stop yourself from going stark staring bonkers?

Well now help is at hand. Here's Polly's tried-and-tested survival tips for what to do with the little monsters.

1. Dump the children with your parents and head for the Med – sorted! It's good for them to bond with their grandparents even if they are not as well as they used to be!?! Buck up Mum!!

2. Dump the children on the nanny and reach for the beach! Honestly – you are doing yourself a favour. She gets to see the heartwarming new movie 'WALL-E' 25 times as well as learning new skills (like industrial-scale ironing and cleaning out the hamster cage) – she even gets to improve her English vocabulary, including useful phrases like "Where do I buy wallpaper paste, your mother has told me to redecorate the nursery?"

3. Dump the children with your friends-with-the-only-child! They are off to Portugal anyway and they'll be only too grateful for some company for their spoilt, annoying brat! No offence Zak and Sabrina but *even you* think Che is a nightmare!!

4. Dump the children in the Pied Piper Children's Hotel near Newbury and fly to Dubai!! Kids *love* it at Pied Pipers – whatever they say!!

5. Dump the children in summer camp. There are hundreds of camps all over England offering a great range of activities – for parents!! Like diving in the Maldives and shopping in New York whilst the kids have an old-fashioned British outdoor holiday and make new friends with some midges.

6. Look after the children yourself – only joking!

Happy Holidays!

© P. Filler 2008.

CHAPTER 7

Meet the Essential Hugger

If you are a Hugger, you may well have found the Polly Filler spoof newspaper column (reproduced from *Private Eye* magazine) amusing, but Organisers beware! You might not think it was so funny and it could be a foretaste of this account of mothering which may make you furious or filled with disdain. The mothering described in this chapter may seem like a prescription for a spoilt brat, or at other times, it may make you question whether you have got the right ideas. Some Fleximums may have similar reactions, some of the time. My plea to you all is to open your minds and do your best to see if you can find anything in what follows from which you can learn, as well as the completely natural response, which will be to find fault. Just as the Hugger needed to grit their teeth when reading about the Organiser, if you are an Organiser and want to improve your mothering, you have to keep challenging your prejudices.

Few Huggers will find the account completely accords with their experience, but do not let that put you off. Hopefully you will recognise aspects of yourself and your approach in this chapter, setting us up for the subsequent ones in this part of the book, which explore the potential difficulties of Hugging.

THE ESSENTIAL HUGGER*

During the pregnancy you feel you have a relationship with the foetus, that it already has a character. You look forward to the birth with excitement, usually hoping for a natural one. If a great deal of medical intervention is required, you may feel angry or disappointed, but in most cases, the joy of being able to see, smell and feel the baby soon enables you to stop thinking about your ordeal.

The baby often seems strangely familiar. Deep down it may be that its presence ignites a profound memory of what it was like to be a baby yourself. That may be distressing if you felt neglected but you convert the feeling into a powerful impulse to give your baby the experience you never had. Alternatively, you may have had a wonderful infancy yourself and simply be trying to reproduce that experience for your baby, reliving it in the process – there is evidence showing that monkeys duplicate the amount that they were loved* and that the same is true, intergenerationally, for human mothers* (see page 139). Either response creates an intense feeling of connectedness and, early on, an actual resentment at being separated, even for a few moments.

After the birth you are happy to be sealed off from anything that diverts your attention. You may well feel on a bit of a high. You are blind to any imperfections of either the baby or your own state, exactly the same as when one falls in love with an adult – they can do no wrong, even their faults seem like reasons for adoration*. This infuses the baby and the state of motherhood with an aura of perfection, superlatives flooding from your lips – 'I adore ...', 'it's fantastic ...', 'incredible ...'. Lack of sleep or difficulties with breastfeeding are troubling but you can cope with them from your loved-up platform.

Voluptuous, you luxuriate in sensuality. You are almost repelled by the idea of using perfume or deodorant, acutely conscious of the baby's bodily smells, happily awash in the animal pleasures of closeness and a new beginning. In breathing the baby's fragrance you may feel you are inhaling the pure innocence of an unsullied, authentic, fresh life. You may have a sense that yours is the best, the only baby in the world and you are the best and only mother for this baby, the only one who truly understands what it wants.

For you may be determined to be the sole source of goodness, aiming to provide an ideal experience. You may jealously guard the baby, demanding exclusive contact at first because only you have the intuitive understanding to interpret the baby's nonverbal messages, acquired, you believe, during pregnancy. The uterine connection has created a perfect synchrony and now this link is physically sustained by breastfeeding. Nothing must get in the way. Your partner may feel a bit excluded but the baby knows best, subtly communicating its needs, and you must be on hand to be attentive to every sound and gesture. It's as if you are in a dream. Or, as one mother put it (as reported by Joan Raphael-Leff), 'I was swimming underwater with the baby, completely sealed off from the world … other people feel like intruders – distracting me with their prattling conversations. I so enjoy this time of mooching around at home, just the baby and I, no pressures, no people, no outside world.'

While by no means invariably the case, some Huggers can find it easier to develop full-scale huggy tendencies towards a girl. A certain amount of the passion that many Huggers feel is generated by seeing themselves in the baby. Deep down, in such cases, in Hugging her baby, she is Hugging the baby she once was. If that baby is a girl, it's easier to see it as herself.

You prefer to be in physical contact at all times, whether holding, or in a sling against your stomach or back, or the baby lying on you. Other kinds of mothers place the baby in diverse containers, like prams, carrycots and bouncy chairs, but you never feel very happy with those alternatives early on. Only after about four months are you willing to lengthen the psychological umbilical cord.

Every cry is a poignant appeal for help, an urgent message. Each wail cuts right through you and continues to do so after it has ended.

For you, there is no such thing as just noise; all the cries are real, signifying something important. You may sometimes feel the cry implies you have failed to anticipate and pre-empt the meeting of a need. Your goal is nothing less than a perfect environment, although you know nothing can be absolutely perfect. Whether it be hunger, pain, cold or fear, you would like to anticipate the problem before cries are needed. You carefully scrutinise the baby's face to guess the next need.

Feeding is on demand, whenever, wherever and for however long. Only when sleep arrives or sucking stops of its own accord, does it cease. Your breasts may leak in public and may spurt milk in response to cries, but you do not care. Day and night, the breast may be best for the first year and you may carry on for another year or more. If you have other children, the night feeds may be especially treasured as a quiet time together, undisrupted by noisy demands. Closeted in the darkness with your sweet-smelling, cuddlesome chum, a special fusion and communion may be conferred. Your routines may become synchronised, sleeping, eating and bathing together at the same times, only gradually returning to separate regimes as the baby gets older. Naturally, the baby is liable to share your bed, with broken nights until well into the second year.

Daddies with Hugger tendencies feel pretty much the same as mummies, without the breastfeeding. Their motivations are the same: either they long to ensure that the baby receives the good-quality, responsive Hugging experienced in their own infancy, or they are compensating for lack of love then.

Hugger daddy was right there for the birth and he just can't wait for mother and baby to get home from the hospital so they can become a sealed-off, loved-up little world. Because he has strong Hugging tendencies, he may feel a twinge of jealousy when he sees the baby merrily suckling away or entranced by its mother – he would like to be mothering too. But he does his best to get in on the act, holding and (where bottles are involved) feeding at every opportunity, more than happy to change nappies, bathe and caress. He wants to be a receptacle for the baby's feelings and to soothe away any distress, to envelop it in love. If not beaten to it, he is up at the night-time crying, never happier than wandering around darkened rooms in the small hours, jiggling and singing.

As can be imagined, Hugger daddies who become the full-time carer (most commonly because the mother is the higher earner of the two) can be in a seventh heaven. While it can be tricky for them to gain acceptance from other mothers, they quickly become indistinguishable from female Huggers in the kind of care they provide.

As we shall see in subsequent chapters, while Huggers are generally reluctant to do any paid work during their children's early years, some do. In a few cases, the daddy stays at home. In most, however, this either is not feasible or the man does not want to do it. As we shall see in Chapter 9, so long as the substitute care is good, it is perfectly possible for a Hugger to do a paid job and feel happy with the arrangement. Where the worker identity is strong, it conflicts with the Hugger desire to care for the child. But once infant has become toddler, from around the age of one, some Huggers feel the best way to reconcile the conflict is to return to work, at least part-time. They just feel it is not enough to be permanently at home, they want the feedback which comes from the workplace, things like having their own money paid into their bank account, the fellowship of employees, the status and satisfaction of their employed role. They may also miss the enjoyment of using hard-won skills to achieve satisfying, measurable goals. Nonetheless, this is relatively rare. The archetypal Hugger is a woman with no paid employment.

Jo, a Classic Hugger: No Paid Job, the Child's Needs Come First

Jo is a sharp-witted, shrewd, outgoing 37-year-old who lives with her husband Will in a small terraced house in the city of Nottingham. Having been a bit of a rebel in her teens, she left school with some low-grade A levels, skipped university and did well-paid casual jobs in IT for most of her twenties to pay for her love of travel, only settling back in Nottingham in her thirties, when she met Will, a self-employed plumber. One thing led to another and today they have Oscar, aged five, and Agnes, aged two.

Like so many women of her generation, Jo was far from confident that she and motherhood would be happy bedfellows. During the pregnancy with Oscar, there were times when she felt quite depressed. 'I wondered "Oh my God, what have I done? Whatever made me think I could look after a baby?" I realised I had barely ever held one, never babysat, never shown any special interest in them, although I liked particular children, obviously. Oscar was not a mistake – we had decided to get on with it – but I hadn't felt particularly broody, didn't think my life wouldn't be worth living without a baby.'

Depression was a cause for particular concern, having suffered quite serious bouts since her teens (indeed, in this she was right – one of the strongest predictors of post-natal depression is having been depressed before*). 'I thought I was a shoo-in for post-natal depression. I'd seen it happen and it looked scary as hell. I had periods of feeling low during the first few months of the pregnancy and I would think to myself, "shall I just check into a clinic now? What's it going to be like with a baby to look after! God help us all."' She knew she was 'pretty rubbish' when short of sleep, liable to become tetchy and preoccupied. Nor did she fancy the practical side. Although highly intelligent, she had never been domesticated or good with her hands.

A great lover of fiction, it was a non-fiction book that proved to be the turning point in the pregnancy. Browsing in a second-hand shop she came upon Jean Liedloff's *The Continuum Concept*, never having heard of it before. Some of it struck her as a bit dubious, 'like the idea of letting your child play with mud on the edge of a precipice', but there was one key idea that transformed her feeling, as well as ideas. 'Liedloff said it was a good idea to have the baby sleeping next to you in the bed. For some reason, when I read that I just thought "God, that makes sense, that makes things easier, that would work, in every way." It touched a chord and when I explained it to Will, he agreed.' They were highly sceptical of medical advice that shared sleeping could be dangerous, feeling that a cot death (only possible in babies not sharing with parents) was a much scarier idea. In fact, there is strong evidence that medical opposition to bed-sharing is quite simply wrong and that a much sounder scientific view is that, rather than being dangerous, it is natural*.

She did not have the classic Hugger's feeling of a strong bond with the baby in the pregnancy, but she hoped the birth would be as natural as possible. 'I wanted to do it with my eyes open, not drugged. It was going to be a trip, good or bad, I didn't want to miss it. I thought "billions of women have done this since time immemorial; I'm going to do it too". However much it hurt, I wanted to feel it, not be numb.' Luckily for her, this proved possible. Although it was enormously painful, she was particularly glad of having felt able to yell her heart out during the process. 'It was liberating, animal. Because it was a natural bellowing I didn't have a trace of a sore throat afterwards. It put me in touch with my feelings which was the perfect preparation for what followed.'

She was 'screaming blue murder' when Oscar came out but like most Huggers, from the first moment she clapped eyes on him, she was in love. 'I remember thinking that I didn't know he would be so beautiful, had never thought of babies like that. I was overwhelmed, total euphoria, a falling in love out of all proportion to any I had felt. Despite all the pain and difficulties of a long birth, I specifically and immediately thought, "God, I want to do this again."' It had been only during the labour that Jo really felt she had got into the 'mother zone'. As soon as she put him to her breast, 'it immediately was going right. I felt "I can do this, this is great". That seemed the irreversible moment. From then on I knew what I wanted, felt a confidence and clarity about everything concerning him. I'd always been liable to doubt, now I was certain. For instance, I would not let them cut the cord right away, refused to let him be taken off and washed and put in something pretty. From then on I felt completely sure of myself.'

Jo was fortunate insofar as she was able to avoid medical interventions during the birth – if that happens, some Huggers get off on the wrong foot afterwards, feeling resentful or sad, the process of tuning in interrupted or delayed. She was also lucky that Will completely supported her decisions. Like most parents, they had never really discussed how they would care for their baby beforehand, but he not only hung in there with her during the screaming and shouting, he completely endorsed what happened next.

For, like most Huggers, Jo was convinced that she was as critical for Oscar's forward momentum as wheels to a car. 'I remember thinking during that first week, "this is the most formative one of his life". I really did think that every little thing, every moment, was critical.' No studies have ever been done to test whether responsiveness of mothers during the first week has greater effect on well-being or other outcomes than, say, the second or fourth or sixth weeks. However, overall, there is a huge amount of evidence supporting the basic Hugger prejudice that the earlier the experience (good or bad), the greater its subsequent impact*. They are also correct in assuming that genes are very rarely a big influence on what a baby is like, that the kind of care provided is critical*.

Back home, Jo hunkered down in the bedroom with Oscar. It was a month before she left the house, six months before she drove a car, feeling she was a case of 'do not operate heavy machinery' because she was so focused on her baby. Will cut back on his work to be on hand as much as possible, doing all the shopping, cooking and washing. Jo didn't get out of her nightdress for weeks, greeting her guests in bed. 'I was very, very unambitious. I didn't give any thought to getting into a routine of any kind, didn't worry much about washing him or myself – the pictures bear witness to how little I cared about what I looked like!

– and ignored my clothes. You can't fit into anything, anyway. I aimed low. When people came round, Oscar was the star; this was his big moment. His needs were absolutely paramount.'

She had a novel experience of feeling very in touch with her instincts. If something felt wrong, she didn't do it, if right, she did. Feeling exceptionally open and susceptible, she stopped reading if a book was upsetting, stopped watching if what was on TV was nasty. She had strange ideas, like when watching the news she thought, 'Blimey, Trevor Macdonald: he was a baby once! Someone must have loved him as much as this (or not).' Instead of taking the tragic view of life, it became the comic one. 'It felt like a tidal wave. If I fight it I'm going to drown, if I submit and allow myself to be swept along, I'm going to enjoy the ride.'

Her fears of lack of sleep proved unfulfilled. If he dropped off, instead of getting out of bed to organise the house, she just joined him, luckily able to leave the housework to Will. Oscar never slept for many consecutive hours but so long as she avoided 'rushing about and doing things', that was not a problem. Also fearing that she would have no chance for her favourite pastime of reading, she quickly realised that she could do so to her heart's content. 'People don't tell you just how many hours a day you are going to spend breastfeeding. If you are in for a long session, you get water, the phone, go to the toilet and line up your book. You're in clover; what could be nicer?'

She did not find his crying a problem either. 'If he did so and I couldn't stop it, I would assume there was a reason. I was careful not to put it down to some unchangeable trait in him, like that he was depressed or in a bad mood. I took the view that however distressed he was, all he primarily needed was to be right next to me, with bodily contact.' In practice, he didn't cry much anyway and had very little wind. Jo says she may have been lucky, that he could have had colic, for example, but she was also very careful about what she ate (despite plenty of unhealthy eating during the pregnancy), avoiding coffee, sugar or other stimulants, sticking to camomile tea and bland food. She took the idea that 'what I was eating, he was eating', seriously. Above all, she didn't want anything to come between them, chemically or physically. 'I had been instinctively against all those prams and cots and baby rockers, never went to Mothercare. I slightly smelt a rat there, all that pastel-coloured plastic: it's merchandising and marketing, isn't it? Those objects, like baby alarms, nearly always seem like ways of putting a distance between you and the baby. I found simplicity best: "I don't need them. He doesn't." Not relying on those sorts of commodities helped me stop feeling this was something I didn't know how to do. Beforehand, it seemed like others knew best, were on a plan, and I wasn't. Now I thought, "No, this will be our way." I had a definiteness which wasn't my normal way. I knew what was right and wrong, felt authorised because this was such important work.'

It never occurred to her to think of paid employment. Will's work brought in enough money because their mortgage was small and she had completely lost interest in new shoes or upgrading her mobile or kitchen furniture, so expenditure was low. She had vaguely assumed before the birth that she would probably go back to doing the odd IT job for a bit of extra cash. Instead, 'I didn't have any feeling that I wanted to get my old life back. I completely stopped thinking like that, I never thought about the future, was in the present.'

By six months after the birth she was beginning to make regular forays beyond the house, Oscar attached to her on a sling. He started on solids about then, began crawling a couple of months later. He was never out of her sight but very gradually the transition to toddler was underway. At that stage, Jo could not imagine ever feeling cross with him. While the vast majority of mothers will sometimes feel irritable and get annoyed, usually because tired and feeling they have no time for themselves, Jo had tremendous support from Will.

The first time Jo recalls feeling a flash of anger was when Oscar was 18 months and he kept chucking his beaker on the floor. Before that, he could do anything, from splashing her in the bath to spitting food on her. Now it was subtly different, she was taking the first steps towards asserting that her needs and feelings had to be considered.

For Huggers, this process is generally later and slower than it is with other approaches. In the great majority of matters, Jo continued not to impose anything on him. By 18 months, he had voluntarily discontinued breastfeeding during the day, only doing it at night. This continued to be the case until he was three, at which point Jo gently insisted on stopping. By then it was largely done to get to sleep. Noticing that a couple of times he had fallen asleep without a feed, the next night he was clearly thinking, 'come on then, where is it?' Jo was already keen to end the feeding because their second child, Agnes, was imminent and Jo did not want the difficulties that two breastfeeders would entail. Having made her mind up not to go back, she stuck to it. But she did not want him to feel pushed away, rejected, so at nights she walked him around the patio, rocking and singing. He did kick up a fuss but she decided 'he's right there with me, he's got everything he needs bar the breast, it's OK to deny him that'. She felt she was giving him a single message, 'you've still got me, you're still sleeping in the bed, everything else is the same as ever except the feeding, which is history'. She was willing to stick to this as long as it took and after a few nights of pacing about with an outraged and vexed child, he just stopped demanding it.

However, this did not mean he started sleeping through the night. That did not happen for the first time until he was three and a half. The price Huggers pay for their approach is that their children tend to wake more and to demand attention during the night*. This is too high a price for many parents. But the counter argument is that if it can be endured, there is good evidence that the child may feel more secure* and sleep easier in later life*.

Nappies ended more voluntarily than the feeding. Aged two and three-quarters, Jo was getting quite a lot of 'oh, is he still in nappies?' from other parents, although she did not care about that. She had read somewhere that children will let you know when they have had enough of nappies. One day, Oscar was playing in the garden with a slightly older, nappyless boy who whipped out his willy and had a pee. Seeing this, Oscar thought 'way to go!', pulled off his nappy and never looked back.

Like most Huggers, Jo was not totally permissive. She knew a few who felt it was a point of principle never to try and impose anything on their children. The result was children who were without boundaries, unaware of the consequences of their actions for others. It made them enormously unpopular, not only with adults but other children as well.

To learn the best methods for helping Oscar to relate happily in social situations, Jo actually went on a parenting course. It taught that the parent needs to have authority, without being a dictator. As much as possible, consistency was encouraged regarding what behaviour was unacceptable. Explanation of why the parent was intervening should be as full as possible, once everyone has calmed down a bit. Jo was also one of those Huggers who felt that an automated please and thank you did no harm (see page 187, Chapter 11 for advice on toddler care).

Jo's story is exceptional in the extent to which her partner was both able and willing to help out in every way. He earned enough to satisfy their material requirements while still taking a lot of time off. He was more than usually willing to shop, cook and clean the house, and he also was very comfortable looking after the children himself, mainly required after Agnes was born.

More common is for Huggers to find that there are severe impediments placed in the way of their desire to devote themselves completely to their baby. The two commonest of these are the need to earn money and conflict with a partner who does not support the Hugger approach, illustrated in the next chapter.

CHAPTER 8

Where the Hugger's Partner Objects to Her Hugging

Jo's story, described in the last chapter, is all very well, but how many Huggers have as supportive a husband as Will – one who removes the need to worry about housekeeping in the early months and earns enough for them both? Since most couples give little, if any, time to discussing how they would go about caring for their children before the birth, plenty of Huggers end up with a partner who either does not really get it or is actually fiercely opposed. Huggers may also find themselves surrounded by other mothers who feel actively hostile to Hugging. To top it all, their own parents may be horrified by the 'indulgence' and 'lack of discipline' of this 'permissive parenting'.

Pam, aged 30, is in this position. On first meeting her you might be forgiven for supposing she is a model or a footballer's wife, but her designer kit and well-groomed appearance are misleading. Get chatting and you soon realise she is a straightforward, uncomplicated person who cares little for the status and money which so dominate the lives of her neighbours in the rich suburb on the edge of Manchester where she lives. She is passionately loving towards her children, a decent, warm person, highly inquisitive about herself and willing to challenge her own ideas. She brings a rare honesty to her evaluation of the ways in which her mothering may have affected her children and her marriage.

Many of the whys and wherefores of Hugging emerge in the story of her relationship with her husband, Brian. Although they are not poles apart in some of their attitudes to parenting, and although he is a loving father, he has been opposed to Hugging throughout. Coupled with the fact that Pam and Brian's friends in their Manchester sub-culture all side with him, she has had to fight tooth and nail to do it her way. It raises the question: at what point does concern with the needs of small children tip into neurotic, smothering mother-love that is more about the mother's needs than those of the child, albeit dressed up as meeting the child's?

Equally interesting, she did not use Hugging with all her three children. She raised the first and third with that approach, but in an attempt to compromise with her husband and to conform to the advice of her friends and father, she tried to be an Organiser with the second, who had a maternity nurse, nanny and childminder before going to nursery school at two and a half. She believes this different approach with her second child had adverse effects. Her story is therefore a natural experiment in the impact of Hugging versus its absence.

The divorce of her parents when she was aged seven left her with the powerful determination that if she got married, she would stay married. Not much motivated to work hard at school, she still did well enough to go to university where, aged 17, she met Brian. University was about having fun, not building a career, just a thing you did next after school. Pam is among that one third of women for whom succeeding in the workplace has always had a much lower priority than getting married and looking after their children*. She did just enough work towards her degree to get by, but partying with Brian was the main focus. 'I didn't do enough work. And I have to say Brian bloody led me astray so badly with drugs and drinking. But it was all good for you. If my kids do that, completely fine: get it over with when you're young.' On graduation they set off for a year's travelling, mostly spent taking drugs (cocaine, hash, LSD and ecstasy) in South America.

Returning to England, she found a job as the PA to an advertising CEO. She split up with Brian for a year, feeling she had had enough of their druggy life. 'When I came back to the airport my parents picked up this bedraggled wreckage. The drugs were doing my head in.' At that point she had only slept with one person but 'boy, I made up for all those years of monogamy and explored what it was like out there in the big wide world'. Meanwhile, Brian did well in his career and at the end of the year they got back together ('it felt like coming home'), married and along came Tim, their first child.

He had been preceded by a miscarriage, making Pam very anxious during the pregnancy. Subsequently, the birth was difficult. Soon afterwards, she found herself in a hospital bed with Tim screaming in an adjacent cot. A midwife said 'why not put him next to your skin, go skin-to-skin, in your bed' (interestingly, a review of 21 studies of hospital maternity wards confirms that when this advice is given it promotes successful breastfeeding outcomes*). From then until he was three years old, he was in his parents' bed. A colicky, easily distressed baby, Pam felt Tim's pain keenly: 'He was really difficult but I was completely attuned, even though he was crying for hours on end.' Having expected to continue the busy round of partying with Brian which normally occupied them, she opted right out. 'I was just so not interested in that, which was really hard for Brian. But he was understanding and went alone.'

Being just 22, only one of her friends was also a mother. That woman used a maternity nurse and au pairs, and her baby ate and slept to order. Although Pam was worried at the contrast between this 'good' baby and her tearful Tim, she was determined to keep doing it all herself. She felt his suffering, that there was something horribly wrong and only she could be the antidote. People would come over and suggest they hold the baby while she took a shower but she would prefer to be with him at all times early on. After three months, the screaming stopped and they settled into a mutually satisfying round of breastfeeding, sleep and cuddles. This is exactly what the studies suggest will happen, sooner or later, if a difficult baby is given undivided love.

The definitive study* selected 100 infants who had been measured as highly irritable immediately after birth, easily upset and annoyed, harder to cope with than smiley, placid babies. If the irritability was an immutable, genetic trait it should translate into insecurity a year later regardless of the kind of care received.

When the babies were aged six to nine months, 50 of the mothers received counselling sessions to increase their responsiveness and sensitivity to their difficult charges. Prior to the help, these mothers tended to have become discouraged by their baby's lack of good cheer, sometimes ignoring or blanking them. Custom-building the help to the particular problems, the researchers taught techniques for soothing the baby, encouraged play and helped the mother to connect, emotionally.

Meanwhile the other 50 mothers and their irritable babies had received no extra help. When the level of emotional security of the two groups were tested at one year old, the contrast in outcomes was remarkable. In the group who had had no help, 72% of the children were insecure, whereas in the assisted group, only 32% were. The only difference was the counselling sessions, so the implication was that even the most difficult babies can be turned around by their mother.

Other studies show that although children born with low birth weights are at greater risk of inattention and hyperactivity at school age, this is less likely if the mother is warm and supportive in early life*. Children whose mothers drank a lot during pregnancy are generally at greater risk of a low IQ – but not if the mother is emotionally sensitive and mentally stimulating*.

Most recently, a study of more than 1,700 maltreated children showed the crucial role of nurture. Measured before two years of age, 85% of the sample were neurologically impaired and at high risk of behaviour problems and language deficits. Followed up 18 months later, it turned out that the more sensitive and responsive the mothering, the greater the likelihood of them having overcome their initial impairment*. Above all, there is good evidence that infants whose mothers were strongly prone to Hugger ways are nearly all emotionally secure, compared with only half of infants not given this kind of care*.

For obvious ethical reasons, we cannot conduct experiments with humans but they have been done with monkeys*. Those monkeys born highly reactive were fostered to either averagely or exceptionally nurturant mothers. The average ones turned out to have the usual problems of the highly reactive, being overly reluctant to explore their environments and very easily perturbed by noises or other shocks. The exceptionally nurtured ones turned out even better than monkeys who had not started out highly reactive. Furthermore, when they themselves went on to have babies, they mothered in ways that resembled their foster mothers, not their original biological mothers, proving there is an intergenerational transmission of mothering responsiveness that has nothing to do with genes.

In accord with this evidence, Pam's care of Tim seems to have overridden his initial distress. Tim is now aged eight and Pam believes that there are no traces of his colicky first few months. 'He is a very calm child, quiet but confident, not in the least nervy. He is sometimes cautious about new people or activities, but only sensibly so. He only needs a little encouragement and he will happily get stuck into a party with quite a few unfamiliar children.' In support of her feeling that the care she provided is the reason he is so well-balanced, she has seen what can happen from trying it another way, with her second child, Sarah.

The change in approach came about because Brian and all her friends badgered her constantly to stop Hugging. While a highly stimulating playmate for their children, Brian longed for her to be like the other mothers in their social circle. For example, every year they would share a Spanish villa with the friend who also had a baby, along with some other friends. Everyone except Pam would smoke marijuana and get drunk. The au pair did much of the daily care for the other mother. Complete strangers would be hired to babysit so they could go out to dinner in the evenings. Pam was not happy with this, refusing to leave Tim. Brian would ask 'Why can't you be like everyone else?'

One evening they were all about to go out. 'The other mother just dumped her baby to scream for at least half an hour while I tried to get Tim to sleep. Everyone was looking at their watches, Brian was furious. Eventually Tim dropped off and we went out but an hour later the babysitter called the restaurant to say he had woken and was crying. The others looked at me as if I was completely mad when I insisted on setting off home. All they seemed concerned about was their supper but what about Tim? What was it like for him?'

During the daytime, Pam recalls the other mother leaving her six-month-old screaming its head off in a bouncy chair surrounded by a playpen. 'Something was viciously wrong with it, wind or maybe just wanting to be picked up. But the mother was out by the pool, the au pair in the kitchen and no one reacted. They just left it bawling its eyes out in a darkened room. Apparently, so they explained, that was the right thing to do if the child was going to learn to be independent, it was best for it. Brian would yell at me constantly for holding Tim wherever I went. But I would only go in the pool if he was asleep in the buggy beside it.'

Brian was convinced that Pam's approach would spoil Tim, making him insatiably greedy and over-dependent on her. He also maintained it was bad for Pam, claiming she was depressed by the exhaustion from lack of sleep and the relentless attention Tim demanded. He insisted she go to the doctor, who sent her to a counsellor. This did not have the consequence Brian hoped for. 'The counsellor told me I had to leave Brian! She insisted that I had to get away from him, that he was bad for me. I probably did feel depressed after all my babies, but so what – doesn't everyone?'

Pam is right: between half and three-quarters of mothers report some kind of baby blues within a few days of giving birth (page 322,

R8). Less commonly, full-scale post-natal depression occurs in about 13% of mothers (actual psychosis, in which the mother suffers delusions and total loss of identity, occurs in only 0.2% – see page 322, R8). However, Huggers do not tend to get depressed during the early months*. Despite the lack of sleep and disorientation resulting from adapting to the baby's routine that their approach causes, overall, most Huggers would not swap it for the world. If serious depression is going to hit them it is more likely to do so when the baby begins to show signs of independence, from about four months. Whether this develops depends on the mother's motives for being a Hugger.

If she had an appalling infancy herself and is desperately compensating for that by Hugging her baby, it can make her reluctant to allow the baby to become independent and separate. Studies show that the most at risk are mothers who have no partner, or have a partner who is unsupportive, or if they had a mother who was very controlling of them – interfering a lot, never letting them be themselves*. Vulnerable Hugger mothers may suffer what is called maternal separation anxiety, in which they continue to feel highly concerned about their baby's welfare in inappropriate situations*. They may fear leaving their 18-month-old even for a moment with its very familiar father or letting a sister, who knows their six-month-old well, hold it. Such Huggers are at greatly increased risk of depression* but it should be noted that they are rare.

Those few Huggers at risk of depression after the birth, rather than later on, tend to have had their dream of how things should be shattered by practical problems. It can start with the birth itself, if they have placed a very high premium on it being natural and they have had to endure a lot of medical intervention. Should the baby require intensive care, the Hugger may feel mortified on its behalf and desperately unhappy to be only able to see the baby through the plastic of the intensive care machine, not cuddle it. If she has cracked nipples or recurrent mastitis and has to give up breastfeeding, she may feel like a failure. If the baby arrives in a cranky state, being colicky, irritable, floppy or standoffish, the mother may be mortified that the blissful union she pictured is not happening. She may ruminate about the injustice of her lost Eden, a rumbling anger that can turn outwards at times in snappy rages or inwards, in depression. If the latter, she blames herself, feeling guilt for something that is not her fault.

Where economic hardship requires her to return to work, she may be tortured at having to do so. Additionally or alternatively, her partner may let her down by having an affair or reacting to the newcomer by working extra hours. Her own mother may be similarly unavailable when the Hugger was hoping she would be there. She may also have not joined any antenatal classes or have recently moved to a new area, lacking other mothers of similarly aged babies. She may have other children requiring care, and no support for doing so, forcing her attentions away from the baby. All or any of these add to the burdens of caring for a neonate but for the Hugger, the gap between the ideal and reality can seem acutely intolerable, triggering depression. The commonest discrepancies between how she would like to be handling things and what is actually happening are having to work or having an unsupportive partner*. The best study on this subject suggests that mothers with small babies who are most at risk are both those who work full-time and those who stay at home full-time – part-timers are least at risk*. But this may not be the whole truth. A proportion of the ones who are at home are long-time depressives, unable to do any work from before they got pregnant. If they are taken out of the equation, then at-home Huggers might be the least depressed group of any – better studies are needed of this issue.

If Pam was depressed, it is likely that Brian's lack of support for her approach was a big factor. It meant that when Tim was three and their next child Sarah came along, Pam felt she had to give way to the pressure not to be a Hugger. For one thing, not repeating the divorce of her parents was 'my big, number-one intention in life', and she was worried that Brian might not be able to stand going through everything that had happened with Tim all over again. For another, the stress of being constantly told that she was wrecking her son was more than she could bear. 'My friends were "what's happened to Pam, she's gone bonkers". Everyone was telling me I was doing the wrong thing. I wanted to do the right thing, to be like everybody else.'

Another factor was that her own mother had wished she herself could be a Hugger when Pam was small but had gone against this inclination because of social pressure, leaving Pam with numerous different carers. She was always very supportive of Pam's Hugging with Tim, the sole person to be so. But when the next child came along, just having her mother's support became insufficient. 'I had had so much grief, Oliver, from friends, from Brian, but also from my father. He was "You can't do this! What is the baby doing in the bed, what about your relationship?"' With Tim, Pam had done what her mother wished she could have done. With her next child – even though it had not saved her parents' marriage – she decided she had better do what her mother had actually done and use lots of substitute care.

First came a maternity nurse, then a nanny, then a childminder. At two and a half, a nursery accepted Sarah because she was potty-trained – 'nursery was a big mistake, she was far too young'. While still being a responsive, attentive mother when with Sarah, that was inevitably for much less of the time because she took up regular lunching with her friends and, with Brian's encouragement, set up a small business.

To begin with, she felt that Sarah did well. Tim had been a difficult baby and this had activated deep-seated desires to 'nurture, nurture, nurture'. By contrast, 'Sarah was a good baby, and that filled me with confidence. She ate, slept, seemed calm, and I put it down to the fact that we had adopted a strict routine from the maternity nurse.' However, at 18 months there was a sudden transformation. 'I remember it so well. It was as if something went off in her head and she thought "hang on a minute, what's going on here?" And it all flipped upside down and she started screaming like a banshee. She would never go to bed, having been as easy as pie.' From then on Sarah stopped being a 'good' toddler. The transitions to a childminder from the nanny and then to the nursery were both accompanied by a lot of signs of distress.

Pam is convinced that the different early regimes account for differences in personality between Sarah, now aged six, and Tim. 'I feel it's payback time now with Sarah, she wants so much attention.' Whereas Tim is calm and confident, she is very worried about Sarah. 'I think she just learnt very young to put a brave face on everything but that deep down she was panicking and furious. She was left to cry, only fed every four hours; it makes me incredibly sad to feel that she just gave up protesting, and to think of all the other babies out there who have also done so. When she was small my heart told me what to do and I ignored it and listened to everyone around me. That means now she is incredibly good at covering up what she really feels.' While Sarah seems unusually grown up at times, Pam encounters a very different side at others. 'She does her best to seem good but then comes the meltdown, she turns into an absolute baby every so often. Like last week we tried to go swimming and she suddenly put her foot down. She cried and cried and cried. She was testing my love, meaning "if my mummy really loves me she will wrap me up and take me home".'

In general, Sarah is much more prepared than Tim to set off to parties or events involving strangers, and often seems to be getting on fine in these settings. However, Pam has gradually realised that this is a false patina of well-being, a fragile one. Often, for no apparent reason, Sarah dissolves into inconsolable tears or becomes furiously angry, like a toddler having temper tantrums. Her façade of friendliness and compliance collapses and a very insecure person is exposed. Pam believes Sarah will go to great lengths to please her. 'She makes a big thing out of how much she loves her younger sister but I'm sure it's just that she knows it's going to make me feel happy – it's people-pleasing. She does that in all sorts of ways.'

This is very much what the scientific evidence would predict. Children who have multiple carers who they do not feel safe with are sometimes liable to 'indiscriminate friendliness' (page 294, R3). They show similar reactions, to familiar and unfamiliar people, a gloss of positive smiles and niceness. But it is important to stress that if Sarah has been damaged, the harm came from the constantly changing and unresponsive substitute regime Pam introduced, not simply from the fact that Pam ceased to be the main carer during the day. As explained in Chapter 1, what babies need is an adult present at all times who is completely tuned into them* but that does not have to be its biological mother. Likewise, a toddler needs a highly responsive adult at all times who is very familiar with its little ways, who is able to gradually introduce some boundaries using explanations and loving care, and who is not distracted by the needs of lots of other toddlers. Again, that does not have to be its mother. If at all possible, you need to find someone who is not, for example, going to disappear off back to Poland or the Philippines after a year, as Sarah's nanny did, even if it entails offering a bonus at that point. If it's an informal arrangement with a friend, be equally careful to assess how temporary this is going to be. You are looking for set-ups that will last to age three.

As indicated in the sections on substitute care in Chapter 6 (page 104), where Pam went wrong was in starting with a nanny, moving on to a minder and then sending Sarah to a nursery. In itself, this runs a considerable risk of making the child anxious, because the carers keep changing. In theory, it would be possible to arrange without problems, but in practice, it will only work if the handover between each carer is gradual and if the carers in each setting are responsive. That is not easily achieved. In Pam's case, she did not realise how important these things were and anyway, and equally significant, none of the substitutes was very responsive.

The other problem lay with the rigidity of the feeding and sleeping regime introduced at birth. While a measure of routine is harmless, it is undoubtedly best of all if it is infant-led – stuff like noticing that the baby gets antsy at lunchtime and that it really wants a sleep at that time. There are now quite a few studies demonstrating that if babies are left to cry and to soothe themselves, they eventually sleep in their cots better than if the parents go to them and offer nurture*. This suits the parents very well but it is not good for the child. The studies suggest that if you do not go to crying babies at night, responding sensitively, usually by picking up, and instead just leave them to scream, they are more likely to be insecure at age one*. While it is true that responding to the cries promptly and sensitively may mean the baby is less likely to have a sleep routine which suits you, there is also good evidence that babies who are responded to at night from birth, rather than being left to soothe them- selves, are less irritable and fussy at three months*. So books which advocate leaving babies to cry are sowing the seeds of bigger problems; it can create babies who are unhappy and insecure, ones who tend towards a surly aggression, joyless lifelessness or withdrawn depression when they get to the age of three, four and five*, and possibly to more serious problems in later life related to lack of early responsiveness*.

Being a highly responsive mother, Pam was never comfortable with Sarah's regime. Her view today is that it was responsible for making Sarah want to regress to being a baby again, to get the care she never had. Without any knowledge of theories, Pam has worked out for herself that Love Bombing is the best solution (this approach really can repair a lot of damage). 'If she wants to sleep in our bed, even now, I let her. I do lots of little things. Like when she sees her younger sister having a beaker of milk, she wants one and she gets it, in a beaker too. I let her be a baby if that's what she seems to need.' Jill, their lastborn's story, only serves to increase Pam's conviction that her Hugger approach was the right one all along.

Although Brian insisted on a maternity nurse, Pam sent her home after a couple of hours. Jill breastfed happily, sharing the marital bed. Now aged two, she has all the calm confidence, the security, that Tim has. Pam can see that the difference between these children and her daughter Sarah has nothing to do with what they were like at birth. Indeed, their personalities at that stage strongly support her conviction that her mothering approach is the key. Whereas Tim was difficult, developing colic, Sarah started off easy. Although Pam knows nothing about the scientific evidence, there is good reason to suppose that Sarah's early care established abnormal levels of the fight-flight hormone cortisol. Being constantly nervous about whether she would be responded to and having several different carers, it is likely that she has high levels, making her hyperalert to the danger of something going wrong, unable to relax (page 279, R3). By contrast, Tim probably started with high cortisol levels which his care normalised. Pam had an anxious late pregnancy (stress in the last three months), made nervous by her miscarriage. There is powerful evidence that high cortisol levels in anxious mothers at this stage are passed through the placenta to the foetus, still showing up as abnormal levels at age 10, even after all the other factors (like maltreatment) are taken into account*. This evidence strongly suggests you should do your best to take it easy during the last trimester of pregnancy.

In Tim's case, having had a difficult birth and suffered colic, he would have been at high risk of subsequently being jumpy and insecure in relationships. But because Pam Hugged for Britain, he has none of these problems today. By contrast, just as the evidence predicts, Sarah does have them – because of the changing and unresponsive care she received. Put crudely, Tim started off with high cortisol levels and his care balanced them. Sarah started off balanced and was imbalanced by her care.

Interestingly, though, Pam still has quite contradictory feelings about her worth as a mother, despite having proved herself right twice over. After nine months there was a scare with Jill's heart that turned out to be groundless but Pam feels this has 'turned me into an ultra-anxious mother again'. She keeps feeling that everyone else deals with babies much more easily than she does, that she is overly worried. In fact, she is simply very well attuned to her baby's changing states of mind. Some of the mothers she compares herself with sound as if they frequently ignore their children's signals and indeed, Brian strongly advocates this, admonishing her, 'Don't go into Jill's head', which is precisely what Jill needs Pam to do, like all toddlers. Yet to this day, so great has been the pressure on Pam to see herself as a bad mother, part of her still feels this.

She believes that her acute sensitivity to babies and toddlers resulted from her own early childhood. 'All I can think is that perhaps I was left constantly with changing carers and perhaps it really upset me and I'm remembering it, what that was like.' This is certainly very possible. A proportion of Huggers are motivated above all to provide the care to babies that they themselves did not have. In meeting the baby's needs, deep down, the Hugger can be giving herself the feeling of safety and love that she missed out on. But that does not make Hugging a sick compensation for deprivation. Rather, it often enables mothers to be supremely talented at meeting their baby's needs, even though those around them paint this as neurotic over-concern.

Pam needs reassuring that, even if her Hugging is a compensation for her own infancy, that does not make it pathological. Her sensitivity is just what her babies needed. Recently, a babysitter had arrived. The woman did not strike Pam as very sensitive and Jill did not seem to be keen on her – sometimes Jill warms to them, sometimes not, and Pam uses this as a sign as to whether the arrangement will work. This is not excessive concern, it is a well-judged method for deciding what is appropriate care for a vulnerable two-year-old. But Brian was adamant Pam was being over-fussy in worrying about the babysitter and refusing to leave their daughter with her.

At one level, Pam sometimes goes along with this verdict, denigrating her own mothering. Because she has been stigmatised by everyone in her social world other than her mother, Pam quite often joins the chorus depicting her as 'bonkers'. She speaks of herself as disorganised, a poor timekeeper, anxious. But at another level she strongly disagrees with this account. 'I just feel I know when my children need me. Like we were driving down the motorway and I insisted on us stopping. I had to scream at Brian to stop the car and if he didn't want to stay, he could head off without us. I got Jill out of her seat because I knew something was really wrong and she needed to be calmed. Other people apparently wouldn't do that.'

One of the most heartening aspects of Pam's story is the way she and Brian have managed not to fall out over her Hugging. 'To be fair, he tolerated what he believed to be complete madness, and he does so to this day. Thank God he stuck by me. I don't know what I would have done if he had walked out.' It is an interesting question why he did not, one that illustrates different ways the partnerships of Huggers can work.

There is not usually much or any problem if the partner is also a Hugger, as we saw with Will and Jo in the last chapter. They are mostly happy to act as a support system and put their self on the shelf for the good of the baby, as they see it. They may not be happy about the lack of opportunity for sex which bed-sharing causes. They may not happen to be very domesticated, in which case the endless shopping, cooking, tidying and cleaning may get on their nerves. But their Hugger tendency overrides these dissatisfactions because, deep down, when their partner feeds and caresses their child, they also feel mothered. The only real problem arises if they feel competitive with the mother, wanting to do more of the Hugging themselves than the mother is willing to allow.

But where the partner strongly disagrees, it can lead to divorce. In the case of Brian and Pam, on the surface, their view of each other is toxic. He believes that her mothering has depressed her and that she needs treatment, although the visit to the counsellor has taught him not to hold out too high hopes of that. But she is no less sceptical of him. 'I really do think he is genuinely crazy. He's incredibly clever, I know. I think I'm shallow and he's deep. He will analyse everything to the very bottom and beyond. He gets incredibly depressed sometimes and still takes drugs quite a lot. He is a total control freak when it comes to me, reading every text message I get; I don't know why because I would never go off.' She admits to having considered this. 'In the darkest moments of our relationship I think "maybe there's this other man, a less complicated one, successful and so on", but then I don't want that. This other man would expect things I cannot give whereas I can give Brian what he needs. There were so many others I could have had, but I wanted him, and he wanted me. Why did we want each other?'

In her case, the answer seems clear: her parents' divorce made her absolutely determined never to divorce and her childhood insecurities make her feel safest with someone who is as fragile as herself – she fears that a more secure, more balanced man than Brian would not need her, would see her as inadequate. In Brian's case, something very similar happened.

An only child, Pam says that 'he was neglected from the day he was born'. His mother was coldly unresponsive, probably depressed, and the stories of his crying and tantrums throughout childhood are legendary in his family. This made Brian nervous about needy babies and inclined to the view that they must be controlled lest they become insatiable. However, he knew Pam extremely well by the time they were married, knew she was loyal and that she had, in some respects, mothered him through a stormy late adolescence and early twenties. Deep down, as well as feeling neglected and left out by Pam's Hugging of their children, Brian does also feel the baby in him gets hugged when he witnesses it. That is why, despite feeling strong intellectual objections to Pam's approach, he has stuck by her.

This is similar to the situation in a great many relationships, best encapsulated by the joke with which Woody Allen ended his film, Annie Hall. A man goes to a psychiatrist saying, 'My wife is mad. She thinks she's a chicken.' The shrink asks, 'So why don't you leave her?' to which the man replies, 'I need the eggs.'

Pam's story has two very important morals for Huggers: that your approach is a good one for meeting the needs of babies and toddlers; however, that if your partner is dead against it, you can expect a great deal of turbulence. In an ideal world, we would discuss our approach to parenting with partners before getting pregnant, but the world is not ideal. By no means can either of you accurately predict how you will feel when the baby is there, before the birth, let alone before becoming pregnant. What Pam's story shows is that even if your partner is giving you hell for Hugging, deep down, he may be on your side. If he is not, you are faced with a horrible choice: deprive your baby or risk your relationship with your partner. If that is your predicament, I can only suggest that you ask him to read Chapter 1 and then to read this one. More detailed suggestions for help are provided in Chapter 11.

We come now to the other main force that can come between a Hugger and her baby: the need for money or the other rewards which come from a paid job.

CHAPTER 9

Huggers Who Do Paid Work

Since Huggers believe that they, and only they, can meet the needs of their baby and that doing so is imperative, there are almost no circumstances in which they will go back to paid jobs in the early months. However, by the age of one, a proportion will countenance it. Mostly, financial necessity is the main reason. This contrasts with many working mothers.

The majority say that they do not return to paid work primarily for the money*. In quite a few cases, the financial gains are negligible after the childcare costs are paid. By far the commonest reason given is the enjoyment of sharing life with peers in the workplace*. For that minority who have professions and careers, rather than just jobs, the feeling that they have worked hard to get the qualifications and do not want to waste all that effort is also important.

Rarest is the Hugger who comes to the conclusion that she can find someone else who can do the job as well or better than she can, after the first year or so, and who also feels a strong sense that her worker identity is not satisfied sufficiently by mothering. Often possessors of advanced qualifications and jobs that pay well above the national average of £24,000 a year, such mothers feel it will be better for their toddler if they work because it will make everyone happier – happy mother, happy baby.

More usually, Huggers work to pay the mortgage, especially if they earn more than their partner. Of course, it could be argued that hardly anyone absolutely *has* to work if they have an under-three. They could buy a cheaper home, cut down on outgoings and, if necessary, get welfare benefits. But this is a lot to ask for most people raised in our Affluenza-stricken society. The vast majority take for granted as basic needs that we must have a car, TV and so forth, and a good many of us come to regard as *needs* things that are really *wants*, resulting in a steady trickle of outgoings – unnecessary clothing, gadgets, coffee habits and the like. While Huggers are probably more likely than most to question our addiction to these things, the bottom line for all of us is that we do need a roof over our head. For those on the property ladder, their savings and pension are often bound up in the bricks and mortar. The average parent is already in a house that is small for bringing up children and they are hoping for somewhere with separate rooms for the children, a garden or bigger garden, or proximity to relatives or preferred schools. They are hardly looking to downshift to an even smaller place.

In what follows, I present two illustrations of working Huggers. The second is one who feels it will be best for her child if she works. The first does it solely for the money.

Sam: A Hugger Who Needs the Money

Sam has had to make her own way in life, overcoming considerable adversities. A delightful, sunny and determined 33-year-old, she had been with her partner John for three years when their son Richard was born, now aged two.

She has the Hugger's adoration of tiny babies. 'I am a smelling person, it means a lot to me – I told John not to wash once we got together, I like him to smell like a man. When I think back to the sour-milk smell of Richard's neck, Oh gorgeous! It's my favourite smell in the world. I will always miss and cherish it.' She feels passionately that nothing is more important than mothering but unfortunately, John does not earn enough to support the family. After a year, she returned to work for two days a week and also does several hours' overtime in the evenings and at weekends. Although she finds this life incredibly tiring and although she would vastly prefer to do no paid work until Richard goes to school, financial necessity would seem to dictate that there is no alternative. The devil is in the detail.

First and foremost, they live in London. They moved into their modest three-bedroom house on the outskirts just before Richard's birth, at the top of the property boom, requiring a £900 monthly payment (on a £220,000 mortgage). But this is not a wild extravagance: it would cost even more to rent. Nor do they have much choice. At the time of the interview (March 2009) it looked as if it would be quite a few years before prices rise sufficiently for them to sell and not lose money.

John's steady bookkeeping job provides £500 a week after deductions. If he was the sole breadwinner, after paying the mortgage that would leave £225 a week for all their joint outgoings. It's hard to see how that could that be enough, even after cutting back to absolute essentials; £50 a week alone goes on John's travel to and from work. Once all utilities and other fixed costs (like Sam's pension and life insurance, which she prudently keeps up) are paid for, it would leave only a bare minimum, with no slack for even minor emergencies, like needing new shoes or if the washing machine broke down, let alone big capital outlays, like a new boiler. They have done the bare minimum to their house and Sam's claim that she is not a big spender is borne out by the absence of any designer possessions.

In general, it is a peculiarity of English-speaking national economics that they foster home ownership and high levels of consumption. As I described in my books *Affluenza* and *The Selfish Capitalist*, the enormous mortgages that we take for granted make dual-income earning more necessary. This is exacerbated in many cases by high consumption expectations, feeling that we need things that we only want, like a 'better' car or kitchen. Addicted to spending, it becomes impossible to maintain what we regard as a basic lifestyle without both partners earning. In America, families with a single earner have 60% lower incomes than ones with two*. Lacking a National Health Service, your very life is at risk there unless you can keep paying your private health insurance.

What startled me about Sam's case was that she is not addicted to consumption and her housing arrangements did not seem grandiose. Even without needing the latest and the biggest and the best, she did seem to need to work. The only ambiguity of their finances lay in John's expenditure. Although he was upset at the idea of Sam returning to work, convinced he should be able to be the breadwinner, his real love is making films and he does spend a certain amount every year on equipment and travel, pursuing this hobby.

As soon as she became pregnant, therefore, Sam realised that she was going to have to return to work. Unlike John, she had been thrifty, having been raised with an ethic of 'save, save, save'. These savings supplied the down payment for their mortgage and she used them to supplement their income during Sam's first year, when she did no paid work.

As we shall see, Sam has managed to find very satisfactory substitute care for Richard. However, she is emphatic that she would prefer to do it herself. 'The bottom line is that, ideally, I should be at home for Richard. I find my work interesting and absorbing but I would not do it if we didn't need the money. The good thing is that I feel proud of having managed to cope. But it just keeps on going, relentlessly; I never thought I would be able to survive. I'm knackered to my bones. I feel like a runaway train, keeping on rolling, but the train wreck could happen soon, hitting the wall and going to pieces.'

The research bears this out (page 328, R8). If a mother has arrangements which she feels deep down do not suit her, she is at greater risk of depression. If her husband also feels that, the risk is even greater, for both of them.

One moral of this story for other Huggers who feel they want to be at home full-time (mostly the case for this type), therefore, is that it is particularly important to stare the economic realities hard in the face well before you start having babies. Obviously, all parents are better off doing so. But if you are a woman who particularly feels your baby needs you until it is three, it is concomitantly important to thrash out the minute details with your partner, which takes long-term planning unless you happen to have a large trust fund or have earned squillions in the City.

This is inevitably often very tricky. For plenty of couples, either one or other of them may be reluctant to get on with having babies and, therefore, be reluctant to get into the nitty-gritty of how it is going to be paid for. Quite a few women do not really know how they are going to feel until they become pregnant or give birth. In Sam's case, for example, John had been in favour of waiting two more years before having children and it was Sam who made the running. It was only after a few months into the pregnancy that John suddenly clicked into feeling strongly paternal and wanting to be a breadwinner. However, despite this turnaround, his feelings were still a bit mixed in that he continued to spend on his filming hobby when they needed to be saving every penny.

Fortunately for all concerned, Sam found splendid substitute care when she did return to paid work. This took a lot of research. While working as an au pair herself, she had developed a very negative view of childminders: 'They often seemed like lazy cows who sat on their bottoms all day drinking coffee while the children fought, occasionally slapping them over the head if it got out of hand.' Since day care nurseries were all the rage, she visited several with Richard. However, this did not please her either. 'Richard did not like there being so many children, very noisy. When other children bashed him over the head he never hit back. He would have been swamped.' She disagrees with mothers who say that it's healthy for them to learn independence at such a young age. 'Some mothers say "let them deal with it, they've got to learn to sort themselves out". My personal opinion is "No, you can't do that. It's not possible because before three they don't have the skills."'

One day, by chance she encountered a childminder in her street who solved the problem. 'I saw her at work and thought "although she is a minder, she seems really nice, actually". She was loving with the children, cuddling, kissing them, playing and observing and monitoring them, all the stuff that I would do. So I asked to see her home and it was just right.' There is only one other child present on the two days she works, and she is four years old. 'Richard absolutely adores her. When he returns he's always happy, never overtired. It's a long day but I can't say how pleased I am with it.' Not all mothers find it easy to see their child being kissed and cuddled by the substitute. Huggers can feel jealous, Organisers can feel criticised. If so, you need to square up to your feelings honestly and realise that a loving substitute is essential for your child, that you have to override your feelings and put the child's first.

But the main moral of this story for Huggers is that, although not easy, it is possible to find substitutes who may be able to be just as good as you, painful though that may be to admit. It can take a lot of looking and you will need to take a lot of trouble because, as a Hugger, you will take a lot of satisfying and quickly become very unhappy if you feel the arrangement is not good. Usually a minder or possibly a neighbour is going to be best, assuming you have no close relatives who are willing and suitable (see page 106, Chapter 6). Very few, if any, day care nurseries will satisfy a Hugger. However, there is one further potential alternative for the employed Hugger, not yet considered: your partner.

Sheila: A Hugger Who Believes It's Best for Everyone if She Goes Back to Her Career

Sheila, 35, lives in a modern one-bedroom flat in south London with her partner Jim, 38, and Samuel, their 10-month-old son. Somewhat self-disparaging, modest and friendly, she has been a conscientious hard worker since her first day at school, achieving high grades. After many years as a social worker, she now has a senior teaching post in a university, one to which she will return in two months' time, ostensibly because

Jim does not earn enough to support the family. While he has a low-paid, steady job in local government, his real love is writing novels.

Sheila is an unusual Hugger in that even if Jim did have lots of money, she would still want to work part-time. She has the classic Hugger enthusiasm for 'snuggly buggly' time in bed with her son, and demand-led breastfeeding and sleeping patterns. But there are several reasons why she feels that even if money were not an issue, she would still go back to her job.

While she was visibly loving her son's company and meeting his needs, she is also quite an anxious person, especially so when it comes to mothering. This started with a miscarriage, where she had to have the foetus removed surgically at three months, it having died at nine weeks. With Samuel's pregnancy she was understandably nervy during it, but this continued after the birth. The self-critical, rigorous intellect which served her so well in her career was less helpful when dealing with the chaotic, messy business of infant care. During the early months she became hypercritical of herself, full of self-doubt.

Unfortunately, Samuel suffered colic for the first five months and this made him grouchy, reducing the amount of sleep she got. 'There would be a lot of screaming in the last three hours of the day, total melt-down. Whatever you do doesn't work. You feel "is it me? My baby doesn't love me, am I doing the right thing?"' For a Hugger, there's nothing worse than the feeling you are not meeting the baby's needs. When she went to see other mothers from her NCT class, all their babies seemed to be smiling and happy. 'I thought I am the worst mother in this room, my baby hates me. It happened every week, I must be an awful mother.'

In fact, she was nothing of the kind, very sensitively and intelligently getting to the bottom of the problem. She realised that he was 'knackered' and needed a lunchtime nap. Being an insecure person who is also quite scholarly, she had spent quite a bit of time reading stuff about mothering on the net. She had rejected Gina Ford during the pregnancy but 'I didn't know how to be myself. I was casting around for someone to tell me.' Ironically, the book which did so (by Donald Winnicott, *The Child, the Family and the Outside World*) helped her to realise she did not need books. 'I found it very reassuring when he said that you only have to be good enough, find out what is best for yourself, others can't tell you, trust yourself. After that I stopped any reading and felt much more confident.'

In terms of her attitude to returning to work, she feels that she is tremendously prone to guilt and finds it hard to believe she is a good mother, even now. She knows she is liable to get bogged down in details, overly concerned sometimes about safety or practical stuff. So the first reason she would return to work, even if money was not an issue, is that she is doubtful she is the best person for Samuel. The second is that she feels Jim will do a better job.

This option emerged after a possible nanny-share fell through and she had visited a lot of day care nurseries. They seemed unbearable. 'Since having a child I have an overdeveloped sense of empathy. I cry at the most ridiculous things – adverts, I couldn't read anything about babies who were in the news because they had been maltreated, watching nature programmes. At the nurseries I thought "these poor little babies are being deprived of their mothers". Watching them, you just feel this total sadness. You see *very little* babies, like one that was only three months old.' Since neither of them has relatives living nearby, she was stumped.

This was the point at which Jim happily volunteered. They had never discussed it before and, being somewhat perfectionist, she does have her reservations. 'A part of me wonders if he knows what he's getting himself into. Because he's steeped in literature, his head is in the clouds. So will he be practical and will he tune in?' As Huggers are wont to be, even with their partners, when Samuel was small she was particularly doubtful about anyone else looking after him, including Jim. 'I watched him like a hawk when he was looking after Samuel. Wherever he was, I was, whether he was changing a nappy or whatever,

I was extremely sceptical. I'm a lot easier about that now.' In fact, she is confident it will work. 'Jim's fantastic at play, a lot more creative than me, I'm too knackered to think of new games. Samuel absolutely loves him, which drives me mad. You spend a whole day with a child who's been grouchy and whining all the time, and then the minute the father walks in it's all smiles. You're bitching about the day you've had and they're wondering what the problem is, he's just perfect. I'm looking forward to that being the other way around. I wanna be the good guy who gets to swan in and do the creative play, the interesting stuff.'

In fact, since she is so given to self-doubt, 'there's another side of me that thinks he will be better than me. He's a man and good at rough play, he's quite warm, affectionate, loving and creative with Samuel. He might not attend to the details as I do, but the love is there and sometimes I think I get caught up in the details. I think Samuel will definitely grow up feeling loved by Jim and, being creative, Jim wants to take him to all these places, like museums and zoos, whereas I might struggle to get out of the house.'

Interestingly, she does not fear that Jim will feel a loss of status in doing the job. 'I'm going to be paying him to do it, essentially, but I've always been the breadwinner in our relationship, which has been tricky at times. But his identity is less with his paid work than as a writer. Putting that on hold for a few years he will still be able to feel good about himself. We have done a trial run, which was fine, and he really wants to be a stay-at-home father, so I think he will make it work.'

It's some achievement to have had the insight and honesty to see that she is not necessarily the most effective Hugger in the world and, on top of that, to have overcome her doubts (perhaps understandable, including elements of rivalry and jealousy) about Jim's suitability. But there is a final reason why she is returning to work. Sheila has also come to understand that her worker identity is a powerful one which needs to be satisfied, along with the Hugger-mummy one, and that if she does not pay it heed both she and Samuel would suffer.

Like many modern women she would feel uneasy about not earning her own money, even if Jim could keep them both. She also feels she has worked extremely hard to reach this point in her career (although she says, 'it's amazing how much less ambitious I am than when I was 18; I realise that I have my limitations and working too hard is stressful. Doing a few things well is enough, being a good parent the most important.') But the most influential thought is that a happy mother brings a happy baby, and she would not be content feeling she was missing out on being part of a team at work and the satisfaction of helping her students. Although she has felt very fulfilled caring for Samuel, Hugger care – being child-led – is especially draining if you are naturally someone who likes order, as she does.

For reasons that are not fully understood, men are still reluctant to be full-time mothers, even in Scandinavian societies which go to enormous lengths to encourage it. In Britain it is still only a small minority of under-threes who are cared for during the working week by their fathers, even for a few hours, let alone all the time. Most fathers still crave the status of paid jobs and want to be a breadwinner*. More mothers than is often admitted are sceptical – as Sheila was – whether men can do it properly. But as women become increasingly liable to be the higher-paid parent in a couple, it is hard to doubt that there will be a steady increase in male mothers. While it is easy to understand why women will continue to be the main carer for the early months, it is hard to see why more and more men will not find themselves holding the baby from the age of one, whether sharing the care or doing it full-time. If so, it would be a splendid partial solution to the meeting of the needs of under-threes, far preferable to day care nurseries (see R3).

Having dealt with the two commonest impediments to the Hugger's mothering – their partner and needing to earn money – we come to the final one: the kind of care they received in their childhoods.

CHAPTER 10

How Huggers' Childhoods Can Help and Hinder Meeting Their Children's Needs

While a few Huggers may choose their approach after reading books or through a cerebral appreciation of the evidence presented in Chapter 1, very deep down, most do so as a result of two prior extreme experiences in their early life: either unusually good early care, or unusually bad.

The first group, whom I shall describe for the next few pages, had their needs met as babies and toddlers, and feel that it is natural to be a Hugger. Prior to pregnancy or the birth, they may have never given this much thought. They may be rather astonished at their reaction to the arrival of the baby, suddenly discovering a serene confidence that they know exactly how to fit into the baby's life. Some of these women may have had high-flying careers and find themselves completely swept up in the Hugger project, only just remembering to tell their former employer that they are not returning to work. Their motivation is to repeat for their baby what was done for them. At a deep level, the reason they get profound fulfilment out of meeting their baby's needs is because they can identify with what it is like to be that baby, recapturing what it was like to be loved like that themselves. When asked why they hug, while they may pepper the answer with scientific evidence or the importance of being natural (especially if they have read Jean Liedloff's Hugger bible, *The Continuum Concept*), they will also often mention that they just know this is the best way because it's like returning home.

The experience of having needs met does not have to have been created by their biological mother. As mentioned in the last part of the book, when I was in China researching *Affluenza* I asked everyone I met there who had cared for them in their early years. I only met one person for whom it was their mother; nearly all had been cared for as babies and toddlers by their grandmothers. It really doesn't matter who was responsive to you as a baby, so long as that is what was done. If so, the odds are that this will be your approach when you become a mother, as the following story illustrates.

Charlotte: Her Grandmother Hugged Her

Charlotte never felt her mother was particularly loving or responsive: 'She could be very distant, remote, away with the fairies.' Consequently, when pregnant, Charlotte was jumpy about having a girl. She feared that a daughter would trigger the same kind of feelings her mother had about her, whereas with a boy it might be easier to come at it afresh. It so happened her best friends felt similarly. 'Doubtless it was no coincidence that they all seemed to have mothers who were pretty sticky about them – I daresay I naturally inclined towards friends who had similar problems with their mothers – and they also had mixed feelings about daughters. I thought that went with the territory. What was more, I didn't think I was a natural-born Earth Mother anyway, so I was pretty anxious about the demands mothering would place on me.'

But when a daughter duly appeared, none of the problems she anticipated came about and today, she thinks she knows why: as a baby and toddler herself, she saw little of her mother; she was cared for largely by her father's mother, who was a Hugger. She believes this is why she naturally clicked into Hugging as soon as she clapped eyes on her daughter. 'It felt as though this love came from things in me that stretched back earlier than I could remember, before I had words. My dad was quite a wise man who knew a lot about himself. He had talked to me about how his childhood – including his infancy – had influenced him. He could distinctly remember the atmosphere of his earliest times, even if he couldn't describe specific incidents. I could feel its effect on him and that effect in me, coming via his mother's care of me. They are experiences that are very hard to reach or describe, but I suspect the mood and timbre of our earliest experiences still live on in us.'

This might sound like hocus-pocus to some readers but it is scientifically plausible – there is strong evidence that very early levels of attunement to the baby have a big effect*. By videotaping mothers with their babies, it has been shown that the extent to which the mother coordinates her responses to fit in with the actions of the baby profoundly affects its mood and personality. As babies, we have no words for our surroundings, or our internal thoughts and feelings. That means our memories of them are inchoate, necessarily at the level of basic sensations, basic emotions, pre-verbal. It may be that much of the power of music derives from its capacity to reach this level, likewise some paintings or other plastic arts, likewise our responses to natural phenomena, like the sea, or a turbulent or clear blue sky. Charlotte believes that many negative aspects of experience also have these infantile roots. 'Any kind of nameless fear, like of the dark, or of abandonment or loneliness, probably stretch back to the earliest years. I think these are the sort of fears that a horror film plays on, like a shot in which it seems you are seeing the back of the head of an old lady but when they turn round it's a snarling man or terrifying monster. It must be very like that for infants, constantly expecting one thing and getting another, or else, not knowing what to expect and getting big shocks.'

Charlotte's theory is that, just as bad infantile experiences can accumulate, creating a much greater propensity in adulthood to have a primitive set of fears which have to be kept at bay, so good experiences could create a calm, rich set of expectations which underpin a secure, fulfilled adult. Very detailed analysis of what goes on between mothers and babies supports Charlotte's theory*. When subtleties of the interaction are dissected, like the level of harmony or the extent to which a mother reacts quickly to her baby in ways that produce pleasure, it seems as if this creates an emotional climate which may affect the basic perspective with which the baby comes to view the world.

THE SECOND MOTIVATION FOR HUGGING: COMPENSATION FOR A LACK OF HAVING BEEN HUGGED

Plenty of Huggers are not like Charlotte. Whereas she is almost automatically providing the good experience she had, they are on a mission to give their baby the love they felt they never had. A few will be very aware of this, able to talk cogently about the difficulties they have suffered in later life as a result of their early deprivations. But most will not realise the extent to which their Hugging is impelled by a desire to repair their past. Also identifying strongly with the baby, they are acutely aware of its vulnerability and of the distress it will feel if needs are not met. In Hugging, they are giving the baby in themselves the experience of love, safety and identity which it missed out on first time round: they hug their little baby to satisfy and soothe that dependent, needy part of themselves. They will probably not be conscious of just how frightened, upset or desperate they felt as babies, and just how much these feelings continue in them now as adults. But once you understand this, you can see just how blissful it must feel to them to be able to meet their baby's needs.

Mothers from the first group, the ones who are only repeating the good care they received, are unlikely to encounter the problems described below. It is from the second group that the ones who get into difficulties tend to come.

Tessa: An Anorexic Turned Hugger

Tessa has a normal weight for a woman of her build in her thirties but when she was 15, she was anorexic. At one point she was so undernourished that she was only days away from death. 'I hated everyone and everything, I didn't want anyone around, including myself. I literally wanted to disappear.'

She was raised on an island in a tiny community in northern Scotland. Her mother was a teacher at the only school, Tessa in her class for three years with four other pupils. She was cared for primarily by her mother as a baby and toddler; her grandmother was tremendously supportive in later childhood. 'Looking back, I think my mother was depressed. One of my earliest memories is of my brother singing "You've got the whole world, at your feet" to cheer her up.' She witnessed many very painful rows between her parents, sitting crying at the top of the stairs listening to the rancour. Sometimes the family went on caravan holidays and at night her parents would have vicious whispered rows while the children were supposed to be asleep, six feet away.

Her recovery from anorexia and depression took years and only really happened when she moved to Liverpool and worked with cancer patients. Suddenly she realised the value of life and escaped from a tremendously bleak view of the world and herself. Newly confident, since she was attractive and, despite all her troubles, had done well academically, she had no difficulty finding a boyfriend and forging a successful career.

Now the Hugger mother of two small children, she believes her Hugging is a reaction against the way her mother related to her early in life. 'I'm still working it out but I am sure it has to do with that. The words I would use for what she was like when I was small are "non-available". I wanted it to be a pleasurable experience to have me there.

Instead, I think she dreaded having to deal with me. When I was old enough, she never read any books to me, never played with me. I think she was just too dead and miserable.'

During the pregnancy with her first child, Tessa was very aware of a determination to give her child a different early experience. 'I said to myself "you cannot be doing what your mother was doing". I was absolutely driven to be emotionally available, to provide all those kisses and cuddles I missed. I know all about that deadness which I felt in my teens and which nearly resulted in actual death, and which my mother felt. I can feel how it originated when I was a baby with someone who did not respond. I have reacted against the way I was mothered in a deliberate fashion.'

There is no good scientific evidence explaining why some mothers respond with Hugging to this kind of childhood, while others just repeat the unresponsive care. These latter have a fear of the neediness of babies, a discomfort at the relentless demand for love, a dislike of the emotional and practical chaos that the first year of the child's life inevitably brings. Many factors come into play, but there is some evidence that a crucial one is whether or not there were other people in the child's life who did provide some love*. In Tessa's case, for example, her granny provided a consistent source of kisses and cuddles, and she may have been the reason why Tessa was able to carry out her plan of being a Hugger. Some other women find that, although they want to be Huggers, it does not come so easily.

Joyce: A Hugger Whose Desire to Differ from Her Mother Included Needing a Paid Job

Joyce is wholly committed to the Hugger approach, including breastfeeding, bed-sharing and putting the child first. She did her best to Hug her son and succeeded for much of the time. However, when he turned one, having found a superb nanny, she went back to her professional career, although she did not need the extra money. There were two reasons.

Her first was that she never felt comfortable Hugging. She has a very mathematical mind, is a highly skilled user of numbers, and her scientific, tidy mentality did not fit well with the emotion-driven, apparently shambolic life of a Hugger. Luckily, she had had love and was able to give it to her son. The love had come from her father, who was warm and affectionate, come what may. So she was able to provide lots of love to her son but the niggling problem was that she found the constant disorganisation of the household trying. While she could cope with it, and with the bed-hopping that having her son in the bed required (her husband often bailing out to the spare room in the middle of the night), the life was far from being her natural yen.

She puts the love of order down to her mother, a woman who liked things neat and tidy. Although she wished she was different from her in these respects, it simply was no good pretending she was – try as she might, she could not help feeling her life needed to be more organised than Hugging permitted, because she had learnt to think that way from her mother.

'She is quite a hard person, a regime person, highly critical and perfectionist, difficult to please. She would often speak about how great my friends were, never me, despite the fact that I got fantastic grades, was best in sport – I couldn't have been a better performer in those respects.' Her mother was opposed to Hugging. 'She was against messy breastfeeding; the children must slot into your life, be seen and not heard. Keep the clean, tidy home, no toys left lying around. I didn't want to be that person. I wanted to be more child-centred, less author-itarian.' In most respects she succeeded, but enough of the other traits had rubbed off on her that she could not eradicate them. 'Sometimes when I get frustrated with my son I hear myself using the very words my mother would have done and I get guilty: Oh my God, it's happening, I'm turning into her!'

So the first reason she went back to work was that she hated becoming like her mother and, in some respects, that was what was happening, despite all her best intentions. The second was that her career clearly demarcated her from her mother. 'She had never worked when we were children and I loathed the feeling that she was stuck at home, contributing nothing. I did not want to just be a housewife like her. I did not respect her when I was small.' By returning to her career, Joyce could convince herself that she was different from that.

In the cases described so far in this chapter, the Huggers managed to provide excellent care for their babies and toddlers. However, a small proportion – how small, we do not know because no studies have been done of this issue – of Huggers find themselves unable to tolerate their baby growing up. This small minority are often cited by the critics of Hugging as being representative of all Huggers. This is a grotesque distortion of the truth. While many Huggers are impelled by a desire to compensate for their own unhappy childhoods, most manage to provide excellent care.

HUGGERS WHO CAN'T LET GO

Hugging only goes wrong for those few who cannot accept the baby's gradual need for separateness and independence, from around four months onwards and into toddlerdom. These become the minority of Huggers who find it too painful to tolerate their baby growing up because their own need to be mothered has not been sufficiently satisfied by Hugging. While the blissful union with the neonate has compensated for their own unhappy experience at that age, it is not enough. They find it very hard to let go. Some get pregnant again as soon as possible, desperate for more love (via a baby they identify with). Others get depressed. This can be exacerbated by practicalities interrupting the bestowal of love, like partners letting them down or desperate lack of money forcing them back to work.

The illusion of being one person joined together, emotionally, starts to dissolve. It's much the same as when people fall in love as adults and one of them finds the gradual or sudden shift from in love to just love (or even just friendship) unbearable – the absence of the white-hot ferocity and passion can make adults suicidal*.

These mothers are liable to become irrationally anxious when separated from their babies, imagining dangers, becoming oversolicitious*. They are reluctant to leave the baby with a partner or relative who knows it well long after that could pose any problem for the baby or toddler. They may feel rather empty and lost when the baby is asleep, missing its company. There is a tendency to feel tinges of anger at the baby when it displays undeniable signs of separateness, like wanting to end a game of 'round and round the garden' or showing interest in their partner.

The Hugger baby may sense its mother's distress*. It may learn to avoid upsetting its mother if she displays pain on hearing its cries, by just whimpering or even offering reassuring smiles. The baby's signals that it has done enough feeding may be ignored. The breast may be offered at the slightest sign of trouble, making the baby over-dependent on it as a consolation. Generally, Hugger babies are less likely to suck thumbs*. This could be a sign of a problem in that minority of Huggers who are actively discouraging their baby from developing any habits that enable it to console itself: a forced over-dependence on mother.

As baby becomes toddler, with this minority of Huggers there may be big problems by the age of three, the child unable to sleep alone, irate if not fed on demand and resistant to toilet training. Although such cases are very rare, if the mother is exceptionally reluctant to tolerate the toddler's independence, it can seem worryingly dependent on the mother, 'enmeshed' with her, unable to disentangle what is her and what is them. This results in later life in serious problems for the child, such as inability to accept authority, the autonomous rights of other children and the normal limitations of the social world.

Of course, it is important to realise that most Huggers manage the transition of their baby to separateness and toddlerdom fine, and their babies thrive. The average Hugger may feel a little twinge of sadness around the four-month stage, when the baby shows interest in a stranger or is perfectly happy in its own company. They might mourn the cosy hours of breastfeeding as that slowly tails off or ends. They might feel wistful as they look down at their toddler, now finally sleeping through the night in its own bed, recalling the cuddly year(s) of three-in-a-bed.

Huggers who cannot let go need help from a psychoanalytic therapist who is expert in 'attachment' problems (see the last section of the next chapter for details of how to find one). With the right help, the mother can quickly see that she is suffocating her child, impairing its need to explore beyond her. It becomes apparent that her anxieties, rage and sense of loss when her child displays independence are directly caused by feeling deprived of love in her own childhood. While it may take many therapeutic sessions, both mother and child hugely benefit. It is near scandalous that this kind of help is often only available to people who can afford to pay for it. In its stead, all too often some form of Cognitive Behavioural Therapy is offered, as part of a parenting programme concentrating exclusively on the mothering behaviour and deliberately excluding the mother's own childhood from consideration. Such behavioural programmes, in which the mother is taught to suddenly dump the child in its own bed and leave it to cry, or to use naughty chairs, or other common training devices, confuse human children with rats or monkeys requiring behaviour modification. By only addressing the symptoms of the problem and ignoring the causes, a trauma can be inflicted on the child while the mother misses an opportunity for a life-changing insight into herself.

CHAPTER 11

Practical Hugger Top Tips

STAND UP FOR HUGGING AND FOR YOURSELF

You are absolutely right in believing that there is a strong bias against your approach in the media (R4). Most TV programmes, like *Supernanny*, revile Hugging: when was the last time you saw a programme in this genre which advocated having your child in the bed during the early years? Likewise, parenting pages in newspapers favour simplistic 'rat training' methods over love. New Labour shelled out billions to lure you to put your child in day care. I believe that very few members of the ruling elite either had Huggers as parents or favour it themselves. As a result, politicians and journalists (many of whom do not look after their children) continually misrepresent the proportion of mothers of under-threes that work. Although there are excellent organi-sations like Full Time Mothers and Global Women's Strike (which campaigns for carers to be paid to look after their children), the facts are almost never presented in newspapers:

⟨ Only 18% of under-threes in the UK have a mother who does paid work full-time (R1)
⟨ One third of under-threes have a mother who has done no paid work by the time of their child's third birthday (R1)
⟨ Nearly half of mothers of under-threes have no paid job on the third birthday (R1)

As we have seen, some Huggers do paid work, and it is fine. But most do not and their status is less than that of a street sweeper. So do not hold back when defending your decision to be a Hugger:

⟨ Far from nurturing a spoilt brat, your approach is much more likely to produce a calm, satiable, fulfilled adult*

⟨ You are quite right to believe that in most cases, genes probably play a negligible role* in how our children turn out and that you are indeed crucial for their welfare

⟨ Critics who suggest that you are being selfish in staying close to your child so much of the time, including breastfeeding much longer than the national average and having them sleep in your bed, should note the strong scientific evidence that your approach is very good for the well-being of babies*

⟨ It is not you who has anything to be guilty about – probably your critic is the one with the problem (and maybe, with the problem child).

KNOW THYSELF 1: YOUR CHILDHOOD

If you feel you need to know more about the impact of your childhood, my book *They F*** You Up* may help. It includes an opportunity at the end of each chapter to carry out an 'Emotional Audit' of how specific stages in your early childhood may be affecting specific features of your adult personality. There are many other good books explaining how your past may be affecting what you are like. Notable examples are *Banished Knowledge* by Alice Miller, *The Politics of the Family* by R D Laing, *Dibs in Search of Self* by Virginia Axline and a novel, *Mother's Milk* by Edward St Aubyn.

Beyond this, if you are willing to have a bit of therapy and are in the early stages of pregnancy or still considering or awaiting pregnancy, for a rapid way of discovering a great deal about your childhood, spend a week doing the Hoffman Process (see www.hoffmaninstitute.co.uk).

If you are already in the thick of parenthood, a short-term therapy, which is both practical and will uncover some of your childhood, is Cognitive Analytic Therapy (CAT; not to be confused with Cognitive Behavioural Therapy – CBT – which is to be avoided unless there is nothing else available). This takes 16 sessions – go to www.acat.me.uk to find a therapist.

If your taste is for something which goes deeper, you can find a psychoanalytic therapist by taking the 'find a therapist' option at www.psychoanalytic-council.org. However, see below under Huggers Who Can't Let Go: Finding a Good Therapist if You Need That Kind of Help for advice on ensuring that the person really is right for you and your problems. In most major cities there are fully qualified therapists who do offer this on the NHS; the trouble is finding the places and that you will not have any choice whom you see and for how long. In north London, for example, there are the Tavistock Centre and the Anna Freud Centre; in south London, the Cassel Hosital. To find places outside London, you could use the 'find a therapist' option to find someone in your nearest city, then contact them and ask if they know where NHS provision is in that area – they probably will.

KNOW THYSELF 2: RECONCILING YOUR WORKER AND MOTHER IDENTITIES

This is usually much less of a problem for Huggers than mothers with other approaches*. For most Huggers, at least during the first year, you are completely convinced that being a mother comes first.

However, you may be in that minority who, while feeling this, are also desirous of what their worker identity provides. This could be as trivial as being able to have an uninterrupted visit to the lavatory or a trip to your favourite shoe shop, to more substantial matters, like feeling uneasy about not earning any money of your own, or missing the status and respect that your career provided. You may also miss the fascination or buzz of daily work decisions.

If you really are a Hugger, in most cases, these hankerings will quickly disappear as you fall in love with your baby. However, if they endure or return as the first year progresses, as in the story of Sheila in Chapter 9, do not worry. It may be that a return to (often part-time) paid work is indeed best. It may also be that your partner is only too willing to take up the slack. Failing that, fear not, you will use your Hugger nose to sniff out a suitable substitute.

THE (UN)IMPORTANCE OF NATURAL BIRTHS

Huggers tend to prefer minimal medical intervention in births. This is understandable and, in general, in all aspects of life, not just this one, the more you can feel in control of what is happening, the better. There is, of course, a lot to be said for natural birth and there is plenty you can do to make it more likely, including attending natural childbirth yoga classes and taking care in what you eat. If you can get through undrugged, instant bonding with the baby is easier because both of you are not in a chemical fog. Recovering from a major operation – which is what a Caesarean is – is hardly the perfect preparation for motherhood.

However, some Huggers get the issue out of perspective. The danger is that you can feel so upset and annoyed at having had to undergo interventions that it distracts from your feelings for the baby, making it harder to tune in and feel loved-up. It's best not to get too obsessed by the manner of the birth if you are going to feel deflated or a failure if things do not go according to plan. So long as the baby is healthy and you are in one piece, it's what happens after the birth which matters most.

Obviously, if the birth proves very difficult, you will need lots of support afterwards. Hopefully, you can draw on relatives and friends as well as a partner for pampering and support, practical and emotional. But what is avoidable is to have too big a feeling of being let down if it goes badly. The more you have set your heart on natural birth, the greater the potential for disappointment.

COPING WITH DIFFICULT BABIES

Huggers tend to believe that their baby's momentary, second-by-second states are the mother's responsibility. However, there are cases in which you must be realistic about this.

In the tiny proportion who are born with a (probably genetic) difficulty, like autism or Asperger's syndrome, the mother cannot wholly reverse the problems, although, interestingly, even in these very extreme cases, how these children are cared for throughout their childhood can make a big difference to their level of functioning*; likewise, if your child is born with a severe limitation to its cognitive potential*.

Much commoner is colic. About one fifth of babies cry more than three hours a day for more than three days a week at some point between the early weeks and three months old*. Such babies are a handful to any mother. Likewise, the 15% of neonates born floppy, irritable or fussy*. In all these kinds of cases, the cause is rarely genetic, it is an imbalance resulting from the pregnancy and birth*. Your Hugging is exactly what the baby needs and it will work. However, it is vital that you understand you have to be patient and not on any account blame yourself. If your baby is a difficult one, creating a strict regime would not help: you are doing the right thing. It's incredibly tiring and stressful, but give yourself a huge pat on the back for making this gargantuan effort and try not to worry: it's going to be all right by around six months, hard though that may be to believe. Whatever you do, do not imagine the child is against you, is deliberately winding you up, or actually dislikes you (page 315, R7). It's nothing personal, just a bit like when you have to spend the day with a colleague who got out of the bed the wrong side – not your fault and they eventually cheer up.

BREASTFEEDING

As with natural births, Huggers tend to be very keen to breastfeed. Again, that is fine and good, but if, after you have moved heaven and earth to succeed, you cannot make it work, you do not want to feel so let down and so self-blaming that it throws you into despair. So, as with natural birth, do not pin your whole mental health on having to breast-feed. You can Hug successfully with and without breastfeeding.

In case you missed it, detailed advice on how to make breastfeeding work is in Chapter 6 (page 99).

THREE-IN-A-BED

Deborah Jackson's book *Three in a Bed* (Bloomsbury, 2003) tells you all you need to know about making this work. There is now strong scientific evidence that this really may be both a natural and a beneficial approach*. It demonstrates that having babies or toddlers sleeping in a separate room is completely at variance with human history and the behaviour of most mammals. In 127 cultures surveyed around the contemporary world, 79% of the societies normally have their infants in the same room, 44% in the same bed. Despite social and medical pressures against co-sleeping in developed nations, as much as half of babies do so sometimes in the first months. Some developed nations still do co-sleeping normatively: 59% of Japanese under-fours are in the bed (vs 15% of Americans).

The new evidence challenges medical advice on the danger of cot death, showing that co-sleeping may actually be safer. It promotes more and easier breastfeeding, and although both partners wake more frequently, when carefully observed using physical measures of sleep, they get more hours overall than if sleeping alone.

In practice, a lot of Hugger couples eventually resort to bed-hopping, with the partner climbing into a spare bed to avoid being woken. However, it does not have to lead to feeling lonely. So long as everyone realises it is a temporary arrangement to prevent the family being destroyed by lack of sleep, it can seem happy enough. Indeed, the mother may sometimes bed-hop if the baby likes cuddling with the dad. The main thing is not to imagine you are doing something weird or that it means your partnership is a failure.

It is also liable to correlate with not a lot of sex. However, again, if you are a demand-led Hugger, baby tends to come first in all areas. Dads who are Huggers tend to be understanding about that and such couples grab what chances come their way, in among the exhaustion and relentless demands of the baby. Since both Huggers tend to be completely shagged out anyway, in the early months actual shagging may not be high on the list of anyone's priorities.

Problems are much greater if the dad is not a Hugger. Not only may he feel that the mother is spoiling the baby, creating a selfish monster, he will point out that it is wrecking the relationship. Since couples with small babies, especially the first one, tend to find themselves screaming at each other from time to time, largely because of lack of sleep, if one of them is feeling furious at the lack of sex it makes matters even worse. If possible, you need to somehow carve out a few 'special' times amid the chaos and demands of the baby to satisfy both of you. Hopefully the man will appreciate that less frequent sex does not mean none and that he does get priority sometimes.

The more the woman is able to convince the man that she still loves him and that she can easily understand how neglected he must feel, the better it will be. Some men will not be pacified by this. If they suffered infantile neglect, it may be unbearable to see their child (especially a son) apparently getting all the love there is going. Such men are the obvious candidates for flings with other women at this point, particularly if they are the earner, as they are very liable to be.

Alas, the combination of a Hugger mother with a man who is dead against it is potentially explosive. As the case of Pam shows, described in Chapter 8, it is possible to survive. But both partners are going to have to work very hard at it. In these relatively rare cases, a Relate counsellor may be worth talking with, if either of you have the energy to find the number, make the appointment and find someone else to look after the baby while you go and thrash it out. A surprisingly helpful self-help method is the Imago technique. This is easy and clearly explained in Harville Hendrix's book, *Getting the Love You Want* (Pocket Books, 2003).

TODDLER DISCIPLINE

A sensible book for helping you to use words rather than blows is *How to Talk So Kids Will Listen and Listen So Kids Will Talk* by Adele Faber and Elaine Maslish (Piccadilly Press, 2001). Disciplining toddlers is never easy and some Huggers can have a tendency not to create clear rules and limits because their instinct is to be led by the needs of the child. This can lead to an ill-behaved child who is doing itself, as well as you, no favours. It can also result in the Hugger suddenly losing their temper, feeling that she has 'given everything and look what I get in return – a wild beast'. The next few pages suggest some reliable principles for avoiding this.

Not just in theory, in practice it really is the case that you should refrain from hitting your children. I realise this is easier said than done but I have somehow managed it, despite having been frequently thwacked about the head by my mum when I was small – and having been a nastily aggressive boy, partly as a result. I mention this because I do not regard myself as a particularly calm or sensible person, but if I can manage not to hit, it probably means you can! In fact, I can remember occasions when it occurred to me that maybe all this child psychology stuff was just too precious, and surely it would not harm to hit occasionally. Looking back, I am very glad I never did do it. Perhaps it does no permanent harm to do it once or twice. The trouble is, you can see how easily the odd slap quickly inflates into a regular habit, as is suggested by the evidence*.

The Hugger approach is pretty full-on and usually requires a lot of patience from exhausted parents. You should not worry if you have seriously pictured killing your baby – half of mothers have done so*. When they become toddlers, allowing them to become independent is hard to gauge and often entails periods in which, compared with other children who have been raised by strict regimes, they seem to be less socialised and less nice to know in social situations. This is because you have given them a more gradual introduction to the fundamental truth that the world does not revolve around them, that there is a separate reality out there which frequently does not do as the toddler wishes. You have to keep your nerve and stick to Hugging. The pay-off is that you will have a toddler who does not lose the sparkle with which it was born (or which developed after a difficult first few months, as a result of your nurture). Let us take some of the big issues for a Hugger (or any parent) trying to civilise their toddler.

Choose Your Battles Carefully

However conventional or unconventional you want your child, it is essential that all parents decide on the absolute no-nos. These should be as few as possible in number because if you have too many, you will rapidly find yourself just 'nattering'. The child will hardly be able to do anything without you having to restrain it by word and deed. Very quickly, any punitive currency becomes devalued*. If you are spending most of the day beginning sentences 'don't', 'be careful of' and 'watch out', the child increasingly ignores you. Your voice will become correspondingly hoarse, your vocabulary ever sterner. It is easy to shift from words to slaps and from slaps to blows. Above all, when one of the universal no-nos that all parents must impose comes along, like running on to a busy road, the parent's screams will be impossible for the toddler to differentiate from the same yells that greeted its recent chucking of the apple on the floor at teatime.

Failure to prioritise what needs to be restrained and what can be let go underpins a common form of damaging early parenting, overcontrol. We talk about perfectionists and 'control freaks' in offices. If you are that way inclined, a toddler is your worst nightmare, potentially. Because they are not doing it exactly right, the way you think it should be, the number of no-nos grows uncontrollably. Either you find yourself becoming like Basil Fawlty, permanently on the verge of apoplexy, or you become devious, having to come up with ever more ingenious ways of tricking the child into your way. Such overcontrol at any stage in early childhood puts the child at risk of feeling powerless and prone to depression in later life, as well as, of course, becoming a perfectionist control freak themselves*.

Equally, the opposite of overcontrol – extreme permissiveness – is harmful. While you cannot spoil a baby and the more you allow its needs to teach you what is required the better, once they can crawl or toddle, at a very simple level it is unacceptable to give them their head in every way in all situations: there are no circumstances in which you can be relaxed about them approaching the busy main road alone. What is more, toddlers given no boundaries will become asocial. As they move from one to two towards three, very gradually they must acquire an understanding of the consequences of their actions for other people. To do so, they need to realise others have feelings and different points of view. No-nos are the foundation blocks of that development and extreme permissiveness does not include any.

Once your few no-nos are identified, you need to be as consistent as possible in making it clear to your toddler that certain things are never acceptable, being as consistent as possible in doing this – no has to mean no each time, applied to the same issues, agreed by both parents. How you go about communicating the issue is debatable but the fundamentals are:

⟨ Anything entailing risk of serious physical injury is a no-no, the key word here being serious. Parents can safely vary regarding minor matters like picking up food off the floor to eat but when it comes to falling down stairs or into full baths, there is no room for debate
⟨ No violence. Hopefully, you are providing a good model in this regard, so the commonest context for this issue concerns other children. Again, there is considerable room for debate about the best way to handle it but handle it you must, usually by keeping a close eye on the child when it is with others

Beyond these, it is very much a matter of preference what you choose to impose or not, but it is crucial to remember that the more you add no-nos, and the younger you add them, the greater the risk of spiralling into a devalued punitive economy. On the whole, it is far preferable with a one-year-old to keep them to a minimum. If it's incredibly important to you that they do not chuck the food on the floor, fair enough, make a big deal out of it. But if, say with your 18-month-old, you also insist on no splashing in the bath, no wiping of dirty hands on clothes, instant obedience when you say it's time to leave your friend's house, and there are dozens of other such rules, do not be surprised if you find yourself running out of punitive coins. With one-year-olds, it's best to choose your battles particularly sparingly. If you are going to want to impose feeding, sleeping and potty-training regimes during that year, good luck to you. But before you go down any 'absolute no-no' road, always ask yourself 'is it *really* necessary?'

On so many occasions when I have worked with parents of supposedly difficult children, the solution has been to simply stop trying to impose the desired behaviour. That does not mean adopting a wholly permissive, boundaryless approach: there are fundamentals. But questioning your powerful sense that this or that minor habit is a major one can greatly improve the quality of everyone's life.

Even if you do follow my advice and loosen up as much as possible on the non-essentials, that still leaves plenty of potential for conflict.

Basic Discipline

The truth is that the word 'discipline', with its connotation of enforcement of a known rule, is inappropriate for a one-year-old and of not much value for two-year-olds either. For discipline to work, a child must be capable of understanding a principle of right and wrong, good and bad, behaviour. This leads to a distinction between one- and two-year-olds.

While one-year-olds are able to understand desired and undesired, insofar as they can see that a parent is pleased or displeased, it cannot be expected to comprehend that principles underlie these reactions. Without that comprehension, they cannot be expected to apply the rule to slightly differing contexts. For example, if an 18-month-old toddles in the direction of a road, it is impossible to explain to it that cars are dangerous and to be found on roads. On average, children of this age have two-word utterances, like 'mama, milk'. Their receptive understanding is much more sophisticated but they are still a long way short of being able to grasp and remember principles. While you can possibly succeed in a Pavlovian imprinting of the idea that it should not go towards a particular piece of road, like the one outside your house, there is no guarantee the rule will stick and no likelihood it will generalise this case to all roads. Indeed, if you try hitting the child or some other extreme measure, there is as much likelihood of merely making it extremely fearful every time it goes out of the front door, potentially creating a phobia. For these reasons, when it comes to safety fundamentals in one-year-olds, there is absolutely no point at all in becoming irate or perplexed or earnestly explicatory of dangers. The same goes if they are violent to you or another child, insofar as it arises this young.

So what is required at all times for children of this age is supervision by an adult. An internal capacity to regulate behaviour safely is simply not possible; the regulation must be external.

Regarding the terrible twos (actually, children vary enormously as to whether they have tantrums and at what age, although the twos are the commonest period), there is only slightly more possibility for nurture that resembles 'discipline'. Once a toddler has become blind with rage, ostensibly, the first step is to take the heat out of the situation. 'Ostensibly' because very often the first person who needs to calm down is you. Until you have got yourself under control in these often highly charged situations, you can be of no use. Once calm enough, some experts advocate a naughty chair or time out in a bedroom alone. I suspect that this kind of coercive separation is often done because the parent cannot trust themselves any more not to lose their temper. Fair enough, it's preferable to that. But far better is to take a deep breath and use gentle force to hold the child in your arms. If you have to be quite firm in your grip initially, so be it, to prevent kicking and slapping. Held and hugged in this way, the child will always eventually quieten and cease screaming, as studies of this method have demonstrated*. You are giving the message that the child is still loved but that it has to be restrained for its own good. The alternatives give the message that the child is unloved and leaves it to stew in its own juices, liable to feeling abandoned and rejected, creating resentment and surly anger.

Contrary to claims for naughty step methods, when used on such young children it actually often results in repetition of the undesired behaviour, rather than successful management. If you are not careful, you are just creating a guaranteed method for your toddler to wind you up. If they do eventually modify their behaviour what is the lesson they have learnt? That might is right and that they need to be more devious to avoid being coerced.

As a parent of a child of this age, you need to realise that if things go pear-shaped it is actually always your fault, in the sense that if you keep a close enough eye on them you can prevent atrocities. Inevitably it's some-times going to go wrong, but do not assume the child is wilfully trying to annoy you. Calling them bad and naughty is completely inappropriate at this age and only serves to make them feel unhappy, rather than learning any useful lesson (page 314, R7). The unhappier they are, the more they are likely to go around upsetting other kids, trying to offload their anger or misery on to others, just as adults do in offices (or partners at home).

Once you have calmed the situation down it becomes possible to really create a useful lesson from it. Two-year-olds usually have a much greater ability to understand than parents realise, and a greater willing-ness to try, as well. They really do want to get to the bottom of what is going on, although their capacity to do so before three is limited. Critical is if they can comprehend that an action of theirs was a bad decision for which they must take responsibility. Only if that happens are they going to be able to learn that there are classes of behaviours, rather than just specific individual instances, which are right and wrong. If they have just bashed another child over the head with a plastic hammer because they were trying to take it from them, they need to learn more than just 'doing that with this object against this child when it is trying to take away the toy, is the problem'. The lesson is that inflicting any violence is wrong, regardless of the toy, other child or provocation. While they may not get the hang of it before three, the foundations for doing so are laid before that age.

As much as possible, in explaining the situation you need to do it in a way that is not an obsessive recitation – treating them like idiots and endlessly elaborating the same point in empty words. It's no use saying 'I told you before, it's wrong to hit other children. Hitting other kids is bad. So don't do it. It's wrong. You really must not bash them like that, it's very naughty. You must learn to behave yourself.' If this just goes on and on and on, the child starts to think 'Etc etc, blah blah blah, oh do shut up.' You also need to avoid covert aggression. You may well still be feeling steamed up, so wait until calmer because if there is a menace of reprisals or a cold rage in your tone of voice, it will not help. You have to really mean it, not just be going through the motions.

What you are seeking is enlightenment of the chain of events leading to the aggression. Give them the bigger picture: other children have feelings, your child's actions produced these feelings; since the other child annoyed them, perhaps they can see that what one child does affects the mood of another. Avoid sentences beginning with 'don't', avoid negative attributions. Words can be very injurious indeed. Telling them they are a ghastly little brat, or worse, is the collapse of your capacity to offer them a good model, not a helpful response.

A sentence structure which works well is 'This is why you did X, I felt Y, because Z.' For example, 'When you hit your sister Annie with that brick, I felt angry and upset because I love her and don't like seeing her hurt.' While it may only be at the emotional level that they get the message, that is a lot better than just leaving them feeling like a rubbish person, which is the danger of naughty chairs and time out alone in the bedroom. Very often, that is how we were disciplined and we are having to fight the temptation to say to our children what was said to us – 'you're bad, naughty, sly, wicked, selfish'. If you do not know what to say, often it is best to say nothing for the time being, reducing the risk of collapsing into condemnatory mode.

In the end, the reason children obey parents is love. If they already feel pretty unloved by the age of one and continue to do so, you do not have much to work with. At the extreme, people grow into psychopaths because no one loved them much, if at all, and as a result, they simply lack the capacity to feel for others – called empathy. If they have also been exposed to a great deal of hate, no wonder they become killers, whether that be greedy chief executives intent on destroying the competition or serial killers like Fred West, desperate to excrete his loathing by enjoying others' suffering. Thankfully, this is rare. More normally, toddlers do feel loved as well as sometimes hated (actually, there are no parents who never hate their small children). Having disobeyed you repeatedly, the ultimate reason your toddler finally starts behaving in a civilised fashion is because they can see that uncivilised behaviour makes you unhappy.

This is not visible at age one but around about four you can see it clearly enough. As one mother of a child of that age put it to me, 'he kept on and on niggling his brother and I kept on trying to explain why that was not the way to go. One day, finally, he turned to me after my attempt to explain it and said, "Mummy, you are making me unhappy. Do you want me to be unhappy?" So I said, "No, I don't want to make you unhappy but I want to be happy too." That seemed to do the trick. He was old enough to grasp that I had feelings too and that other people's needed to be taken into account if he was to be happy.'

Not All Automation Is Necessarily Bad

Parents will vary greatly as regards what they feel happy making into a habitual reflex. A prime example is please and thank you.

Adults like being thanked after handing a visiting toddler a cake. They like being asked by the child if it can please have some more orange juice. Instilled early, by frequent prompting, it becomes as second nature to the child as going to the loo or getting dressed in the morning. If it is not sincerely meant, arguably that does not matter. The child does not have to think, costing it nothing, and in return, adults will generally feel better disposed.

Conversely, if a child consistently does not log that something has been done for them, it eventually gets noticed by adults, galling them. Given that such customs seem to matter in British society, or at least in some sections thereof, it helps the child to conform. Other examples in much of Britain might be interrupting adults when they are in mid-flow and not picking your nose in public. Being nice to know does no harm, even if it has an element of falsehood, so long as the person is authentic in the many other areas that count.

A distinction can be drawn between please and thank you for

insignificant matters, like passing potatoes or sugar, and important ones, like thanking an adult for laying on a big treat. For these, you might hope that your child says please in recognition of the possibility that the request could be denied and cannot be taken for granted, and thank you because it appreciates the benign intention and effort required in making the donation to them. Expensive birthday presents, special treats, unusually thoughtful compliments would qualify for this. An important part of the child learning to mean it is if you explain why this is different from normal: that it cost a lot of money, that it required the donor to put themselves out on the child's behalf.

Apologising is another candidate for automation. Initially it is best taught by example. It is fine for you to apologise to the child if you get something wrong. In teaching them, before they go off and say sorry, they need to actually feel they got something wrong, from their point of view. If you force them to go and make a false apology, it turns into a wipe-the-slate-clean, say-three-hail-Marys ritual and they learn no lesson, no principle. So as already noted, in explaining the context you can use quite adult language even when they are as young as aged two, although most of the understanding will be on the emotional level. Using dumbed-down baby language is curiously ineffective.

Whether it's sorry, or important please and thank yous, you should not expect them to manage a proper understanding much before three. When so small, they usually feel completely justified in having lashed out at another child, even though it was their fault, and was unprovoked. At this age, it is expecting too much for them to understand the wider context and their responsibility within it and if they do lash out, in a sense it is always your fault. The lashing out will be happening because they are tired, or hungry, or envious of a sibling, and although the victim is guiltless, so is this perpetrator: it would not have happened if you had kept a better eye on the situation, which, of course, we cannot be expected to do at all times. It is for this reason that it really can make sense for you to be making the apology, and doing so to the appalled other parent. Not only is this the truth, it provides a good exemplar to your child. Some might think it is namby-pamby craziness to do this, that you are merely teaching your child never to be responsible for their misbehaviour. In fact, you are acting as a good model and, if fully explained, it helps them to grasp that they are surrounded by a fine-grained web of social obligations when in the company of others.

DEALING WITH OTHER MOTHERS WHO DISAPPROVE

When you first hook up with the other mothers from your antenatal group after the birth, there is a big risk of feeling you are failing, especially if most of the other mothers are adopting a different approach. You are likely to be in a fragile state and comparisons in this area are as personal as can be. If you criticise someone else's parenting practices, it is as rude and potentially hurtful as saying to someone who is conspicuously overweight, 'why don't you stop eating so much, you are making yourself much too fat' or to someone who is ugly, 'you really have got an unattractive-looking nose and your chin is almost invisible – yucch!' Some mothers are feeling so vulnerable at this stage that they can accidentally upset each other. Others are feeling so defensive that they may try to make you feel bad by claiming what they do is best and by implication, that you should do the same.

Two golden rules:

1. Although it seems as if the mothers you meet all have perfect babies who are not crying, are feeding happily, are calm and cheerful when awake, tell yourself that the other mothers are probably feeling like failures every bit as much as you.

2. When asked if your six-week-old is sleeping through the night, keep it simple and if pushed, just lie. You can start with 'it's going OK', even if you spent the whole of last night jiggling. Pressurised to supply more detail, say 'his eating and sleeping is going fine' and change the subject. You may not realise it, but

there is a tremendous amount of lying going on already: many mothers who claim their baby is sleeping right through the night on a regular basis at six weeks are either lying or displaying an exceptional level of neglect. Even small babies that have been given pints of bottle milk before bed usually need another feed after four hours, although there are a few exceptions.

Early on, there are particular problems for Huggers. It becomes apparent that you are breastfeeding but others have gone straight for the bottle. You have the baby in the bed, they are using cots in another room at night. They are sticking to routines, you are demand-led. You have not any intention of thinking about paid work for years, they are lining up a day care nursery for three months.

The best thing is to completely avoid the subject of your approach with mothers who differ from yours. That way, you minimise the risk of making them defensive and them attacking yours. If you can subtly nudge them towards a non-aggression pact by never discussing these tricky areas, you reduce the risk of losing that oldest friend. Of course, if you head off on holiday with them, it will be very tricky indeed. What you need in the way of intimates are mothers who share your approach. Anything else is liable to end in tears. This may mean a loosening of some of your friendships but it is better than the out and out enmity which easily springs up.

HOUSEKEEPING: THE UNENDING BATTLE

In the early months, many Huggers are so besotted that they do not care if they live in a tip. Those who have always preferred cleanliness and tidiness may rapidly begin to get bugged by the mess. But most are able to turn a blind eye.

Obviously, for those able to afford a cleaner, that helps, and if you have the money, spend as much as it takes to remove the housekeeping as a worry, even including the shopping. But interestingly, this is easier said than done. Even rich Huggers often find it hard to identify a helper who really does achieve what they would like.

For most Huggers paid help is anyway not an option. Potential problems with ratty partners arise. If they are fellow Huggers, usually they are prepared to muck in with cooking, shopping and so on, in some cases breaking habits of a lifetime involving ironing and shirts. The problem is worst with partners who are not Huggers, often already feeling starved of love and sex. Some pretty nasty scenes can occur, as the pans and plates fill the sink, and the unwashed clothes mount up on top of the washing machine. In those cases where the partner makes a point of not upping his domestic game as revenge, if you want your partnership to survive, you are probably best advised to dig deep and try and get bits and pieces done while the baby sleeps, although a lot of the time, especially early on, you will probably need to sleep when they do, to catch up after broken nights. In the end, the children will not grow up thanking you for having had a spotless house in which they wore only freshly washed and pressed clothes; it will be the love you showed them that counts. Practically speaking, this is a situation in which you should not be proud, calling in every favour you can from siblings, parents and intimates. As mentioned above, if the situation really does seem to be spiralling into full-scale warfare, a visit to Relate may be required.

HOW TO EVALUATE WHETHER YOU REALLY NEED TO GO BACK TO WORK FOR THE MONEY: HOW MUCH WEEKLY INCOME IS 'ENOUGH'?

I was quite startled to find that Sam, the Hugger who went back to her paid job in Chapter 9, really did not seem to have enough money despite a partner earning £500 a week after deductions. Some readers might have pointed out that she could have sold her house, removing the mortgage. But there would still be at least as much to pay on rent as her mortgage (£900 a month) if she did that, so long as they continued living in London, and they would only be able to rent a much less pleasant home for that money. The reader might persist by saying, in that case move out of London – you can rent two-bedroom houses for as little as £400 a month in the countryside. But then in Pam's case, her partner would have been paid less, always assuming he could find a job.

And this is a couple where the man is earning miles more (net) than the national average wage. While that is £24,000 (before deductions), more than half of the adult population earn less than £10,000 (including many part-timers). That shows how relative the concept of 'enough' is, even before we start thinking about the billions who live on less than a dollar a day in the developing world.

The truth is that you must accept that you cannot have your Hugger cake and eat it too. As I have tried my best to explain in my books *Affluenza* and *The Selfish Capitalist*, two particular trends have got in the way of parenting.

Nearly all of us have developed some bad values in placing too high a premium on money, possessions, appearances and fame. As a convinced Hugger, I doubt you need persuading that your little lovely comes before those things. Nonetheless, do not be surprised if you suffer a certain amount of cold turkey after you give up your job and exchange it for a status-free, invisible, often isolated and incredibly demanding role as mother. Not only may you miss the status it gave you, now you have no money to contribute to the household and decades of independence suddenly seem under threat because you can no longer afford to go on shoe-buying sprees without considering what your partner might say. Tough though that can be, however, I am sure that most Huggers can cope with this stuff.

The other huge change is what Avner Offer labels in his excellent book, *The Challenge of Affluence*, the 'disinvestment in the domestic household economy'. Men never were much invested in it in the first place, so the more they can buck up the better. But it is women who have particularly changed. The present generation of mothers were encouraged by our culture to be Bridget Jones (the chaotic heroine of Helen Fielding's *Bridget Jones's Diary*), not a Hugger. Unsurprisingly, a fair few do not feel either very able or willing to do cooking, darning or tidying for themselves, let alone for others. Many were strongly encouraged by their full-time housewife mothers to avoid that role, a case of 'do as I say, not as I do'. Where their mother would like them to follow in their footsteps, some daughters are reacting against that. Taken as a whole, if you used to be Bridget Jones and are reacting to your mum (either way), it creates problems for following through in your desire to Hug.

But now you have read this, at least you understand the dynamic better. You should say to yourself 'sod my mother, sod Helen Fielding, I am not going to let my dislike of housework and my previous addiction to the money and status of work get in the way. Above all, I am going to get on top of the cooking and cleaning to a reasonable extent without feeling put upon because *I am doing this stuff with my baby by choice, it is what I want and it is necessary for my baby's sake that I do it.*'

Of course, it is very important to also stress that a significant number of Huggers will not be having this problem. One third of women are not modern in the sense that they have never imagined they would have a career rather than a job, or that they would do anything other than look after their children*. These women need to be recognised as well, to be accorded the status they deserve. Just because it is fashionable to want to be Nicola Horlick or Kate Moss, does not mean you deserve to be seen as letting women down. Both other women and men need to start respecting you, realising how shallow it is to only be interested in someone because they have a high-status job.

HUGGERS WHO CAN'T LET GO: FINDING A GOOD THERAPIST IF YOU NEED THAT KIND OF HELP

Defining whether your Hugging is a problem is not easy. If the average Hugger was assessed by a conventional clinical psychologist or psychiatrist, in many cases they would be deemed overly involved with their baby. This is because conventional child psychology conflates babies with rats or monkeys. It is liable to ignore or, worse, be ignorant of the huge body of scientific evidence supporting the account I gave in Chapter 1 of the needs of babies and toddlers.

However, as already explained in previous chapters, from around four months, a small minority of Huggers find it increasingly difficult to tolerate the growing need for independence. At four months, this might show up in your reluctance to allow even your partner to hold the baby, despite the fact that he is responsive and well-known to the baby. Around nine months, when the baby may be wanting to sit up on its own or even to crawl, if you are unable to relax at all because the baby is 20 feet away and if the fears you have are completely groundless, like that the baby is about to turn a heavy armchair over on top of itself, or that it may somehow crawl through a shut front door on to the road, clearly you are having trouble tolerating its separateness. By 18 months, if you are continuously and minutely monitoring every little foray it makes as it toddles around the living room, that may be excessive. Certainly, if it is a year older than that and you cannot feel comfortable when its much loved and very familiar grandmother offers to help with getting it to eat its food with a teaspoon, perhaps because you fear it will choke, there is a problem.

In such cases, you do need to visit a therapist, possibly with your child present, to discuss how your childhood is affecting your nervousness about these things. As listed above (Know Thyself 1), with any luck you can get this help from the NHS.

The way to check that you are talking to the right category of therapist is to ask the following questions, to which the answer needs to be yes:

'Do you have one of the trainings in psychoanalytic therapy listed on the British Council of Psychoanalysis website?'

'Are you familiar with Attachment Theory, and is it help with my attachments that you will provide?'

'Will you focus primarily on the way my childhood is interfering with how I am caring for my child?'

Even if the answers are all yes, that does not mean this person is right for you. I would further recommend that you define three things you would hope that the therapy will achieve and right at the outset, tell them to the therapist and ask directly whether they believe they can help you. While they will probably hedge their bets in answering, which is fair enough in that there are no guarantees in this business, you should get some kind of feel from their answer as to whether this is someone who you feel is warm, on your side and really wants to get involved in your problems – those are the criteria. If you are not really convinced, even if this is an NHS provision, you do have the option of saying to your GP that you did not feel this therapist was the right person for you and that you would like to try a different one, even from the same institution.

CONCLUSION: POTENTIAL PITFALLS OF HUGGING

⟨ *Fixation on Natural Birth*: the more you raise your hopes of an intervention-free experience, the greater the risk of feeling let down or a failure. It's more important to focus on what happens afterwards, getting your house, partner and family prepared

⟨ *Maternal Separation Anxiety*: if you cannot leave your 18-month-old with your responsible, responsive partner, whom it knows well, while you go for a short nap, you have a problem. Brief parent–infant therapy should quickly fix it

⟨ *Lack of Willingness to Seek Support*: this is the royal road to depression. Fine to tune in for 24 hours a day to the baby for months on end, but you really do need intimates for regular moaning sessions. Ideally, you already have these from your antenatal class but, if not, and you feel yourself getting very lonely during the days, why not contact Homestart UK?

‹ *Excessive Household Chaos*: everyone has a different threshold for what is 'excessive' but if yours is being broken too much, for too much of the time, it will wear you down. Your baby or toddler can probably entertain themselves while you do a bit of ironing or cleaning, after the first few months are over

‹ *Insufficient Relationship Maintenance*: you may be in love with the baby, but do not forget your partner. He may not be too bothered to be excluded from your embrace for a few months, but depending on what he is like, serious problems may arise if you do not set some evenings aside for him

‹ *Permissive Toddler Discipline*: do not be scared to set boundaries. Being authoritative is not the same as authoritarian. So long as you are consistent and keep the rules to the minimum, the child will eventually see the point. You want to adapt to the child, fair enough, but from two onwards, it needs very gradually to understand that there is an external social and physical world to which it must sometimes adapt

‹ *Using Toddlers for Comfort*: if the toddler is still breastfeeding or in your bed to keep you company, it's a problem. Fair enough, if they want it and you are happy to provide it, but beware of seducing them to stay close to you after they are looking for a bit of independence

‹ *Forgetting Which Shelf You Left Your Self on*: as the toddler years pass, occasionally apply your mind to what happens when they go to school. If there are no more children coming along, you need to be able to remember who you were beforehand, and what ideas you have about who you will be in the future, other than their mother. Nothing wrong if it's only that: just do not completely lose track of your needs

Part Three

THE FLEXIMUM

CHAPTER 12

Meet the Essential Fleximum

THE ESSENTIAL FLEXIMUM*

If about one quarter of British mothers are Organisers and the same proportion are Huggers, the remaining half are Fleximums.

The Hugger adapts to her baby, the Organiser believes it's best for the baby to adapt to her. Fleximums (henceforth Flexis), as their title suggests, oscillate between these approaches, depending on the circumstances. On the surface, at least, they seem calmer and less intense. Whereas the Hugger's response to the baby's total dependence on them is literally to embrace it, and the Organiser's is to nurture independence as fast as possible, the Flexi is comfortable varying her approaches in quick succession, as and when required. She is a supreme pragmatist. Above all, unlike the other kinds, she is less likely to be plagued by guilt or fear of getting it wrong, because she neither blames herself nor the baby for how things go, she accepts things as they are.

Flexis shy away from getting too tied to fixed ways of doing things. They develop patterns, like of feeding and sleeping, but if something throws the plan, they are not thrown emotionally and make necessary changes. When the baby develops diarrhoea or a cold, they quickly identify what is wrong and find it easy to adjust, perhaps spending the day at home despite having planned a walk in the park. They manage to hang on to their own needs and their baby's, not liable to lose track of either as much as other kinds of mother. They may be able to empathise with babies and toddlers, be good at picturing how it feels to be like that. This is subtly different from identifying with the child. Deep down, identification is actually feeling yourself to be another person, empathy is remaining yourself but recognising what another feels. Many Flexis recognise how vulnerable and needy babies can be, but are able to do so from their adult position. Many Huggers and some Organisers can also do this, but some of both those types can also feel their adult selves dissolve (the Organiser quickly correcting that by becoming super-adult and treating the baby in the same way, the Hugger feeling as helpless as a baby or identifying very strongly with its helplessness). Flexis are in touch with their moment-to-moment adult feelings and, at the same time, may apprehend those of their under-three.

In interacting, the calmest of Flexis will tune into the baby's communications and rhythms, and when the baby asserts itself, like by crying or smiling, she will react appropriately. So do many Huggers, but some are tuning into the baby to meet their own need to be loved, making it hard to react in ways that suit the baby, based on its needs rather than theirs. Some Organisers find the baby's attempts to engage with them too threatening, a dangerously enticing invitation to get involved in a mutual dependence which could suck the mother dry.

Many Flexis initiate communications, expressing what they feel as well as waiting for the baby to do so, and offering new ideas for play. So do many Huggers, but sometimes they are so dedicated to the baby's way of seeing things that they solely look to the baby for the lead. Some Organisers fear the baby's insatiability, so that if they initiate it will be the thin end of an enormous wedge of needs. Outwardly, the Flexi is less vexed than the other kinds of mother, jammed neither on 'transmit', nor on 'receive'.

She comes to motherhood with a pretty open mind. During the pregnancy, she realises that a phenomenal change is about to happen and that she cannot really predict how she will react or approach it. In some cases, this is because her own early years were stable and she was responded to and tuned into, so the idea of either a foetus or a baby does not trigger worrying memories. However, the Flexi pattern can also be a reaction to early distress – either too much or too little involvement with her own mother.

In such cases, being Flexi is a way of keeping scary emotions at bay. Flexis avoid feeling responsible for what happens by a patina of cheerful expedience. In practice, they may supply a bewildering mixture of child-led and adult-based care, like sleeping with them in the bed, yet also having very inflexible feeding routines. Then they may suddenly change the plan if they feel it is not working for them or for the baby.

Flexis are usually good at including others in their life, do not find other mothers as threatening as the other kinds sometimes do. Often they do not adopt strong positions in the Mommy Wars*, a 'live and let live' attitude, less likely to give voice to criticisms of other mothers' approaches even when they do feel critical. If they have more than one child, they may be good at coping with the chaos.

On the whole, they prefer either to be at home full-time or to work from home, although many do so outside the home, mostly part-time. They will do their best to involve partners in substitute care or seek out a similar substitute (relative, friend, neighbour), happy to share reciprocal arrangements.

At their best, they are realists who keep constantly aware of what they and their children are feeling. Difficulties are most likely to arise if they find themselves too flexible, unable to define self or other, skipping between approaches in an attempt to avoid feeling committed to a particular pattern of care which would put them at risk of blame or guilt. They want to feel they are being good and to have an optimistic, positive experience. That becomes a problem if it conceals something darker, is a sheen where true emotions are not experienced. Like some Huggers and Organisers, they may find the baby's extreme dependence a terrifying burden. But instead of seeing themselves as giving the baby what they lacked (Huggers) or keeping the baby at arm's length (Organisers), they gloss over this reality by constantly changing the plan, so they are never a sitting target for their self-criticism or fears.

Mothers who work part-time are less likely to get depressed during the early years than full-timers or at-homers (page 326, R8). Often sociable and often part-timers, Flexis are also least likely to be irrationally anxious about being separated from their under-threes – Huggers fear the baby will not be adequately loved in their absence, Organisers worry that physical harm will come to them, like accidents*.

The truth about Flexis may be that they are good at arranging things so that they feel at ease. In some cases, this may be at the expense of their baby's needs, if their reluctance to nail their colours to any particular mothering mast means they lose sight of how vital responsiveness and tuned-in care are in the early months, or indeed, that a measure of routine or boundaries are desirable for toddlers. What they want to feel is that everyone is happy and the danger is that they kid themselves that this is so, when it is not, organising matters really so that they have a nice life, even if it is difficult for their child.

But that is the exception. Most Flexis react with an earnest thoughtfulness to an incredibly complex modern world which offers horrendously conflicting messages to mothers. Ducking and diving if partners let them down or jobs disappear, their lack of unrealistic idealism helps them cope in the face of severe adversity. They are survivors, but not of the histrionic kind evoked in Gloria Gaynor's song 'I Will Survive'. They are down to earth and do not see themselves as victims, and on the whole, they enable their under-threes as well as themselves to more or less flourish.

Sharon, a Classic Fleximum: Part-Time Job, Mum and Baby's Needs Balanced Out Despite Major Adversities

Sharon, 36, speaks in slow, deliberate, measured sentences, every word carefully chosen. She does a nice line in understatement but whereas this tactic can sometimes sound like dark cynicism or bitterness from some mouths, from hers it comes across as just wanting to see the funny side of life, its ironies. She has a warmth and solidity you can trust. There is nothing flashy about her appearance; she is a cautious woman who you might suppose is overly timid. In fact, she is truly strong, able to stay level-headed even when things go pear-shaped, as they certainly did while her daughter, Celine, now aged three, was still very small.

From a poor background, Sharon was a diligent pupil at school. This enabled her to become a manager in a chain of hairdressers, a career for which she has always had a soft spot. When she was 19 she met Dave, an American. 'It was all about personality with him, he's very charming and outgoing. Everyone loved him because what they saw was this fun-loving guy who makes you feel good.' Whereas she was prudent and sensible in her pursuit of a safe career, becoming a reliable breadwinner, he was a much wilder spirit. The oldest of eight, from a working-class family, he took casual jobs while trying to become a pop musician in his spare time. They had been together 14 years when Celine was born.

The pregnancy went swimmingly. 'As it progressed I felt I had more and more relationship with the baby. Once you can feel it and actually see the limbs poking out, it becomes a reality. I hadn't a clue what sex it was but we went through the book and picked out American names which we both liked.' Flexis tend to keep an open mind about the child's gender or what sort of person it will be. Likewise, they avoid preconceptions about the birth.

Once Celine was back home, a Flexi regime was established. 'I didn't read books because my mother and sister live nearby, and my sister is a nursery nurse who has two small kids. As a first-time mother I didn't really know what to expect so we very much played it by ear.' She breastfed for the first six months, gradually introducing bottles. Celine slept by the bed in a Moses basket for the first three months and was then transferred to the cot. There were some echoes of the Organiser about this change. 'I wanted to get her into her own room before she got too used to us, to being very close to me ... I'd heard it can be difficult once they've formed that dependency on you being there.' On the other hand, there were Hugger elements too: 'Some nights were sleepless, I would take her into the bed.' Flexis are always looking for balance: 'But I would never go to sleep while she was in our bed, would put her back in the cot before that. I varied it according to what was needed.'

Unfortunately, Sharon was about to be put under a lot of pressure. Celine developed colic, leading to a sleepless period and the week in which the colic ended proved eventful. 'It was then that I discovered Dave was having an affair. It was also when the health visitor came for the check-up, so I spilled my heart to her. They were very supportive, along with my family. I didn't want to take antidepressants but I took St John's Wort; I think that helped because I was mildly depressed.' She did her best to keep her husband from leaving. 'Initially, I was trying to rebuild the situation but it was quite clear he was going more and more off the rails. He finally left when Celine was aged one.'

Looking back, she shows no malice or bitterness, although this had been a long relationship and it was a terrible shock. 'I found it really hard to move on, emotionally. I have finally done so and recently developed a relationship with a man who is older than me, 44.' There is the Flexi's realism and balance in her appraisal of what happened with Dave. 'The first eight years were great as far as I was concerned but I think he had been living a double life for quite a long time. He had had to be patient while I did my studying and training. I suppose I had the long-term plan, could see it was going to give us the better quality of life, but he lost patience. He wanted us to start a family long before I was willing to.' This realism was accompanied by a judicious apportionment of blame. 'I did obviously look to blame myself for having been a bit selfish pursuing my career, making him wait. But when I finally was ready to start trying for a child he should have been upfront if he wanted out. It takes two to make a child, doesn't it?' Just as Flexis tend to keep both their own and their baby's needs in mind, losing sight of neither, so she shows that mindset in thinking about Dave: she sees it from both viewpoints, keeps sharply realistic rather than allowing emotion to blind her.

When it came to the issue of returning to work, she displays classic Flexi thinking. For practical and emotional reasons, she never had any doubt that she would continue her career. 'I knew I would do so, three days a week, from during the pregnancy. Shortly after the birth I discussed childcare with my sister and mother. Mum does it one day a week, my sister the other two. I do actually pay her because it's not so easy for her to go to work, having two children herself, so it's a good arrangement all round.' Flexis are especially good at fixing up friends, neighbours and relatives to help with substitute care. In thinking about how this arrangement impacts on Celine, Sharon sees it as win-win (as is the Flexi wont). 'I do sometimes compare with friends who are full-time mothers, thinking of all the different activities they do with their children. But then I think to myself that Celine certainly doesn't miss out. She spends so much quality time with her relatives that she gets the best of everything. She gets the best of me, and then she gets really good one-on-one attention from her grandparent, and when she goes to my sister's, she's got two lovely boy cousins. I just look at it as a whole and think "she's got a good life".' Given that the substitutes are one-to-one relatives, this may well be true. But to what extent is the arrangement driven by economic necessity?

I asked her if she would have returned to work had she not needed the money, say, had married a rich man or won the lottery. Her reply was unambiguous. 'I think I would need to do something. I can't see myself as being a full-time mum. I don't think it would be good for me or Celine, I don't think I'd be happy: I need the mental stimulation. As she gets older there's more interest you can take in her – increasing language, social skills, personality – but I still feel I need something that's just for me. I enjoy my time with her, I just wouldn't want to do it seven days a week. Then there is the fact that I have worked very hard in my career and I don't want to give that up.' This could sound like classic Organiser talk. But the difference is that she is well aware of her daughter's need for responsive, tuned-in care. Hence, when I asked how she would feel if she had to leave Celine in day care rather than with her relatives, she looked perplexed and thought deeply. 'That's a difficult question. I would have to search for an equivalently good alternative to what she is getting, which might be tough – it certainly wouldn't be a nursery. But I am sure I would find a way.'

Luckily, she does not have that problem. Instead, she feels the complete comfort about her arrangements which Flexis so strive for. When asked how hard she finds the transitions back and forth between being mother and being a worker, she says, 'The minute I walk out of the office I switch off completely from the job. When at work, I am totally confident Celine is fine. But it's true that I don't feel as ambitious as I used to in my career, I am just very glad I can afford to support my daughter and have a reasonable standard of living. That's enough for me.'

The classic Flexi: if she works, she seeks more than adequate substitute care and will compromise about how much work she does within the constraints. They do not believe the hype about Having It All, something's got to give. While there is sometimes a danger that they kid themselves about what is going on, be that at home or work, their goal is not to be too greedy and in doing so, to carve out as happy a life as possible for all concerned.

While part-time work suited Sharon, it is in the nature of Flexis that they are diverse. Since some also work full-time and many also are at-homers, I shall devote the next three chapters to how the Flexi approach pans out under these three different conditions: full-time work, part-time and at-home.

CHAPTER 13

The Full-Time Employed Flexi

Most Flexis are either part-timers or at-homers when their child is under-three. Their ideal scenario is to share the care with a partner and to work from home. However, in some cases, they do opt to work full-time – even when there is no financial need. There are intriguing differences between them and the Organiser in their reasoning for this, and how they arrange matters.

Jess is 40, with three children, the youngest of whom is 18 months. Her husband Paul is the successful chief executive of a medium-sized business which he created and owns, in Bristol.

Jess is an intelligent woman who did well enough at her comprehensive to get into Cambridge University without being a workaholic swot – you have to be pretty bright to do that, since 45% of Oxbridge places still go to alumnae of public schools. She probably could have been one of the leading commercial lawyers in this country, earning the millions that they do. Instead, she has always felt impelled not to let her work dominate her life and is satisfied to be restricted in her career horizons by living in a relatively small city, limiting the amount she can ever expect to earn and the degree of challenge she is likely to face.

The subtleties of the Flexi's search for balance permeate her approach. She has several Hugger characteristics when it comes to babies, yet she is by no means so in love with them that she is prepared to give up her career – she has the Organiser's strong commitment to her worker identity. She has wangled things so that even in a very hostile economic climate, she is indispensable to her employers. Twice she has returned to work full-time after maternity leave but with her third child, she has negotiated a part-time job.

Because they have plenty of money, she can choose the substitute care arrangements that she wishes. So can several hundred thousand other mothers of under-threes, but money does not guarantee getting it right. As we shall see, Jess is particularly instructive in how to create a satisfactory substitute regime.

With the first child she took six months' maternity leave, nine months for the others. She ticks the Hugger box in many important respects, although always with a Flexi twist. During each pregnancy she felt relaxed, looked forward to the birth and had strong intuitions about the gender of each child (Hugger). Yet she also says 'I wasn't sitting there talking to the foetus all night, every night' (Organiser). She had the Flexi's open-minded attitude to the birth, not strongly committed to any particular delivery method, finding that all three went without problems (only gas and air in each case). She enjoyed breastfeeding all three children until six months (Hugger) but would have been unhappy with much longer than that (Flexi). Asked about what a baby needs, it's 'someone kind, maternal, giving them love, someone who communicates with them rather than overstimulates' (Hugger) but 'as they get older they need boundaries, you need to give them a nap but not force it, there's no need for strict routines' (Flexi).

When one of her babies was born not very cuddly, she did not take it personally, did not feel rejected. If the baby liked lying on the mat kicking its feet and staring around the room, that was fine by Jess. But equally, after the birth of her middle child, she made a point of doubling up the cuddles and snuggles for the oldest at the times when it was feeling a bit under the weather or snivelly, just to be on the safe side, to avoid that child feeling neglected or unfavoured. Whereas

Huggers adore a hug and Organisers restrict cuddles to what's needed, the Flexi is more driven by what she thinks the particular child requires at the particular moment, depending on what is practically feasible: pragmatism.

She is against being against particular approaches, advocates non-advocacy. 'This is a task where however good you are, you always fail to some degree, unlike your career where you can get nearer to perfection. If things go pear-shaped at the office I know I can regain control, I like to do a good job. But as a mother I'm not someone with a fixed view of how it's going to be. I didn't expect to get the babies into a four-hour Gina Ford feeding regime. It was chaos quite often.'

The pragmatism of her Flexi approach is consistent. After the birth of her third child there were problems with all three not sleeping. 'Some nights I'd be up every hour with one or all three at a time. The lack of sleep was really, really hard and I was in a permanent fug.' The Hugger would take them into the bed, the Organiser would do some controlled crying back in the cot. Jess just kept on ducking and weaving. Some nights it turned out Paul was willing to offer a bit of human sofa service propped in front of the telly in the wee hours, to give her a break. Other nights she would go with a different flow. When her eldest wanted a glass of water Jess would sometimes let her 'snuggle up with me in our bed for a cuddle then after a few minutes, I'd ask if she would like to go back to her bed, take her there, lie for a little with her to cuddle her back to sleep'. She believes that approach meant having them in the bed did not arise as an issue. 'We've never said no. Because it's never been forbidden they don't really know about it as an option.'

Classic Flexi, she completely refuses to be a combatant in the Mommy Wars (R4), neither supporting nor opposing *The Contented Little Baby Book* nor *The Continuum Concept*. 'Women who work aren't evil; home full-time mothers aren't lazy. There is a happy medium.' Her approach is always to look for the middle way, the compromise. 'I accept "good enough" as a mother but there is no book describing The Right Method. The key is to know yourself and avoid the wasted emotion of guilt. If you have decided to go back to your career but wish you could be at home, it's pointless sitting feeling guilty all day so if you possibly can, go and be a mother instead. Equally, if being at home is not for you don't sit in a heap of frustration when you could be back in your career. There's no absolute best way, it all depends on who you are and what's practical.' While she has many times had moments of feeling she is a rubbish mother who is making a mess of her children with the wrong approach, including doubting that it's right to be satisfied by only being good enough, she always comes back to a baseline feeling that her best is sufficient.

At the heart of Jess's successful regime is her nanny. Readers who cannot afford one may be asking 'huh, what's so clever about finding someone else to do all the hard work?' For one thing, even if you could afford to offer your nanny a flat, unlimited use of a Golf GTI convertible, £400 a week pay, with hot and cold running boyfriends thrown in as a bonus, you would be surprised how hard it is to get it right. The difficulty is not so much a shortage of good candidates, as in getting your own head straight about two things.

First, where care of under-threes is concerned, it is vital you grasp that you are looking for someone who is effectively going to be a second mother, not a teacher or life coach or moral educator. As described in Chapter 1, babies need love and subsequently, along with that, toddlers need empathic help with accepting they cannot always get their way. This kind of highly personalised responsiveness is hard to provide even if you are strongly motivated by being the child's parent. It's found even more rarely in unrelated women who are being paid to do the job for the working week. But Jess found just such a woman in Sasha. 'I didn't want someone who'd be the life and soul of the party. I thought "low-key, down to earth, easy, calm", those were more important. She's very nurturing, just particularly loves babies. If they're a bit poorly she'll take them off to the doctor without asking, she's got initiative. If there's anything important that comes up, she will call me, but I could completely rely on her to make the right decisions. It's very important the nanny knows the child, how it likes to settle when sleeping, its favourite food, tiny details that mean everything to them when small.' It was this thinking which ruled out day care.

In typically open-minded Flexi manner, she took the trouble to investigate it. 'I went round a couple of very good nurseries. They were lovely buildings and the art teacher came in and gave a great talk, so did the gym teacher. But it didn't feel right. I know a lot of people think all that socialises them earlier, giving them a head start. But I was going to be working full-time, it would be a long day, and it seemed much too young. My three-year-old is just starting nursery and she only quite likes it even at that age' (this was a rare admission that she was putting her desire to work ahead of the well-being of her child – Flexis are highly skilled at convincing themselves that their arrangements are win-win, even when they are not win for the child).

Jess completely understood the necessity of having someone who was not focused on education or stimulation but on providing warmth and sensitivity. 'You get other nannies who rush about, take them to the Science Museum, with manic play dates twice a day. Sasha does do stuff with them but it's nothing frantic. She knows that home's important, where they mostly want to be at that age.' Jess could feel completely confident that the care was as good as she could have given. 'It was very important to me that they were at home with someone basically doing what I would do with them – pottering, going to the library for a new Babar book, moseying around in the park. From day one I've been able to go to work and not worry at all. It would have been very different without that.' So it's absolutely vital in choosing any substitute care to find someone who understands that the true needs of under-threes are for love and responsiveness, not for stimulation and education, and who is emotionally equipped to supply them. On top of that, you need someone who is going to stick in there right through until the child is aged three, a major issue. While changes of nannies can be done successfully, it is terribly difficult because, in effect, the child is losing a mother if the substitute has really been doing her job.

The second key insight necessary to make substitute care work is that it is actually a good thing if your children really love the nanny (or any other permanent substitute), perhaps even as much as they love you. Jess grasped this. 'I've never had a problem with them being attached to Sasha. I know some where the children run to the nanny rather than the mother but because I've had long periods of maternity leave, we've never had that.' Having established strong personal bonds with each of her children, despite working full-time with two of them, Jess continues to play a pivotal role in their weekdays, as well as weekends. 'I've never felt she's taken over as mother. I get them ready in the morning, put them to bed. I've repeatedly been up in the middle of the night at various times with all of them, I know how important I am to them.' Perhaps that is why she is able to feel unthreatened by their closeness to Sasha. 'You wouldn't want them to be not attached to the nanny. It's obviously right for them to be with someone they love.'

If there are any tiny niggling feelings of rivalry for their love, Jess has a way of reframing it to negate any possible sense that she is second best. 'They know at some level that it's not quite the same, Sasha and me. They can deal with us doing things slightly differently – Sasha is not a duplicate. It's like them having a strong bond with a grandparent.' However you frame it, be very, very glad if your child loves the substitute. That is exactly how it should be and if it is not like that, the arrangement is not as satisfactory as it should be.

It was because Jess had such a clear understanding of these two key points – that under-threes need a mother-substitute, not a teacher, and that they need to love that substitute like a mother – that she was able to find Sasha. She did all the standard things that affluent mothers do to find a nanny; the difference was that as soon as she met one who fitted these criteria, she knew it. Having spoken to many on the phone (making contact via a website), Sasha was the first and only one she interviewed. An hour with her was enough. If you know what you are looking for, you should be able to find it.

Of course, there was always the perennial problem of hanging on to Sasha. In her late twenties when Jess first employed her, she had trained and worked as a teacher in her native Eastern European country and she had a husband. Her love of babies was all too evident and it was obvious she would have her own. Luckily for Jess, it is only now that Sasha has got pregnant.

Jess has found a replacement, who she feels will do just as good a job. Realising that it will be disruptive for her 18-month-old and three-year-old, she is introducing the new nanny gradually, making sure she is always around for the first few weeks. However, given that Jess understands the needs of under-threes so well, I pressed her about why she did not consider giving up her work altogether at this point to save her children the potential distress that a change of nanny could entail. It would only require her to be a full-time mum for a couple of years, four at most, with her youngest being already 18 months. Jess wrestled with the question, her Flexi mind batting the problem around in a typically even-handed manner, but perhaps in this case making it harder to cut right to the truth. She skated around all sorts of reasons, often obscuring from both of us what she really felt although she seemed absolutely sincere in her desire to find it and I think we did get there in the end. It has nothing to do with financial necessity.

Both her mother and her school had had quite a strong ethos that girls were as clever as boys and should be able to achieve whatever they wanted. Giving up work to care for her youngest would betray that and lose her hard-earned place on the career ladder. She worried that she would have nothing very interesting to say to her uber-bright husband and felt she would be a bad role model for her daughter. She didn't fancy sitting around discussing nappies and food with other mothers, or spending so much time cooking, washing and cleaning, none of which she considered herself good at. Although her own mother had a successful career after being full-time at home until she and her sister were well into primary school, she feared finding herself on the career shelf if she dropped out for a bit.

At the same time, Jess would not be heartbroken if she was made redundant tomorrow and she is fairly certain that her present job will not last more than five years – the credit crunch could mean it ends any day now. Especially if she had been having a bad few weeks at the office, she says she would be happy to give up work and get rid of the nanny. But immediately she says this she is plagued by fears. She has a friend who stopped her successful career for a couple of years and cannot get back into the job market at the same level. That means 'she ends up going for coffee mornings with other mothers and wondering what to do with her life'.

This kind of mental to-ing and fro-ing is a risk for a mother with Flexi mentality. While it has the considerable merit of being able to adapt to the real demands of mothering and of life at any given moment, it is also potentially obfuscatory, making it hard for the Flexi to distinguish what is vital from what is subsidiary. Being well-educated, bright and a lawyer can only serve to make this more likely, so that the Flexi can end up seeing too many sides of the argument and lose touch with what is really important. Only by being quite persistent in pointing out that she knew it could be tricky for her 18-month-old to have a new nanny and that it would only entail a few years out of the workforce for her to do the job, did we eventually get to the heart of the matter.

There were two basics.

First, she really does not enjoy caring for three children as much as doing her work. 'Part of what motivates me to work is how hard it is to be at home. It's full-on looking after kids, very hard work.' Whereas some Organisers find it toxic to be at home all day with under-threes, that is not the case with Jess. It's just that 'caring for three under-fives is really, really hard work, physically, emotionally, everything.'

Second, Jess thinks the nanny is better at caring for her children. 'With two children, and certainly three, you can't meet every need they have, right when it's required. It takes a lot of skill and a certain kind of patience. Sasha is very in control, she's fine with them. *Actually, I think she's always found it a lot easier to look after them than I have.*' With all the adeptness one would expect of a lawyer, she quickly tried to backtrack away from the implication that she felt Sasha was actually better at mothering than she was, mainly by saying that it is one thing to do it as a job, nine to five, quite another to be kept up all night and then do it.

Given all this, then, what were Jess's mental acrobatic tactics for reconciling her mother and worker identities? A reported 72% of part-timers repeatedly claim that they have successfully and satisfyingly integrated mother and worker, with win-win 'reframing' as their method – reframing means taking a problem, like that under-threes are hugely dependent on carers, and presenting it in a new light that makes it not a problem, like saying that 'yes, under-threes are dependent but luckily it is not only their mother who can meet their needs'*. While half of them say they have a strong worker identity, they are much less likely than full-timers to emphasise money as their goal, stressing personally fulfilling elements instead*. As we have already seen, Jess genuinely and very wisely perceived that it was probably best for her children for her to have the stimulus of her career, so long as they had Sasha. This was not just a rationalisation, it really may be true that her nanny could do a better job than she can and there is very little doubt that she would be a more playful, loving companion for her children if stimulated (but not exhausted) by her career.

However, the win-win reframing did begin to sound a bit like a way of rationalising things when the need for a new nanny for her 18-month-old came along: it can be argued that that child would benefit if she stopped work for a couple of years. It all depends whether she can make the new nanny work, which remains to be seen.

But prior to this problem, there seems little reason to doubt that it really was win-win. 'Having two identities is something you have to get used to. I was ready to do something when my eldest was nine months old. I remember being quite excited the first time I put clothing other than jeans on, got on the bus, sat and had a cup of coffee, read the paper. I was working 7.30 till 4 so my husband did the morning and I did tea-time. I knew my eldest had had a nice day, was never upset. And I was hugely pleased to see them when I got home. It's a lovely feeling as you walk down the road towards the front door, especially so if you have had a rubbish workday.' Not that it was always like that. 'If everything was a bit slow at work I found it hardest, I would think I was missing out. But I resisted the temptation to ring up because that doesn't do any good for you or the child.'

It was helpful that, just as she has a very well-developed, clearly understood mother identity, so with the worker. 'I like doing things properly. But even in my mid-twenties I was never at the office till midnight, like the most ambitious people. I wanted to be seeing friends, going to parties, having fun – whatever. When I was 30 I realised that you could never be getting the top jobs without working very, very hard and I don't think it's right to if you have children.' In true Flexi style, Jess fully grasped the necessity of compromise. 'You have got to get your head around the fact that, if you have children, some people who are less talented or deserving will get promoted over you. There's one of my colleagues who works incredibly long hours; luckily she has her husband caring for the kids at home. She will go higher than me but something's got to give. You can't do everything and you must not get wound up by that. It's either your home or work life that has to be sacrificed; you must decide which and be honest about it rather than pretend you can have it all.'

Not that Jess is unambitious. 'I never wanted to be a Mistress of the Universe but I do want to get well paid to do something interesting.' It was after she said this that I believe we got to the very heart of Jess's matter. I asked her if she really did find her work interesting, did she feel absorbed and intellectually stimulated by it? To my surprise, after some thought, she replied, 'Well, it's not *really* interesting. I certainly don't have a passion for it. If I stopped I am sure there are many other kinds of things I would enjoy more. I kinda drifted into it after university, got picked up at the university milk round; none of it is close to my greatest interests.'

Of course, Jess is like the vast majority of us, doing work that pays the bills, trying to find something that is as stimulating as possible within that limitation, trying to do as well as possible given the time and energy she is prepared to make available to employers. But right at the very end of our encounter, when I was asking her about her background, she revealed something important about her Flexi motivation.

Both her parents had always stressed the importance of family and hard work. She had completely bought into those values. Then, when she was 17 in her A-level year, in what Jess described as 'an absolute cliché', her father had had 'a midlife crisis' and went off with his much younger, prettier secretary. For the rest of the year after her father had taken up with his fancy woman, Jess stopped working so hard (though she still made it to Cambridge). 'Once he did that, I went out every night. I was quite upset and if it was all right for him to mess around like that, then why shouldn't I?'

This revelation of her parents' divorce occurred at the very end of our interview, so there was no time to explore it further. But I wondered if it might not provide an insight into some of her – and some Flexis' – discomfort with absolutes. Perhaps she had always assumed her parents' relationship inviolate, safe. Faced with the shock of its end and her father's total flouting of his own stern injunctions about the importance of the family, she may have learned a lesson: stay flexible, you never know what might happen.

If so, she has managed to carve a splendid life for her children out of that adversity. While the Flexi's greatest risk is of being inconsistent and too permeable, chopping and changing approaches to fit the circumstances so that the child is never quite sure what to expect, in Jess's hands, she has managed to make compromise into a virtue, almost an art. You might ask Jess, 'Why devote so much of your life to a job that is not really interesting to you?' But such perfectionism and idealism is not for the Flexi. They just know that reality nearly always falls short if you aim too high.

CHAPTER 14

The Mental Gymnastics of the Part-Time Working Flexi

The calm, assured, even timbre of 32-year-old Jane's speech belies her shrewd and determined personality. This is a woman who knows her own mind and is forceful in getting her way, yet in person, she oozes femininity through her figure, manner and dress. She has a way of smoothing away flaws in her arguments or uncomfortable truths, yet she is also startlingly frank and open-minded. She is an independent person who expects autonomy from others. Above all, she seeks balance and in its absence, persuades herself it is there, making her one of the most subtly self-contradictory of the mothers I interviewed.

Balance has made her prioritise a desire for 'a decent standard of living' while convincing herself that she has done the best she can about her children's substitute care. She had the Hugger's intense passion for her two babies but, like many Organisers, she found mothering infants boring if done for more than six months. Unlike most Huggers, she could comfortably leave her son at six months in day care, even though she could tell that he was upset by it. A practical, tough streak enabled an unsentimental approach: they needed her income if they were to afford a certain lifestyle.

As a girl at school she did well until aged 18, when a glamorous and celebrated Australian chef whisked her off her feet. Two years disappeared in a hedonistic blur, instead of university. However, despite being exceptionally attractive, Jane is no flighty hippy chick. Catching her breath at 20, the extent of her dynamism is shown by the fact that in just five years she worked her way up from secretary to account executive in the advertising industry. Along the way, in a London nightclub, she met Trevor, a beefy, solid police officer. Both aged 25, they decided to get married and have children, although they knew no one else who was doing so.

Speaking of her relationship to the foetus during the pregnancy, she sounds like a Hugger. 'He was very much part of me. He seemed like an old friend who had been away for years and who I was waiting to come back. I felt I knew who he was, a placid, calm bump, he did very slow turns in my tummy, no kicking.' Soon after the birth, she felt instant relatedness. 'I remember handing him over to my mum for a cuddle and someone made a joke which made me laugh loudly. His head span towards me: he was very aware of who I was, we had that connection from the beginning.'

The early months also had many Hugger elements. 'I've always referred to him as my ally. He was my mate, involved, close by everywhere I went, sleeping in my arms, folded there. At night he was in the crib by the bed or occasionally in it.' At the same time, there was Flexi expedience. 'I didn't plan anything, we just did what we did. Older, more academic friends had read the books but we didn't have a game plan or any mentors.' Having been advised by the hospital nurse to feed every four hours, instead, she found it happened every two and half to three, going with that flow. 'I just accepted that as what we did to survive, didn't try to impose anything. For the first couple of months it was chaos, I didn't get much sleep, feeding a lot during the night. Luckily Trevor was a star. He would get up and make a cup of tea and we'd sit round chatting, a bit of a family event in the middle of the night.'

Yet elements of Organiser coexisted with these approaches. 'I felt quite lonely. People treat a new baby like a bereavement, say that the mother "needs some space, needs quiet" but actually, you're really bored. You can't get out of the house and you feel quite detached from the world, on your own.' The day after they came out of hospital she received a text offering her a job, but that did not faze her. 'I asked them to give me a few weeks to get my bearings and went for an interview when Sean was seven weeks old.' At the interview she remained her usual unflappable self, getting the job despite lack of sleep and the 'chaos'. Few Huggers would be able to do that so early on, and because many Organisers find the early months so destabilising, they might not either.

From even before she had got pregnant there had been no doubt that she would return to work four days a week because Trevor's income would be 'insufficient'. Starting her new job when Sean was four months, Jane found a nanny-share in a magazine. The trouble was that the other child was a baby of Sean's age. 'I really liked the nanny but she had two four-month-olds at the same time. Having since seen what it's like with friends who have twins, I know that is really not a good move for anybody. It sent the nanny crazy.' She noticed a big impact on Sean. 'Beforehand, he was relaxed, smiley, very rarely crying. During his three months with her he became quite withdrawn. From being very giggly and alert, he was non-reactive to his environment, just not looking around or interested in what was going on.' What happened next precisely illustrates the Flexi's skill in justifying her approach.

Having seen that looking after two four-month-olds is a tall order, she might have concluded that Sean needed a nanny exclusively to himself or, at least, that he would be better off with a minder who had him and an older child. Instead, she arranged for him to be in day care. His carer there had not one, but two other babies to look after, an even worse situation than that of the nanny, she might have reasoned. But her rationale was as follows. 'When I was pregnant my ideal was a nanny. But then my experience was that it's quite an intense relationship for the child to be with one person. If you're a nanny and you have a bad day, the child will have one.' The manager of the spanking new nursery she chose for Sean had a sales pitch which further supported this thinking. 'She said "if you're in a nursery and your carer is having a bad day, there's other adults there who can give you responsive care as well".' But above all, the manager clinched it for Jane by arguing that 'everyone brings up their children differently and the nursery approaches all children differently as well'. Quite how they could do this if there were 10 babies present with three carers was not made clear.

It might sound true in theory, but in practice, if the other adults are busy trying to care for three babies (one more than the nanny who was driven insane by having just two to care for), it sounds improbable. If one of the carers is having an off day, that means the others who are not have nine babies to worry about. It is hard to see how they could really treat each of them differently.

But, typical of the Flexi, Jane can also be very accurate in her perception of the truth. Quite a few mothers would probably fudge the issue but Jane recalls clearly how difficult it was for Sean when he started at the nursery. 'He was always very sad when we left him. We've got a photo my husband took after a week there and he just looks quite sad. He used to cling on when I was leaving, completely. They had to take him off me every time, very much so, it was really hard.' Since it is greatly in their interests, nursery carers or managers will tell mothers that the child recovers and is full of good cheer within minutes of the mother leaving. Jane does not recycle this misrepresentation (see pages 344–55 of my book *Affluenza* for my account of what really happens; remember as well the study, described in Chapter 6 (page 105) showing that cortisol levels are still elevated an hour after the mother has left*).

Later in the interview I asked her if she thought genes largely determine what we are like. 'People are born the way they are,' she replied. However, asked if this applied to the differences in personality between her two sons she was able to consider other possibilities. Whereas she went back to work when Sean was four months, with her younger son,

Max, she did not return until he was aged one. She wondered if the reason Sean is so 'placid and passive' has to do with these different early experiences. 'Sean was in nursery from a very young age and he had to do what was laid on for him that day. He had to go, first to the nanny, then to the nursery, and there really wasn't any choice.' By contrast, she regards Max as more 'confident and assertive' and she pondered if 'having that year at home with me gave him more of a "rule the roost" feeling. I don't know if that's made him a bit more empowered?'

The flexibility of her mind was evident in the way she wriggled her way through the various awkward emotional elephant traps her decisions and their consequences set her, swiftly and smoothly shifting between wish fulfilment and stark honesty. For example, she did nothing to conceal that her reason for going back to work so early with Sean and leaving him in a nursery was a desire for affluence. 'I knew that I had to go back to work, financially, when I was pregnant. We could have settled for a smaller house and got by on one person's wage but that had never been my game plan, really. I wanted to be able to have nice things, like good holidays, a car each and nice furniture.' As noted, she does not pretend Sean was initially happy either with the nanny or the nursery. 'He must have taken time to accept that he was there and that he had no alternative. My thinking was that I had done a lot of research and this was the best nursery I could find. I thought "I've made this choice, I can see he's upset but I know it's still the right plan for the family".'

Yet there may be a bit of positive gloss, fancy mental footwork, when she says of her boys in day care that 'both of them would just rock up and you knew they just owned the space. They'd go straight in, loads of kids around, and when you came to pick them up they wouldn't want to come home they were having so much fun.' More detailed questioning did not always support this account. In Max's case, there were signs of actively rejecting her (known as avoidant attachment*) when she arrived to pick him up. 'One time he was playing with a little girl with a wheelbarrow and he ignored me as if saying "if you want me, you'll have to come and get me".' In Sean's case, 'he wouldn't even stop what he was doing, maybe just say "hi", then carry on without looking at me'. While this might be a sign of his absorption in his game, as a pattern it sounds more like the avoidant cold shoulder.

It's a complex balancing act, mental acrobatics. She keeps awkward thoughts at bay and yet, she also stays for much of the time very close to the truth. There is no self-deception at all about the degree to which she truly needs money from her job. They now have a mortgage of £265,000 because she wants a particular sort of home. 'I don't need to work to put bread and water on the table but I do if we want our lifestyle. We could get by on Trevor's money but only by living much more frugally.' Equally, if funding a certain kind and level of consumption is her priority, she is very honest and exact about how little she really enjoys looking after small children.

When I asked if she would have worked if she had won the lottery, she said, 'I would not have stayed at home. I need a balance, time away from being at home, from the monotony of it. I know their personalities are changing and developing every day but on a housekeeping level, the monotony just kills me. It really doesn't fit my personality.' What would happen if she was forced to stay at home? 'I would make sure I did cope and I would, probably. For the early months with Max, my sense of achievement was very much based on him and I would say to Trevor when he tried to get involved "this is my one chance and you have to let me do it". But around about six months both Max and I went a bit insane really, the pressure on that relationship between us was just too great. He couldn't give me what I needed with regard to organisation and process, and things on an emotional level.'

In so saying, she revealed an Organiser-like focus on her needs over those of the child, yet at other times, she displays Huggeresque empathy for it. That is the Flexi, in touch with her own and the child's needs, not necessarily at the same time, not necessarily in equal portions, but rarely completely losing sight of either for very long. By contrast, extreme Organisers may never much understand the needs of babies or toddlers, while extreme Huggers can completely lose track of their adult needs for years at a time.

CHAPTER 15

An At-Home Flexi Copes with Multiple Adversities

Flexis who might have been Huggers are often edged into the approach by circumstances. Limited money or unhelpful partners or sundry other obstructions can prevent them from Hugging.

Carrie, 45, is an example of a Flexi who never had the slightest intention of doing anything other than becoming a full-time at-home mum – something commoner in Huggers. It took her some time to get round to motherhood, but now that she has, despite some huge adversities, she could not be happier. The adversities have prevented her from being as much of a Hugger as she might have been, but she does not repine about that.

Born to working-class parents in inner-city Liverpool, she lives with Gerald, her middle-manager husband, in a quite prosperous suburb of the city, their modest house overlooking the Mersey estuary. They have identical twin boys (Seamus and Paul, six), another boy (Damian, four) and a girl (Jordan, two). Carrie gave up work as soon as she became pregnant with the twins and does not intend to return for the foreseeable future.

Whereas Jane, described in the last chapter, is at the Organiser end of the Flexi scale, Carrie is an example of a mother who would probably have been a Hugger, had circumstances been different. As noted, this is quite common. Practical problems can force a Hugger to turn

Flexi. In the event, she found herself having to adopt quite a few Organiser tactics. It started with the pregnancies.

Aged 38, she not only found herself carrying twins, she was diagnosed with cancer, a disease she only completely vanquished a year after the birth of her fourth child. It led to excruciating pain, along with great anxieties, and understandably enough, it affected how she felt about the foetus. 'I don't think I ever had a relationship with any of them because I felt so ill. I always thought I would be proud of my bump but I never enjoyed it at all. Every time, I was just concentrating on getting through the pregnancy.' She was extremely ill throughout the first one. 'I couldn't even get out of bed about six weeks into it, and I had to go in and out of hospital throughout.'

For obvious reasons, having twins increases the risk of depression and once they arrived, after a calm first few days, she found herself swamped by baby blues, which thankfully only lasted until they were two months. 'I couldn't stop sobbing. I was ringing my mum the whole time and she was "don't worry, love, it was just the same for me".' Gerald is a traditional dad who expects a wife to deal with the home and children. He was mystified by her mood. 'It was a bit scary, weeping all the time, and Gerald was saying "God, what the hell's the matter with you?" Luckily I had my mum and gran to sob down the phone to.' Gerald was equally thrown by the demands of twins. 'He found them quite hard to cope with; well, he couldn't really cope at all, what with the babies constantly screaming and all the mess.' She did not much like the chaos either.

'I found those first few weeks awful, it was the same with all the babies. I hate it, the normal life going out the window. I like to have my routine. I can't bear that screaming when you are thinking "what the hell is it that you want?".' She had always been someone who liked a tidy, active life. 'Luxuriating in bed until lunchtime is not something I am very good at. I would hate to be slobbing about in my pyjamas all day, I like to get up, have a shower and get dressed. When I go to bed,

I want the house reasonably clean and tidy, with the children's clothes laid out.' Having worked from the age of 16, she had not experienced a student lifestyle. 'I never did any of that sitting in front of the telly watching *This Morning* that they get up to. I wouldn't have been a very good student. When I visited student friends they lived in these filthy places and liked staying up all night getting paralytically drunk. I like to be in bed at a decent hour, clean sheets and clean clothes. I don't like hangovers and I hate chaos.'

The early weeks with the twins were tough. She was feeling extremely ill from the cancer and they had only recently moved to the area. 'My mum came for a few days but after she left I can remember sitting in the lounge and as soon as I had got one of them settled, the other started crying. One time my mum kept ringing and eventually I picked up the phone and shouted "For God's sake will you stop ringing! I can't even get dressed, let alone answer the phone."' The combination of her illness, her husband's discombobulation and the lack of sleep might have led to a strict routine but this was not her choice. While her instinct was never to have the babies in the bed, without the added pressure of two mouths to feed she would have Hugged. Instead she adapted, in true Flexi fashion. 'I breastfed, but by the time you have fed them and topped them up, most of the day is gone, so I introduced bottles as soon as I could. When they were in bed I went down with them in the spare room with a line of bottles and a mountain of nappies. I did occasionally manage a sleep during the day, though that's not my natural tendency.'

She recalls having been 'thrilled to be pregnant and longed to cuddle up with my baby'. But any Hugger desire to luxuriate with them was extinguished by the pressures. 'It was a case of "I can't wait for three, six months, the sooner they are walking and talking the better". It was just getting through, surviving. There were a few lovely moments but mostly they were screaming blue murder. I think the baby blues went because you just don't have time to feel depressed.'

The Flexi automatically plugged into a social network. She had found like-minded souls in her antenatal classes, and her mum and granny kept her going. She would go off to stay with them when Gerald had to be away from home for work. 'Gradually I got into the life of the community, like my mum did when we were small – she was always someone who helped others. There'd be coffee, lunch, tea with other mums. I would never live in the middle of the countryside, I like having people nearby.' She made sure she plugged into every possible support. Even Gerald rallied. 'One night I had to be in hospital and he looked after them. My God, the fuss he made, such a fuss. He had to take one of them to the doctor in the middle of the night and he was saying "oh, I've been up all night, it was dreadful". When I pointed out that was normal for me, he actually got quite bad tempered!' With all the children, whenever possible, he has avoided getting roped into too much childcare. 'He likes going to work before the children are up and coming home after they are asleep. He's a very good dad but he doesn't want to be a mum. At weekends if I get an occasional Sunday lie-in, I will come downstairs and he will be watching the football in the playroom, the children will be doing God knows what, no one's had their nappy changed or got dressed, the place will be a total tip. It drives me mad.' But most surprising of all, her father turned out to be a big help.

Her parents separated when she was young. Her mother had had a series of boyfriends, although she protected Carrie from becoming confused about them by keeping the relationships separate from home life. Her father had been a heroin addict and was now reformed, although still not popular with her mother. To everyone's surprise, he has enjoyed getting involved, coming to stay regularly. 'He feeds them fizzy drinks and crisps, and turns the house into a pigsty, walks dirt all over the place. But the children love him and he loves them, they are thrilled if they know he's coming. My mum disapproves but so long as I give him specific instructions, like to take them swimming, he brings a lot of warmth and I think a grandparent should be a bit indulgent, a treat. It also gives him a purpose. He is incredibly helpful every summer when we go to the Isle of Wight for our summer holiday, plays with them for hours on the beach.' Here is the voice of the authentic Flexi. Despite her dislike of mess in the house and opposition to her father's indulgent attitude, she looks for the win-win: she needs the extra pair of hands, she does not have the spare capacity for much playing on the beach which she realises is good for the kids, she sees that it helps her dad stay sane.

Her desire for order over chaos apart, the extent to which she might have been a Hugger in more propitious circumstances emerged when we discussed what ages she loves best in children. At first, it seemed that, like an Organiser, she preferred them as they get older. 'I love them when newborn for the first few days, before they start screaming, but I'm not very good between then and about six months, it's a bit tedious and it's such hard work. You can't even go to the toilet, you can't get out of the house. I think maybe between two and three when they're talking and walking is more my favourite.' However, when we explored this a bit more, she realised that the combination of her illness, having twins, her husband's unsupportiveness and the fact that she has a natural disinclination towards messy chaos had obscured a love of babies. Talking of her third child and the early months with her much-desired daughter, her lastborn, she described strong Hugger feelings which were being suppressed by the huge demands of caring for a large family with adversities flowing thick and fast. 'With Jordan I loved the first year. I loved her being a baby. On the rare days when I could get time alone with her, I loved just pottering about together. I could run a nice bubble bath, dim the lights, get a nice soft towel ready, it was cosy and cuddly. But it was terribly rare that it could be like that with any of them because of all the problems.' It should be remembered that she achieved all this despite the terrible spectre of an early grave from cancer.

A fascinating aspect was the extent to which Carrie felt comfortable in her skin. Of all the mothers I spoke with, she was the one who seemed most in touch with her moment-to-moment feelings, very alive, and she was strikingly unhampered by theories of how life ought to be, in fact, did not engage in theorising at all. Quick-witted and astute, she also had a first-hand experience which is rare. She does not think of herself as being particularly clever, but she does not run herself down either. 'I wasn't much good at school, but that didn't matter. I would not have ever wanted to go to university, even if I could have, because there was nothing I would have wanted to study. Why do some crappy degree, which isn't going to be any use?' From a young age she knew what she was going to do. 'I always wanted to be a mum, for ever, a wife and a mum was what I was going to be and all I needed was to find a husband.' Unusually for a woman from her background who longed for motherhood, she resisted the temptation to have children young because she always felt she had not met the right man. For many years she went out with more or less enjoyable rogues and it was only in her mid-thirties that she grasped that this had to do with having had a father like that. Talking it over with her ever-reliable and usually very sensible mother, she saw that she was attracted to flaky men and deliberately chose another direction, eventually being very happy to marry the dependable Gerald.

The crucial factor seems to be her total lack of conflict about her mother role (R5). She did clerical work in offices and enjoyed the social life but says 'it's not as if I ever had, or wanted, a career, it was always a job'. Once she became a mother, despite all the difficulties, she felt she was completely at home. 'I recently had to fill out a form and the woman asked me what my profession was. I said "mother, housewife" and she said "House Director?" and I almost shouted, "No, just put mother, for God's sake".' If at the pub or talking to her husband's friends, 'I say I look after my children. It doesn't bother me in the slightest. I've never, ever had any intention of going back to work. I always wanted to be at home cooking and caring for the kids. Of course there are days when I think all I have done is clean the house and wipe bottoms. And tomorrow it's all got to be done again. But it's what I want.'

She is unlike many other mothers in not feeling any sign of concern about what she contributes. 'I've got friends who worry that they are not bringing in any money but I work bloody hard. When I spend our money I feel I have earned it.' By contrast, she has one particular friend who is often discontented. 'She is always talking about what other people do and trying to change things about herself to make them better. I say "I don't care what anyone else does, this is the way I'm doing it". I'm sure my children will have gripes when they are older but I have done the best I can, which is all you can do. I may be right and I might be wrong but that's the way I'm doing it. I'm not going to try something that's not for me.' Old school friends tell her that they have noticed that since becoming a mother she has become less shy and more confident, and she agrees. 'I am more sure of my own mind. I really am comfortable in my skin.' None of these points was made smugly or with vanity, they all emerged purely because of my questioning.

Two aspects of her seem unusually mentally healthy. One is that, unlike most of us, she really has been able to learn from her experience. This is most obvious with regard to her relations with men, so that she paid attention to the fact that she kept picking lovable rogues and was able to kick the habit. The other is that she is what is known as 'self-concordant'. It means having a life and being a person that closely reflects your true wishes. Such people do not feel the grass is greener in others' lives. To do that, of course, you need to know what you really want, which many people do not. On top of that, you need to have matured sufficiently to have learnt not to want certain things – even though they seem tempting – because they harm you. There is a good deal of scientific evidence that being self-concordant may be the single most important feature of women who are truly fulfilled by motherhood (indeed, it may be the secret for everyone)*.

A final fascinating aspect of Carrie's story is how little thought she has given to the nature–nurture debate. She told me in great detail how different her children are, including her identical twins. When I asked what she thought explained this, she replied 'They're all very different, it's just how they are, they were born that way – genes' (it is amazing just how deep geneticism runs in our culture; I recall being at a party many years ago where there were two identical twins; despite being Oxbridge-educated, both were very put out when I said that, whatever else explained it, genes could not possibly account for their (considerable) differences because they had exactly the same ones – despite their expensive education, they still maintained they had been born different). Typical of the Flexi and of her unforced openness, she was not in the least defensive, only curious, when I pointed out a big contradiction in this belief. I said, 'but if genes mean you are just born a particular way, it would not have mattered who looked after your children. Suppose you had gone back to work and sent them to a nursery, if it was all genes, why did you bother to put all that work in?' She was puzzled at this, instantly grasping that, without realising it, she must actually believe her nurture was important, not only genes. She pondered how her mothering might affect what the children are like, saying 'well it makes a difference if a mother works, they need their mum there. If someone is paid to look after them she will not care as much.' Yes, but why would that matter if genes are so important? 'Their general life and well-being will be improved by having the mum there. So it's probably not all genes. Maybe it's not. You mould them? I don't know, can't really think, um, I've completely lost my train of thought.'

Further prodding revealed all sorts of ways in which their different nurture may be linked to why they are so different. But I was fascinated to meet a mother who had genuinely never given this matter a moment's thought. So 'in the moment' does she live, it's not bothered her. Just as she never read any baby books or worried what other mothers do, she just got on with being her.

This might be the only weakness of her approach. In a very short time we identified a number of ways in which, since it was not a genetic destiny, she might possibly be able to help her children with difficulties they have. As all the evidence shows, it's far better to realise that the way you care for your children is highly influential of how they turn out (page 314, R7). It is not that Carrie lacks intellect or imagination. She lives in a rich, vivid present, and is constantly adjusting her mothering according to her highly realistic, accurate appreciation of reality. The only problem I could see was that she was making the mistake of assuming that there were many things about her children that were givens, unchangeable genetic fate. As soon as I pointed out that this may not be so, she was quickly applying the idea and considering ways she could help them. Being so undefensive and uncluttered by theoretical or ideological assumptions, she felt no need to protect herself or deny a useful truth.

While Flexis have many merits, the main risk is that their pragmatism means they need to provide themselves with stories that leave out important truths. As they duck and dive their way to what they perceive as win-win arrangements, perception can eclipse reality. Carrie is the exception that proves this rule.

CHAPTER 16

How Fleximums' Childhoods Can Help and Hinder Meeting Their Children's Needs

Along with keeping tabs on their own and their child's needs, the greatest strength of the Flexi is a willingness to adjust the care according to reality. This applies in their moment-to-moment adaptability to the child's immediate demands: simple things, like being willing to end their phone conversation immediately because the baby is about to go ballistic, or to take the flu-ridden child into the bed even though they may generally dislike three-in-a-bed. They can be equally adaptable in their broader strategy, giving up day care and switching to a minder if the child is clearly not happy, or giving up or taking up work, if that is what seems to be needed for the time being.

However, as should be clear by now, the greatest Flexi weakness is if their mental elasticity – acrobatics – leads them to deceive themselves about the true situation, pretending that win-lose (or even, lose-lose) is win-win. Occasionally, that means they are kidding themselves that they want to be at home when in fact they would be less depressed if they went back to work. Much more commonly, they are glossing a substitute arrangement they have made for their child on returning to work, fooling themselves that it suits the child. Equally, they sometimes kid themselves that they want to be back at work when they do not really – they succumb to peer pressure that they should 'have it all' or that they should not waste hard-won qualifications when the truth is that they wish to be at home. Whichever way, they may portray these situations as win-win when there is actually a 'lose' involved.

As with the other approaches, your childhood history can be a major cause. The most positive version is where the mother has had her needs met in early childhood. This has enabled her to become a highly empathic carer herself who can also keep track of her own needs – she does not overidentify with the baby or toddler, she empathises with it. She is able to respond well at different ages, tuning into the baby and putting her self on the shelf for much of the time, enjoying doing so, yet never forgetting to get it back when she needs to. In practice, that means in the early months being very attuned to the baby and only gradually and occasionally initiating interactions based on her own wishes. So to begin with her games with the baby are based on its favoured patterns, like imitating sticking its tongue out at her, rather than the mother doing that first and expecting the baby to follow. As it gets older, if the mum is feeling particularly cheery, she may smile and talk loving words to the baby, and it may smile and coo back. By six months, they have a whole vocabulary unique to the two of them, with the mother's flexibility greatly enhancing the baby's scope and the pleasure it provides. In such cases, none of the potential problems of the Hugger (difficulties coping with the baby's growing independence) or the Organiser (trouble getting on its wavelength) are present, it truly is win-win. If the mother does go back to work, it is usually part-time for not many hours and she is liable to find a partner or relative or friend as a substitute who is almost as good company for the baby as she is.

Problems from the Flexi's own childhood which lead her to be rather too skilful a mental acrobat, misperceiving win-wins, take four main forms.

As with other approaches, the first is not having been responded to and tuned into as a baby. Instead of reacting to this by Hugging ('I give the baby the infancy I never had') or Organising ('I find babies boring' because distressing or because on a different wavelength), they use being Flexi as a way to keep at bay the distress that the baby's vulnerability and dependence provokes. When something distresses them, under the guise of pragmatism and adaptability, they change their plan, distracting from the unease.

The second problem is if their parents divorced or separated and it left them too angry or scared of committing to a particular approach. They fear that if they get 'pinned down' they will feel trapped, although they conceal this from themselves and others.

The third problem is if their early or later care was disorganised, or if the love they received was erratic or lukewarm. This leaves them nervous of commitment too. They are the Flexis who are most prone to the modern vogue for happiness, the falsely positive optimism which has been imported from America, peddled by the likes of Paul McKenna*. They can be liable to spread a thin veneer of cheeriness over the bleakest of situations.

The final problem is if their parents were authoritarian, harsh or strict. Being a Flexi may be a reaction against such parenting. Rather than being openly defiant, which is what adoption of a Hugger approach would entail, they prefer a middle way. Being Flexi neither openly challenges their parents' dictatorial approach nor embraces it, thereby evading nasty rows with (usually pretty fierce and scary) parents but also satisfying a desire to give their child a different experience. I shall start with two examples of this last kind of Flexi childhood motivation.

Two Very Different Sisters for Whom the Flexi Approach is a Reaction to a Strict Father

Sandra and Charlotte are sisters with contrasting personalities and values, yet a shared Flexi approach to mothering. Aged 34, Sandra is the oldest by two years. She sees herself as having been 'a good girl', saying 'I always used to do as I was told, like my mum, more laidback, will avoid confrontation at any cost'. Raised in the West Country, she has never lived more than a few miles from her parents. She regards her husband's £40,000 income as sufficient for both of them and during her periods of working since having children, has not done so for the money.

Charlotte has always been more rebellious. She was attracted to the bright lights of London and a more ambitious career. She makes no bones about wanting a larger, more expensive house. 'I do like the good things in life and so I have had to work hard. I was careful to find good nurseries for my kids and I realise they may not have been perfect. But if we wanted a decent house and car and all the rest of it, that's what we had to do.' Her husband earns £35,000 a year, she earns twice that.

Despite being so different, both are Flexis. They used some routines for sleeping but were more Huggers about feeding. They would vary what they did with their different children, depending on what was required. What made them such different people but so similar as mothers?

Their factory shop-floor supervisor father was a forceful man, a firm disciplinarian. Recalls Charlotte, 'He was very strict. We were only allowed to watch TV for one hour a day, the one between mum going to work and him coming home. He would feel the back of the TV set to see how warm it was as a way of gauging how long we had been watching. We were only allowed one programme each, so I used to watch *Home and Away*, then I would have to leave the room while Sandra watched *Neighbours*.'

As the oldest, Sandra seems to have been exposed to greater strictness. 'I paved the way for Charlotte. I really wasn't allowed out on my own on a school night until aged 17. Charlotte was let out for longer, from younger. I would have to do my homework in my room with no music on.'

Sandra had two daughters, two years apart, in her mid-twenties. She enjoyed her career as a shop manager in a large chain. Having worked hard to achieve this, she went back to work when her daughter was six months old, handing her over to an 'excellent' childminder. 'It's difficult. I love being a mum but you have to keep your sanity as well. When at work people see you as an individual and you can go to the toilet when you want or drink that coffee while it's still hot.' However, she began to feel the reasons for working were not sufficient to keep her there. 'After a year, I realised I was missing out on all the early stages of her development. Huge chunks of what she was doing were not seen by me, I had this sense that time was slipping away.' Flexis like win-win but 'I was getting the worst rather than the best of both worlds'. Because she did shifts, she was able to see her daughter for much of the day but would then have to do eight hours' work. She felt 'I'm not enjoying (a) handing over my child to someone else, (b) trying to combine shift work and being a mum.' She gave it up and soon after, her second daughter came along.

Despite the experience with her first child, she was tempted back to work again when the second was 18 months old. This time she only lasted six months. She hated hearing her daughter crying when she left her at the minder and she found the mix of shift work and two children 'horrendous'.

In contrast to Sandra, Charlotte used nurseries rather than minders, and worked full-time because 'only that way would I be able to give my children the lifestyle I wanted for them'. However, she did take time out for both her children when they were babies, spending a year at home with each and adopting a classic Flexi 'cut and paste' pragmatism in the care regime. She would have them sleeping in the bed if they were ill, though not keen on the idea. She acknowledges that day care was difficult for them and she did her best to compensate for it at weekends. She always kept her children's needs in mind, as well as her own, albeit putting her desire for affluence ahead of everything else.

As I explained in my book *They F*** You Up*, it is differences in care provided by both parents, and differing relationships to them, which explain why siblings are different from each other, far more so than genes. Sandra and Charlotte illustrate this well.

Already having a daughter in Sandra, their mother hoped for a son with her second-born and that may be why Charlotte is more stereotypically male, having been an assertive, more rebellious child who subsequently refused to allow her children to get in the way of her career. In addition, Charlotte is quite conscious of having had a different strategy for dealing with their strict father, who had also hoped for a son. 'I was more of a "daddy's girl" than Sandra.' Although both girls did well at school, Charlotte did better, knowing this was something he would particularly like. 'I definitely got some Brownie points from dad for doing well academically. I knew how to work the family system, if you like. His strictness didn't sit so well with Sandra, made her a bit anxious, accommodating, wanting to make sure everyone was happy.' It would seem that Charlotte served as the son that her mother wanted and managed to insinuate herself into her father's favour as a surrogate son as well. Sandra, meanwhile, got on with being like her mother, whom she stayed close to, geographically and emotionally.

Almost the only thing they have in common, psychologically, is their Flexi attitude to mothering. In taking this approach, both are aware of having reacted against their father's strictness, saying that they feel they did not want things to be quite as disciplinarian. However, at the same time, neither reacted so strongly that they became Huggers. In both cases, they saw this as excessive, too much putting themselves second. As women raised in an age when they are encouraged to realise themselves rather than 'just' be housewives, they felt that they should not be wholly subordinate to their children's needs.

Hence, in Sandra's case, it is interesting that the key reason she decided to give up work was not that she felt it was going to be best for her daughters, it was that she was not enjoying it and that she was not witnessing her daughter's milestones. She said, 'When I went back to work the second time, it just reiterated to me that I was missing out on my daughter's development.' She wanted to see these changes first-hand, but this was for her own satisfaction, she does not mention the possibility that her daughter might receive better nurture.

In Charlotte's case, her own needs also came first. Like so many people, she wanted more and better possessions. While in true Flexi fashion she was concerned about her children's needs, the priority was what she wanted for herself. She is open about the fact that her children suffered as a result, albeit perhaps unaware of quite how much long-term damage may have occurred.

The key point is that both women were reacting against their upbringing and that this slightly clouded their judgement about whether their situations were truly win-win. In terms of meeting the needs of their children, this might have been more likely if the sisters had been better able to understand how their past was influencing their present. They could have been less likely to use the Flexi approach as a fudged excuse for pleasing themselves.

BEING FLEXI AS A RESPONSE TO EMOTIONAL NEGLECT IN EARLY CHILDHOOD

Now aged 35, Sheila had an emotionally deprived early life. Her mother was depressed and, in later life, was febrile. It left Sheila nervous of commitment to men, something she eventually overcame in her mid-thirties when she settled down with Ken and they had two children, without marrying.

Her approach to the early care was characterised by frequent shifts. In the minute-to-minute mothering, she could be adoring and respon-sive, only to suddenly feel detached and removed, to her baby's puzzlement. In her regime, she started off with the first child in the bed, only to suddenly decide he was ready for the cot. Having been strikingly Huggy, she now adopted controlled crying as the way to get him sleeping. This was presented as being necessary because of traits he was supposed to have been born with – 'he's an independent boy, always has been, it doesn't suit him being in the bed'. In fact, further questioning suggests that she was 'feeling suffocated' and wanted the bed for herself and Ken. A similar inconsistency of regime followed with her second child and in both cases, she bounced like a yo-yo between deciding she wanted to be back at work, first of all full-time, then part-time, then not at all, then back to full-time. On top of all that, during the periods at work she changed her substitute plans several times with both children, jumping between nurseries, nannies and minders.

Her skill in representing these rapid changes as being win-win was impressive. However, unlike most Flexis, it did not seem to be based on the real needs of herself or her children. The heart of the problem was that she lacked much sense of self, was someone who deep down had little idea of what she was feeling or needed. While the rhetoric with which she presented her plans concealed this, at times she could see it was true. 'I wish I was someone else, you know. I quite often feel like a fraud, not a real mother at all. But it's the same in lots of ways, I never feel too sure what I want from my career either – is it for me or for my boss? It's the same with men' (she confided that she has had several lovers since being with Ken, usually one-night stands). Unfortunately, these moments of insight did not last long because they would soon be eclipsed by despair and self-attacking ideas, and then by defences against them, like fanatical jogging or bouts of drinking. To keep the show on the road, she would decide the problem was something to do with her arrangements or a trait in the child, unable to stick to the truth, which was that her own early care had left her lacking much soundly based certainty.

This is an extreme case, of course. More common is for a Flexi to have suffered less early or extreme emotional deprivation than this, but to have suffered enough, nonetheless, to be attracted by the idea of not over-committing herself to any particular approach. Out of a patchwork of Hugging and Organising, she cobbles together something that works for both of them, up to a point, and where it does not, she covers the problems up with win-win discourse.

THE FLEXI WITH DIVORCED PARENTS

There are two main ways in which divorce fosters a Flexi approach.

The first, as we saw with Jess in Chapter 13, the lawyer who went a bit wild when she discovered her father had been having an affair, is when a daughter has felt that one or both parents were hypocritical. The parents have preached family values but acted selfishly. It leads the girl to conclude that she should beware of adopting didactic, bigoted positions about family life in general and parenting in particular. Having seen her parents as idols who forcefully insisted on traditional values only to find that they have feet of clay that pitter-patter into adulterous beds, she swears never to be so sanctimonious – at all costs avoiding black and white about good and bad.

For instance, Heather's father was a classic working-class patriarch who was a stalwart of the local Baptist community. She recalls that 'he quoted the Bible at us, the Ten commandments, the whole works. He was always the first in line to make condemnatory comments when the latest politician was caught with his hand in his secretary's knickers.' When Heather was 11, they went on holiday with some friends. In the middle of the night she went to the loo and is understandably still outraged at having found her father on top of their friends' 16-year-old daughter in the sitting room. 'I felt for my mother but I think I also decided then and there that the only "should" in life is that you should avoid being judgemental. I think that is a big part of how I care for my kids. I try really hard never to get fixed into any single "system", to keep an open mind and react as the situation requires.'

Another example is Clara. 'My mother had the view strongly that before the age of three you should not leave the child with anyone else, including grandparents, for any length of time. She even got involved in a Conservative think tank that says any mother who leaves their child for a moment is evil. We haven't fallen out but I don't like having things slammed in my face. My friends all do different things, and it's a live and let live world.' What really wound Clara up was when, having espoused these views so strongly, her mother had another child and when he was six months old (Clara was now 13), began an affair with a younger man, resulting in divorce. She then proceeded to leave her son in day care and embark on a career in fashion. Clara's conclusion was 'never say never. I just think you owe it to your children to avoid giving them false expectations. Right from the start, whether it was with the breastfeeding or the sleeping arrangements, I was absolutely determined not to be doctrinaire. Balance and flexibility were my mottos.'

The other impact of divorce on the Flexi is at the emotional level, so that it makes them uneasy whenever anything becomes too settled into a pattern. Having become convinced that their parents were a unit and that it could be relied upon, their whole world is shaken when it breaks up. This can result in a woman who does not believe in marriage when she has children. She may expect to have two or more partners (usually serial monogamy) with whom she has children during her reproductive life. Being a Flexi comes naturally to her. She does not like to feel tied down by anything because it reminds her of the illusion of safety that preceded her parents' fissure. Hugging does not appeal because she fears the baby becoming too dependent on her, but Organising seems like too much of a commitment as well – the four-hourly feeds or 'rule' that she must not go if her baby is crying at night. She is much more comfortable responding to each situation as it arises, although there is a danger this is more based on her emotions than on the needs of her child.

THE FLEXI WHO HAD CHAOTIC CARE IN
HER OWN CHILDHOOD

Finally, some Flexis endured erratic care and only lukewarm or unreliable love when small. The punishment they received was inconsistent, so that what was punished last time is rewarded this time, perhaps with parents contradicting each other. As babies, their mother may have blown hot and cold, or have been unable to feel passionate adoration. As toddlers they may have been cared for by a succession of changing substitutes, forcing them to develop an indiscriminately friendly false self, a persona with which to attract scarce attention from the available adults at the nursery or minder. Having learnt at a terribly early stage to put on a face to meet the faces that she meets, this mother is skilled at concealing her real feelings from herself, as well as from others. When she has children, she finds it especially easy to paint win-win pictures out of the most unpromising scenarios, usually ones that really suit her but not her children. Her friends may look on askance at how positive she remains as her children become miserable or withdrawn or aggressive. If the friends get too sceptical, she is as willing to chop and change them as she is her mothering approach.

Unfortunately, such mothers get little encouragement to revise their approach from the wider culture. If she gets depressed, her GP may send her for six sessions of Cognitive Behavioural Therapy. This provides tips on how to 'think positive' but using such tricks is precisely what is causing the problem, and has been doing so since she was tiny. If she is a low-income mother, she is under pressure from the welfare agency to get a job and leave her child in day care, which suits her just fine. If she is affluent, she may feel surrounded by women who are working full-time (not realising that only 18% of mothers of under-threes do so and that half of them are university educated – see page 270, R1) and by women who believe genes largely explain what their children are like (R7). She takes these to be signals that she is doing the right thing if she adopts a chaotically Flexi approach, rather than the more measured one of the Essential Flexi. She believes herself to be taking the needs of her under-three into account but is really just reproducing her own splintered upbringing.

Having delved for the last few pages into the darker side of the less common Flexi, it is important to remember that most are more like the Essential version described at the start of this part, in Chapter 12.

We are ready to get to the practicalities of how to make being a Flexi work best, whichever kind you may be.

CHAPTER 17

Practical Fleximum Top Tips

PAT YOURSELF ON THE BACK FOR CREATING A WIN-WIN LIFE FOR YOU AND YOUR FAMILY

Classic Flexis generally just get on with it, they do not spend much time 'bigging up' their own approach. Well, here's a chance: congratulate yourself for having managed to reconcile a host of seemingly irreconcilable demands. If adversities have come thick and fast, then all the more power to your elbow.

What is so admirable about the essential Flexi is as follows:

⟨ You empathise with your child, whether pain or joy, while never losing sight of the fact that these emotions are theirs, not yours

⟨ You respond to the true situation you are in or the actual behaviour of your child, not what 'ought' to be the case

⟨ You manage to be truthful with yourself about your mothering, and where necessary, in talking to others

⟨ You resist the temptation to attack what other mothers do and waste less emotion feeling threatened by it

⟨ Most important of all, if anyone can create authentically win-win arrangements, it is you

OK, I realise that you do not manage all of this all of the time, but do not let that get you down. No one is a paragon. What we need to consider now are the ways in which it can go pear-shaped and how to avoid them.

First and foremost, what are the merits and demerits of your approach? Since it is based on a mixture of the other two approaches, we have to start with the pros and cons of them.

DOES BEING FLEXI BENEFIT UNDER-THREES?

Overall, Flexis with Hugger tendencies are probably better for the under-three than those with Organiser leanings. This is because classic Huggers are most likely to appreciate the need for responsive, tuned-in mothering that a small baby requires. By falling in love with the baby and submitting to its phenomenal dependency, the Hugger gives the baby an experience of magical union. If the baby's desire for a feed or a sleep is provided almost before it even knew it wanted it, the baby has a feeling of enormous potency and of value. These are the foundations of a strong, enduring sense of who it is, at the deepest level, and of a secure pattern of attachment, as described in Chapter 1.

However, it is important to stress that not all Huggers succeed in their project. As described in Part Two, the potential for the Hugger approach to go wrong, in terms of the long-term mental health of the child, usually starts with the baby's attempts to be independent. The Hugger needs to make the shift from in love to love. If the Hugger does not achieve this, the baby's desire to relate to other people, or to be left alone to just hang out, is not respected and instead, the mother keeps on trying to second-guess what the baby is feeling, smothering it with her prescriptions for what it needs. If so, the baby will begin to feel over-controlled and start to lose its sense of autonomy.

Other Huggers are too permissive, failing to provide proper boundaries. There may not be sufficient safeguards against physical dangers, not sticking to firm rules about car seat belts and the like. When the child is toddling about the place this mother can be too reluctant to let it know where the limits are – that sometimes it has to do things it does not want, like go to bed or stop throwing food on the floor. Such mothers may find themselves losing their temper, having gone to great trouble to cook the child some special food and had it literally thrown in their face. There is a risk that the establishment of basic discipline is done erratically, with what was punished last time being rewarded or left unpunished this time.

Perhaps the commonest threat to the Hugger project is if the mother eventually becomes isolated and exhausted by her focus on the child, resulting in depression. From the child's standpoint, this is as likely to result in serious problems as low-quality substitute care – definitely lose-lose.

As an approach to nurture, the nub of Hugging is the principle that the mother should adapt to the child. This makes practices like demand-feeding and three-in-a-bed commoner, but it is not these practices alone which define the approach, it is the principle of adapting to the child. It may be that it is at least as important what kind of person you are, as what practices you employ, although the two tend to go together. *The kind of person who is attracted to Hugging practices also tends to be the kind who adapts to the baby and toddler responsively.* It's the way she relates which is most important.

Hence, a few unresponsive, not tuned-in mothers do create Hugger regimes that do not meet the baby's needs. Such mothers are using the baby and toddler to satisfy their feelings of loneliness and neediness by having them in the bed or breastfeeding, often until older ages. The baby's need for the mother to respond to its signals of what it wants are ignored, the mother uses the baby to comfort herself*.

However, most Huggers do manage to tolerate their child's independence and their heightened alertness to the toddler's needs often also makes them the best kind of mother for that age group. There is good evidence that they play with their children significantly more than Organisers, for example*. If they do use substitute care, they are much less likely to arrange something which will produce an insecure child*.

Moving on to the Organiser, the problems start in the pregnancy, when she finds it difficult to be mindful of either the foetus or the coming birth, doing her best to ignore the whole thing. But the greatest problem is that she often finds it hard to tune in and be responsive in the early months – her use of strict regimes, as such, is not necessarily harmful. I used the analogy of two people with walkie-talkies that are tuned to different channels. If she does not empathise with her baby, she finds it feasible to impose strict routines, able to ignore the strong signals that they are causing extreme distress. Controlled crying can only be carried through by a mother who is able to convince herself it is for the baby's good. Many mothers abandon the regime not only because they realise it is actually causing potentially permanent harm but, primarily, because they find it too distressing, empathising or identifying with the baby. Her desire to get the baby to adapt to the adult world as quickly as possible in order for her to be able to return to her normal life is potentially disastrous. Never mind that there is good evidence that controlled crying actually produces irritable, fussy three-month-olds*. The key point is that extreme Organisers are only able to stick to the routine because they are so out of touch with the baby's feelings (because of their own distress when tiny, it is unbearable to empathise with the baby's powerlessness). That is why they are also more liable to regard day care as good news and worst of all, not to realise that low-quality day care and constantly switching arrangements badly upset the baby and toddler*.

Organisers who pursue strict regimes and are unresponsive risk creating passive but angry babies who have a weak sense of self*. In later life, this may put them at greater risk of all manner of problems, from severe mental illness to a people-pleasing compliance which leaves them feeling empty and sad*. That is why it is preferable for extreme Organisers to do their best to find substitutes who are Huggers, and having done so, to let them get on with it.

The Organiser's desire to tame the beast in the nursery persists with toddlers. The extreme Organiser's one-year-old is nearly six times more likely to be insecure (45%, versus 8% extreme Huggers)*. Having mostly returned to work, these mothers are at risk of not realising that the toddler does not need education and stimulation, rather, that it wants the security of knowing there is always an adult nearby who is familiar and responsive. It wants a nurturant companion, not a teacher.

It is hard for Organisers to appreciate the kind of substitute care that is best; day care seems so logical to them. They are often Organisers because of the care they received, so their own mother is unlikely to be a Huggy substitute. The good news is that, as we saw in Part One, some Organisers find partners who can do it. Others make good provision through minders or nannies. But to do so they have first got to understand that routinised group care is exactly what a toddler does not need. Most uncomfortable, they also have to acknowledge that their lack of responsiveness exists, without that making them feel like a bad person – it is not their fault, nor does it suggest they are mentally ill or otherwise defective, it's just that empathising with babies is not their thing. We saw some impressive examples in Part One of women who managed to take all this on board and provide excellent arrangements, so it can be done.

Having said all this, as with the Hugger, the real issue about Organisers is not only the regime in itself. A responsive, tuned-in Organiser might be able to impose many of the practices without harm, probably in a softened form. If empathic with the baby they would not be able to persevere with controlled crying but they might attempt a watered-down version. So in the final analysis, the actual approach of the Organiser may not be the biggest issue, it may be that the sort of person whom it appeals to is not necessarily well-equipped to meet the needs of under-threes. They may be wonderful with fours and fives and sixes, but the extreme dependence of the early years is not for them. It follows that Flexis at the Organiser end of the spectrum are less likely to meet the needs of under-threes and more at risk of deceiving themselves as to whether the arrangements are win-win.

So, overall, what is the consequence for the under-three of a Flexi approach?

So long as the mother is able to be responsive and tuned in, the fact that she is flexible could make her exceptionally good. The best Flexi is probably as good as the best Hugger for toddlers. Whether she is as good for babies seems unlikely insofar as she is reluctant to put herself on the shelf: so long as the Hugger can survive it, the self-sacrifice hugely benefits the baby and a mother who keeps bearing herself in mind is not going to be as tuned in as one who forgets that for the early months. But if this is the best kind of Flexi, what of the average?

As we have seen in the examples in preceding chapters, in all sorts of ways, the Flexi approach does risk presenting win-lose as win-win. It seems likely that significant numbers of Flexis do underplay the needs of under-threes and to that extent, their child's sense of self and security of attachment suffer. Either they chop and change their approach too much, confusing the child or making it feel that love is erratic, or they set up substitute arrangements which are too much driven by their self-satisfaction. So the danger of the Flexi approach is that it is a wheeze for putting the mother's needs ahead of those of the child while allowing her to believe she is simply being balanced.

HOW CAN YOU TELL IF YOU ARE CONNING YOURSELF THAT YOUR ARRANGEMENTS ARE WIN-WIN?

Flexis are exceptionally good at being honest but they are equally unusually skilled at persuading themselves they have achieved win-win. As I explained in Chapter 6 (pages 254–60) of They F*** You Up, sometimes honesty is a way of camouflaging the truth from oneself and others. The commonest Flexi trouble is when you have created 'win' for you but 'lose' for your child – it's rare that a Flexi deceives herself into thinking she has won in her own life, when she is losing (e.g., if she stays at home suffering a low-grade, chronic depression and would really like to be working, it's unusual that she tricks herself into believing she is feeling great). A good example of one who may have deceived herself that she is winning for the child as well as herself might be Jane, from Chapter 14, the mother for whom affluence and lifestyle was a priority. How could she see through her own mental gymnastics?

There is a simple test, one that works for all approaches: do the arrangements meet the needs of your under-three? In fact, you may recall, Jane did realise that they failed this test when she described how unhappy her six-month-old son was at nursery: 'He was always very sad when we left him. We've got a photo my husband took after a week there and he just looks quite sad. He used to cling on when I was leaving, completely. They had to take him off me every time, very much so, it was really hard.' The trouble was that Jane did not believe this was going to do her son any long-term harm. Believing that genes are critical, she simply assumed that, perhaps a bit like an adult who is going through a rough patch at work, it was just something he would have to endure until things got better. She did not grasp that the experiences we have under-three are generally much more enduring than those we have as adults. What was more, she made herself feel better about the situation by believing that her sons' subsequent habituation to being left in the nursery proved they enjoyed it – the fact that they were reluctant to leave seemed to prove that. But as I suggested, in fact, their reluctance may well have been signs of an insecure, 'avoidant' way of relating which could continue for the rest of their lives.

It's worth recalling the study described in Chapter 6, in this connection. It showed that there were raised cortisol levels in the first hour after arriving in day care on days one, five and nine. While the levels did subsequently drop, they were still significantly elevated five months after starting day care*. Taken with the other evidence regarding day care and cortisol (page 279, R3), it seems very possible that Jane was mistaken in thinking day care was good for her sons.

Of course, it is vital also to recall that in Jane's case, doing the care herself meant both she and her second son 'went a bit insane ... the monotony just kills me. It really doesn't fit my personality.' So she was right to find substitute care; the mistake was choosing day care. In her case, a key factor driving all her thinking was the desire to save money. But money saved on substitute care is usually a false economy, at least in terms of the child's well-being. It's no use claiming 'win-win' if the person caring for your baby is trying to look after two other babies all day long at the same time. What also threw Jane off the scent of doing the best for her son, therefore, was the extra cost of an exclusive nanny, one she could have afforded.

The implication for the Flexi is that you need to carefully inspect your beliefs about whether the 'child win' side of what you believe to be a 'win-win' really is as it seems. In particular, you need to take the evidence in Chapter 1 very seriously indeed: responsive, tuned-in care is vital early on, and the presence of a responsive, familiar adult who knows it well is essential for toddlers. While nobody gets perfect care, you really do need to ensure that it is good enough, if you possibly can. That rules out day care as the substitute, if there is any choice in the matter, which there nearly always is.

Do not kid yourself that genes are crucial and the early years are like later ones, and do not allow expense to stand in the way of providing exclusive care, if you can afford it. Flexis find plenty of other ways of convincing themselves that 'loses' are 'wins'. In the case of Jess, in Chapter 13, although she arranged first-class substitute care, I could not help feeling that she was making a mistake in putting her not very interesting (to her) career ahead of the chance to make a potentially big difference to her 18-month-old's life. I may have been wrong, but as with the other approaches, the key is to know thyself ...

KNOW THYSELF 1: YOUR CHILDHOOD

As we saw in the last chapter, a number of factors from your own childhood can mean that your Flexi approach goes awry.

Flexibility is one thing, not knowing your own mind is another. If you are a rare example of someone who suffered severe infantile deprivation or harsh parenting, your feelings may flood you at times, though at others you may feel detached from yourself and your baby. Either way, you will have trouble meeting the needs of an under-three and you may find it hard to recognise which substitutes are best. There is a danger that your frequently changing patterns of care reflect these problems, rather than the essential Flexi's openness to reality. If so, you may need a lot of help from a psychoanalytic therapist, as described in Chapters 6 (page 93) and 11 (page 193), or could be helped through parent–infant psychotherapy (page 96).

Less extreme, and more common, is if your Flexi approach is partly a response to later difficulties like parental divorce or overly strict parenting. Again, the danger is you are scared to commit to a particular plan rather than that you are truly flexible. Again described in Chapters 6 and 11, you may benefit from Cognitive Analytic Therapy or The Hoffman Process (pages 94, 174).

KNOW THYSELF 2: RECONCILING YOUR WORKER AND MOTHER IDENTITIES

Flexis are the least likely to report having difficulties with this. Of mothers who work part-time, 72% repeatedly claim that they have successfully and satisfyingly integrated mother and worker, with win-win 'reframing' as their method*. However, as we have seen, a proportion of these are probably fooling themselves, and actually have arrangements which entail more 'lose' for their child than they like to think. In addition, that still leaves 28% who do not feel mother and worker are successfully integrated*. As we saw with Sandra in the last chapter (the sister with the ultra-strict father), she kept bouncing in and out of work precisely because she could not decide what was best.

A key issue here is balance – the Flexi Shangri-La – but what is really on the scales when we use that word? I would suggest it is needs, those of the mother and the child.

On the one hand, it is abundantly clear that it's best for everyone if the mother does not get depressed and feels full of enthusiasm when she does see the children, so if feeding her worker self is part of achieving that, then it is also in the child's interests. However, on the other hand, the needs of the child can get left out if the only thing that is considered is the mother's 'work–life balance'. It was striking in the case of Sandra that she finally left work because she felt she was missing out on her child's developmental milestones, rather than because she felt it would be best for the child. Because she did not realise how important early care is, she did not correctly weigh her child's needs when loading the scales. So a crucial initial point is that you cannot properly reconcile mother with worker if you do not understand the evidence in Chapter 1.

But then comes a new problem. Suppose you can fix up a life which suits you to a T. Let's say you have an interesting job for two days of the week, enjoy looking after the children on the remaining three and have a partner who is an enthusiastic and effective supporter at the weekend. Let's further suppose that you and your partner get on like a house on fire, up to and including the bedroom. What if you realise that your child does not really enjoy the substitute care for the two days of the week when you work but if you were to pay extra to have an exclusive nanny, it would throw the whole plan? This is a situation in which the Hugger might score over the Flexi in terms of the needs of the child. The Hugger would very likely decide to drop her work or would prioritise the need for extra cash over everything, to give the child better substitute care. The danger with some Flexis is that they would put their desire for a nice life above that of the child, *without realising it*. By using mental acrobatics, they would be liable to find a way of thinking about the situation which left their pleasures untouched but which did not meet the child's needs.

The commonest rationale would be that unless the mother feels happy, she will not make a good helpmeet for her child. This is obviously true, but it can leave out the possibility that considerable sacrifices might be necessary in order to meet the needs of the child. While it is highly desirable that modern younger women have become increasingly confident, assertive and report higher self-esteem, it is also the case that the culture constantly encourages them to be more selfish*. So there is a risk for some Flexis that they will reason to themselves that they need to be selfish in order to be good mothers. This is true, but only up to a point. In the case of Sandra, for instance, her selfishness in only leaving work because it would be nice to witness milestones may blinker her from the most important thing of all – the needs of her child. So Flexis have to be very wary of losing sight of these. There is a massive advertising and marketing industry, backed up by implicit role models portrayed all over the media, which suggests that being selfish is a good thing. Making sure that you create a life which truly reflects your wishes and needs is not the same as that – it would take a large account of your child and partner's needs too, in order for you to feel yours are being met. Some altruism may be ultimately the most successful form of selfishness!

Putting your happiness ahead of that of everyone else is not what is meant by balance. Properly weighted scales include the needs of your family. Essential Flexis realise this but others can kid themselves that they do when, in fact, what they are being is just old-fashioned selfish. While Organisers (and mothers of under-threes who work full-time) are by far the most at risk of suffering depression and while Flexis (and mothers who work part-time) are the least likely to do so, if the Flexi's cheerful mood is at the expense of her child, that is not necessarily as good as it seems.

HOW CAN YOU FEEL AS COMFORTABLE IN YOUR SKIN AS CARRIE (CHAPTER 15)?

As we saw, Carrie was remarkable for her clarity about her own needs and her complete lack of interest in comparing herself to others. This contributed to her managing to experience life at first-hand and to her being tremendously open-minded on the one hand, yet exceptionally sure of what she felt, on the other. These things can be said of very few people, but especially younger women. It is a little known fact that the younger you are, the greater your risk of mental illness: older people (11.5% of over 75s) are three times less mentally ill than the young (32% of 16–24-year-olds)*.

It could be argued that the fact that Carrie had opted for a traditional role explains comfort. However, I know women who never had children who are similar to Carrie and I also can think of women who were mothers and in later life became like her. What seems much rarer is for a mother with small children to feel so at peace with herself.

I suspect that the explanation is that her ideas about the life she would like to be leading (a full-time at-home mother) were in perfect concord with the reality, that she was self-concordant. Nearly everyone in our *Affluenza*-riddled society is plagued more or less with a desire to be someone that they are not or to have possessions that they lack. We are expected to be an individual, to identify who and what we are. In theory this is a huge advance compared with the past, when you were under enormous pressure to conform to parental, gender and class norms. In practice, as part of our quest to define our individuality, it means that most of us are constantly comparing our lot with others, trying to work out how we are doing relative to them, and whether there is not a better person to be or better life to be living. There is a plague of Keeping Up with the Joneses (see particularly Chapter 3 of my book *Britain on the Couch*, in which I compare how this has changed among women since the 1950s by contrasting the experiences of the Queen Mother, the Queen and those of Princess Diana and Sarah Ferguson).

When it comes to mothering, women feel very vulnerable. In terms of the best methods, it is a Tower of Babel. But on top of that, women's magazines, television and other media are constantly pushing women towards and away from mother or worker identities (R4). These twin uncertainties make it dreadfully hard to decide what sort of individual to be once you have children.

What was noticeable about Carrie was that she truly did not care what other mothers were doing and nor did she have an internal ideal that she was trying to live up to. She did not worry if she was caring for her children by the book and she did not have any interest in her worker identity, so she felt able to get on with being her. Some might see this as a blinkered approach, partly fostered by the threat of a fatal illness. In fact, her certainty preceded this. Carrie had not been to university and had seen herself in the mother role from a young age, never really questioning it. But rather than blinkered, you could argue that Carrie is simply mentally healthy, someone who, despite a very confusing and toxic social environment, has a strong sense of self, at least as far as mothering is concerned. As she herself said, she is not perfect, but by having access to her true desires on a moment-by-moment basis, she is comfortable in her skin.

Of course, if you are like that, it is not necessarily best for your child. What if you only felt comfortable in your skin if you were an ultra-strict disciplinarian or a chaotically permissive mother? Self-reflection and being able to learn from others seem essential if we are to progress in life. Carrie managed both of these, while also being sure of her self.

The moral of her story is to do your best to identify what you want and who you are, not what others will approve/disapprove, not what ought to be happening in theory. If you can do this, at least it will protect you from being a floaty Flexi, one who keeps changing her mind, and it will certainly increase the chances of your enjoying motherhood.

CONCLUSION: POTENTIAL PITFALLS OF FLEXIMOTHERING

⟨ *Flexi Organising*: this is less likely to meet the needs of your under-three than veering towards the Hugging end of the spectrum. The danger is that you do not responsively tune in enough, letting the infant's needs tell you what is required. If it's a case of 'walkie-talkies on different wavelengths', parent–infant therapy will be a big help

⟨ *Win-Losing*: be careful to check your rationalisations for why your under-three's needs are being met. You may believe it suits your child to have time away from you with that unresponsive neighbour or au pair, but the truth might be that you just want a break – you are kidding yourself it's for the child's benefit and ignoring the fact that it does not sleep or eat properly that evening, is fussy, withdrawn or distressed

⟨ *Lose-Winning*: equally, if you are feeling permanently downcast and your child is full of beans, do not kid yourself about that either. You may need to set up adequate substitute care so you can get a bit of time doing something for yourself. A depressed you is not helping anyone

⟨ *Lose-Losing*: rare, but if you are claiming everything is fine when neither of you is thriving, you need help. Recognising this can be difficult, your Flexi acrobatics can be so good that you can con yourself and everyone else. If you have a sneaking suspicion things are not right for both of you, maybe ask your intimates what they think. If you have not got any intimates, that's a pretty strong clue to the answer

⟨ *Saving Money on Substitute Care*: it's the ultimate false economy to send your baby or toddler to day care because a nanny or minder would use up everything you earn. If you need to do part-time work to be in good form with your child, take the hit. There is no need to feel it makes working pointless: maybe you are one of those women who needs that time away and the adult stimulation

⟨ *Never Saying Never*: while it's fine to be open-minded, it's another matter to have no convictions. Even if it's only what you say to your partner or intimates, do not be scared to have a point of view about what is best for children. Let that govern your mothering rather than a fear of being over-committed to one approach

⟨ *Wanting to Think and Act Positive*: optimism is one thing, hyperactive 'happiness' another. If you cannot bear any negativity in your life, always having to put a positive spin on the most frustrating or saddening of realities, it will get you into trouble. You cannot learn from life without noticing mistakes you have made or adverse consequences from your actions

⟨ *Never Putting Self Second*: a measure of unselfishness is inevitable if caring for under-threes. If you like to think of yourself as having 'a perfect life', in which you never have to put yourself out, self-deception is going on

⟨ *Being Too Flexible*: if you keep changing your arrangements too often it becomes confusing for the child. You have to make some firm decisions and stick to them

Meeting the Needs of You and Your Nipper

To return, for a moment, to the care I received during my early years, my mother wanted to be a Hugger but ended up being a not very responsive and quite aggressive Flexi. She felt lots of love but was rarely in a state to express it. I believe there were good, as well as bad, consequences.

One bad one was that her mothering set my electrochemical thermostat in 'angry', 'risk-taking' and 'sad' modes, fluctuating between them. In later life, if nothing was particularly going on, those were my basic default positions. It is interesting that I did not become a drunk or a drug addict or a criminal, for those are common consequences of that kind of thermostatic setting. Why not is another story (I am, however, terminally addicted to nicotine, nowadays ingested via lozenges).

Another problem was that I did not take well to the inescapable truth that external reality often did not correspond to what I wanted. When I arrived at school, I found it extremely hard to accept that there were rules which had to be obeyed. There were people and social processes that existed independent of my wishes, and because I had not been responded to early on, or loved for much of the time, I tended to deny their power and have a rumbling anger that led me to behave in ways which provoked them to attack or restrain me.

But the consequences of my early care were not all bad. Along with their faults, my parents could be tremendously lively, optimistic and encouraging. From as soon as I was able to play, they rarely failed to show that this was something they approved. I was always allowed to challenge the *status quo*.

Whether we are talking about me or you, little that was done to us is completely irreversible. Where parenthood is so refreshing is that it provides an opportunity to avoid the mistakes of the past.

To this end, I hope to have persuaded you of two things by writing this book.

The first is that babies and toddlers need to be in the presence of a responsive, loving adult at all times in order to thrive. They do not need a teacher, they do not need friends, stimulation or education. Nor does that person have to be its mother.

The second is to help you understand how your past has affected your reaction to motherhood and how best to make the transition from being Bridget Jones to a mother who is comfortable in her skin. Two nuggets of wisdom from the stories of the mothers I met particularly stood out.

Jess, the full-time working Flexi in Chapter 13, said, 'You have got to get your head around the fact that, if you have children, some people who are less talented or deserving will get promoted over you ... something's got to give. You can't do everything and you must not get wound up by that. It's either your home or work life that has to be sacrificed. You must decide which and be honest about it rather than pretend you can have it all.' We live in a society of 'It Could be You', 'Shop Till You Drop', credit-fuelled consumer junkies. Whether at school, at work or on the way to the ballot box, the authorities constantly exhort us to want more and better, and above all, to believe that this is both possible (without limits) and our entitlement. But the idea that anyone can Have It All is completely bonkers: infantile, in fact. While I have no objection at all to my four-year-old son telling me that he is a better goal scorer than Wayne Rooney or that he can fly, it is disgraceful that the leaders in English-speaking nations encourage adults to think magically too, not to grow up. That is what I take away from Jess's comment: that to become good parents we really do need to grow up. As I shall explain in a moment, this applies every bit as much to fathers as to the mothers I interviewed, who were without exception strikingly concerned to do the best by their children.

The other nugget of wisdom that sticks with me is the story of Carrie, the at-home Flexi in Chapter 15 who seemed so comfortable in her skin. She had managed to learn from her experience. By doing so, she was able to see that just because she desired something (like lovable rogues) did not mean she should pursue it. So she had been able to see beyond the many lures of our hedonistic, imprudent, short-term, 'be yourself' culture to identify what would actually be good for her. Having established this, based on real experience rather than envy of what others have, she was able to place the limits on what she wanted that are required if we are to put into practice Jess's advice not to want to have it all. Unlike most of us, Carrie doesn't just want to be herself, she actually is herself. That means she has a strong basis for turning things down, for deciding what direction to take, and it results in the ultimate hope of being not just a good mother, but of being a good person, of self-concordance. If you can get to a state where what you do and who you are for most of the time corresponds to what you want to do and be, you have cracked it, in my book.

That is why, ultimately, as described in the last chapter, I contend that what matters most is not what mothering approach you have. It is what kind of person you are. If you sort that out, you will be able to be responsive and attuned to your children, or arrange for others to do so.

Putting it like this places all the burden on you. My final conclusion concerns me and mine – men.

I believe that in the future (whether that be 20 or 100 years' time), men will be as likely as women to be wrestling with the issues addressed in this book. When a baby comes along, men will feel as torn as women between the desire to work and their responsibility to ensure that the needs of their under-threes get met. This will be a hugely significant improvement in humankind's prospects. When the father appreciates that it is his pigeon as much as his partner's that these needs get met, society will adapt to maximise the chances of this happening. I predict that about one quarter of men will be caring for their children at home from soon after the birth. Maybe half of couples will share the care, with the woman as likely to be working as the man. And maybe one quarter of women will do the care full-time. Rather than nationwide networks of day care nurseries, the money will be spent on parent–infant therapy and practical support at home for those finding it difficult. If substitute care is best, it will be provided by nannies or minders, one-to-one. Huge efforts will be made to help disharmonious couples to resolve their problems, with a strong focus on the way that each individual's childhood is disrupting the relationship. Before even getting pregnant, it will be routine for partners to have discussed in detail what approach they are going to take to the nurture.

But that is for the future. In the meantime, let me end with this thought. What kind of person do you want your under-three to be aged 45? Will they have gone to university, what will they have studied, what career will they have followed? What sort of partner do you hope they have chosen? When will they have started having children? As to the sort of person they will be, it is not enough for you to say that you want them to be happy. Just as it behoves all of us to work at defining what we mean by this for ourselves, so with our children. Do not be scared to admit that how you care for your child is going to hugely influence how it turns out. Then work out how you can become comfortable in your skin because that is likely to ensure that you meet its early needs … which is what will ultimately decide whether your child has a fruitful, sane life.

MOTHERING:
THE EVIDENCE

Mothering in the UK: The Facts About What They Want and What They Do

There are many misconceptions about mothers and work, fostered by inaccurate or selective statistics in the media and in popular books. A true picture of what is normal and average enables you to compare your aspirations and actual lifestyle to that of other mothers. This is helpful because all too often, studies show that mothers of all kinds tend to feel the wider culture is against them – full-time working mothers and full-time at-home mothers alike feel they live in a society that is hostile to their chosen approach (Johnstone et al., 2004). In what follows, I shall use the words 'at-homers' to refer to mothers of under-threes who have no paid employment, and for those who work, either 'part-timers' (mostly less than 30 hours a week, three-quarters of mothers of under-threes doing less than 20 hours) or 'full-timers' (meaning those working 40 or more hours a week).

1. All the increase in women's employment since the 1950s has been in part-time jobs

In 1950, only 30% of all adult women had a paid job, today more women than men have one (Offer, 2006). However, there has been little or no increase in the number of women working full-time (Hakim, 2000). *All the increase in female employment has occurred in part-timers.* This is true throughout the developed world, including

Scandinavia, where governments make every effort to ease maternal employment. A key reason that more women do not work full-time is that when they become mothers they actively favour mothering over paid employment.

2. 82% of under-three-year-old British children have a mother who is not employed full-time

If you rely solely on newspapers, radio and TV for your information, you could be forgiven for believing that the majority of under-threes have mothers who work full-time. In fact, one-third of mothers do no paid work at all from after the birth to the child's third birthday. The proportion who work full-time when their child is under-three is 18% (Dex et al., 2007), so the great majority of working mothers of under-threes are part-time. On their third birthday, half of children have mothers who do no paid work (Dex et al., 2007). Only one third of under-threes' mothers have a job continuously during the first three years, mostly part-time (Dex et al., 2007).

It is interesting that full-timers very much tend to be highly educated. Half of them have university degrees (Dex et al., 2007); only a quarter of 25- to 40-year-old women as a whole do so (ONS, 2010). Full-timers tend to have relatively well-paid and interesting jobs, which makes them more reluctant to go part-time or become at-homers. They also tend to place a higher value on their worker identity than at-homers or part-timers (Hakim, 2000; Hakim et al., 2008).

3. The vast majority of mothers of under-threes would prefer to work less

In survey after survey, when mothers are asked what they want, it is usually to look after their children until they are in their teens. For example, in a 2001 survey (Hakim et al., 2000, page 20) over 3,000 mothers were given three choices: to work more hours if they had access to good-quality, convenient, reliable and affordable childcare; to reduce their working hours in order to spend more time with their children if they could afford to do so; or to give up work to stay at home to look after their children:

⟨ Half of working mothers with one or more children under 15 said they would prefer to give their job up altogether
⟨ The great majority of those who were working full-time (76% of those in two-parent families, 85% of single mothers) said they would prefer to work fewer hours
⟨ Overall, two-thirds of working mothers would prefer to work fewer hours or not at all

In another study, 90% of women – whether mothers or not – said they would prefer to do no paid work or to be part-time, if they did not need to earn any money (Hakim, 2000) and more recent surveys have similar results (Odone, 2009). This is not terribly surprising. The great majority of women (77%) have low-paid, low-skill jobs which most say are not stimulating or fulfilling in themselves (Hakim, 2000). When asked what they enjoy about work, they are far more likely than men to say that it is the social element, such as the companionship and amusement gained from interacting with other employees if working in an office or a shop (Hakim et al., 2008; Odone, 2009).

The most recent evidence (Dench, 2010) reveals that there are sharp differences in attitudes to caring for small children and to working, between middle-class women and others, with traditional roles being much more favoured among lower-income women. This author proposes that, because it is largely middle-class women who occupy senior roles, their views are very disproportionately reflected in government policy and media coverage related to mothering.

Mothers' Preferences When Choosing Substitute Care

Mothers who work far prefer to use their partner as substitute carer, then grandparents, friends or other relatives and only if they have to, in most cases, do they pay someone else to do it. Both state-provided and private nurseries for under-threes find themselves with spare places because parents are very clear that, in most cases, they do not want their baby or toddler being looked after in group care (Hakim et al., 2008).

In practice, nursery day care is least often chosen, not because of cost or availability but because mothers feel that group care for small children is inappropriate. In an English sample of 1,000 children (Sylva et al., 2007), at the age of 10 months, half were still being cared for at home by their mothers, 22% were cared for by relatives or friends, 15% by paid childminders and only 10% were in nursery day care. Since 1997 there has been a huge, government-sponsored increase in the number of nursery day care places but the option has been widely rejected by mothers. Occupancy rates in day nurseries fell from 95% in 2002 to 79% in 2007 (Hakim et al., 2008, page 33).

It is interesting to see what happens in countries where parents are given a real financial choice between home and high-quality state-funded day care. In Finland day care was offered by the state until the late 1980s and the great majority of small children were put into it. But in the early 1990s mothers were given the alternative of taking an allowance to stay at home instead. By 2002 only half of mothers of children aged 0–3 were in work, the other half were at home (Hakim et al., 2008, page 29). Similar policy changes have occurred in Sweden and France, with similar results.

The Pros and Cons of Day Care

Introduction

Since this is such a controversial matter, I will devote much greater space to it and provide much greater detail than the other reviews.

In what follows, I provide evidence that high-quality day care can increase the cognitive skills and academic performance of children of low-income parents, especially parents who are not very sensitive in the way they relate to their infant and toddler. There is also some evidence that emotional problems, such as depression, may be reduced in the long term for children from high-risk families, if they are in day care combined with interventions that improve parenting skills.

However, there is no evidence that day care is advantageous to children from middle-class families, and there is considerable evidence that it increases the risk of dysregulated cortisol levels, aggression, disobedience and emotional insecurity, especially if the care is of low quality. Unfortunately, this latter is the norm in the United States and the UK.

High quality is defined as follows (Daycare Trust, 2009):

⟨ For under-twos the ratio of children to staff should be 3:1
⟨ For under-threes the size of core groups in which children are cared for should be eight

- ⟨ For children aged two years and over, half of staff should be graduates and the remainder should be up to Level 3 qualification
- ⟨ For children under two, one third of staff should be graduates, the rest up to Level 3
- ⟨ Pay scales should be based on equivalent roles in schools
- ⟨ Other non-staff costs (e.g. premises costs) should be one-third of staff costs

Whether applying these or looser criteria, the quality of the vast majority of care provided by British (and American) day care centres falls far short of high (Leach, 1994, page 88; Daycare Trust, 2009; UNICEF, 2008). In the case of the United States, an authoritative researcher stated that 'the vast majority of American child care is of unacceptably low quality' (Ramey, 2005, page 432), estimating that only 9% of day care for American under-threes is high-quality. The author pointed out that there is a strong tendency to ignore, perhaps even to suppress, this very vital fact for anyone who wishes to be an advocate of day care: 'many of the studies ... gloss over the basic finding that so many children spend so much time in low- to medium-quality care, and such a small percentage are in consistently high-quality care' (Ramey, 2005, page 432).

These facts are worrying. Nearly all experts agree that low-quality day care is harmful and medium-quality often is as well. Only a small proportion is high-quality. Follow through the logic, and the vast majority of American and British children in day care today are put at risk of emotional problems from being there.

1. The Pros of Day Care

Overall, there is a large body of evidence spanning more than 20 years and from many different countries suggesting that children whose mothers work in the early years achieve less, educationally, than those whose mothers do not work (Hill et al., 2005). For example, a study of 516 pairs of siblings born in the 1970s found a causal relationship between full- or part-time maternal employment before the age of five and lower educational achievement in young adulthood, such as a reduced likelihood of obtaining A levels (Ermisch et al., 2000, 2001). This was especially likely if the mother was of a high income, possibly because the child sees less of its usually highly educated and intelligent mother, so it has less opportunity for these attributes to be passed on to them. If a mother returns to work full-time very early, before the child is three months, there is a substantially increased risk of a number of problems in later childhood (Berger et al., 2005).

However, these adverse effects of maternal employment are not necessarily connected to day care. In fact, the strongest case in favour of it is the evidence that high-quality care leads to good cognitive outcomes in children from disadvantaged homes.

Like many previous studies, the American National Institute of Child Health and Human Development (NICHD) longitudinal study of 1,000 children found that at 15 and 24 months, the more attentive, responsive and stimulating the day care, the higher the cognitive and linguistic functioning (Belsky, 2008, page 9). Similar findings occurred at age four and a half, and high-quality early day care predicted higher maths, reading and memory scores up to age nine. When quantity was measured, there were similar gains – the more hours spent in day care, the more that the same cognitive and linguistic benefits were found, until age nine (Belsky, 2008, page 14). However, the boost to achievement had almost completely disappeared by age 11, except for vocabulary.

If this proves that high-quality care can be beneficial for cognitive development, at least until middle childhood, it is also the case that low-quality care is as bad for it (Peisner-Feinberg et al., 1997). This is unfortunate, since the quality of the vast majority of American and British care is either low or medium; it follows that the vast majority either do not benefit cognitively, or are actually impaired. But be that as it may, there is no question that when day care is done well it can benefit mental development, at least in the early years.

By far the greatest benefit goes to children of low-income mothers, many of whom are single, and this may be at its most providential when considerable care is also taken to improve parenting sensitivity skills. Where government has forked out for full-scale early intervention of this kind, its impact on the outcomes of the children of low-income or single parents is considerable (and not just on mental ability, possibly on emotional development as well).

The evidence for the American Head Start programme is unequivocally positive for disadvantaged children (Love et al., 2001, 2005; Administration on Children, Youth and Families, 2002). This is likely to be because these programmes do a lot more than just provide (often second-rate) day care. A great deal of help is provided to mothers to increase their sensitivity to their children, as well as more practical and social support from child centres. The sensitivity therapy may include weekly home visits for the first year, and fortnightly ones for the second and third (Love et al., 2001, 2005).

Thus far, results from Britain's Sure Start programme have been desperately disappointing, apparently actually leading to worse outcomes for children from the most disadvantaged homes (such as low-income single mothers) and only marginally improving functioning in some better-off families (Belsky et al., 2006). A possible explanation is that, although it was originally intended to be much more than just day care, Sure Start rapidly turned into a method for cheaply enabling low-income mothers to discard their under-threes and return to work (even its apologists admit this – see Sinclair, 2009, page 44: with the expansion of the Sure Start programme 'came a reduction in spend per child and an increased emphasis on day care to help women, particularly single mothers, get back to work').

However, overall, there is no question that in America, as part of a comprehensive package, high-quality day care can significantly improve the short- and long-term ability and educational performance of children from low-income families. As Heckman (2006) has shown, the earlier you intervene with disadvantaged groups, the more effect your money buys. Spending money on unemployment benefit or imprisonment is far less effective as a way of helping someone to become a solvent, law-abiding member of society than spending on early intervention.

Heckman (2006) is notable for his criticism of the overemphasis placed by American and British interventions on intelligence and cognitive skills as targets in the early years. Most European nations make no attempt at formal teaching and curricula until age seven. Prior to that they regard the promotion of social skills, play and fun as primary (Heckman, 2006; UNICEF, 2008). It is also important to always look closely at claims made for the benefits of intervention programmes in terms of the age at which the child starts and whether it entails therapy for sensitivity of the mother. There is very little doubt that out-of-home educational programmes increase academic performance when they begin after age three, much more debate regarding the benefits for under-threes.

The long-term advantages of high-quality day-care-based intervention programmes may extend beyond cognitive advantage. A study of 104 infants from high-risk, disadvantaged homes (nearly all African-American) randomly assigned half of them for full-time day care and parental assistance to the age of five years, the other half having no intervention (Mclaughlin et al., 2007). Measured at age 21, the children who had been helped were significantly less likely to suffer from depressive symptoms. The more the children had a low-quality home environment, the greater risk of depression at 21 where there had been no intervention. A striking finding was that negative effects of a low-quality home environment were almost completely neutralised by being in the intervention group. While there is little other evidence that day care is beneficial for emotional outcomes in adulthood, this study does prove that it can be so for children at severe risk: where a child's home environment is very liable to create both low cognitive performance and emotional problems, there is a case for providing an extensive intervention programme which includes day care.

However, there is no evidence at all that this model is better in the long term for the children of educated middle-class mothers. In practical terms, if you are a disadvantaged mother there may be a case for putting your child in day care if it really is high quality (very rare in the United States or Britain), if improved cognitive performance is what you want. There is no scientific basis whatever for doing this if you are middle-class: all the evidence shows that the more your child is exposed to you the better, unless, that is, you are depressed. Hence, by the age of three and a half, large gaps are opening up between high- and low-income children, due to very different levels of education and social skills in the parents of the different social classes (Feinstein, 2003). What makes the middle classes perform so much better at school is contact with their parents. This may help to explain the overall finding mentioned at the start regarding working mothers – where they are middle-class, in most cases they leave their child in the company of substitutes who are young women, usually with much less education and lower IQs than them. All the evidence on what enables a child to perform well would predict that doing so would reduce its performance – as it does.

That high-quality day care, alone or in combination with an intervention programme, can improve cognitive performance in children of low-income families is not a case for middle-class parents to opt for it. The fact is, anyway, that most day care is not high-quality. When you put this together with the evidence you are about to read about the proven emotional problems caused by day care, there seems no case whatever for opting for day care if you are a middle-class parent and seeking substitute care.

2. Cortisol Levels and Day Care

Cortisol is the stress hormone secreted when a person feels under threat, leading to fight or flight in animals, and to aggression or hyperactivity, or withdrawal, in humans. As we shall see, there is now overwhelming evidence that day care causes children to have abnormal cortisol levels, probably increasing the risk of behavioural problems like aggression, fearfulness and hyperactivity.

It has been established for some time that maltreatment in early life, like neglect or abuse, causes children to be hyper-responsive to threats. They have either high levels of cortisol, so that when feeling threatened they get quickly jammed into an aggressive, defensive state, or else exceptionally low levels (Dawson et al., 2000). In these latter cases, the child has become so used to feeling insecure or under attack that its system has closed down, is blunted, so that even quite extreme threats no longer affect the child: it has given up reacting to threat by secreting cortisol (Tarullo et al., 2006; Gerhardt, 2004, pages 78–83). This damage to the cortisol system may endure into adulthood if the maltreatment is not reversed (Graham et al., 1999; Tarullo et al., 2006). Where maltreatment is extreme, such as in cases of sexual abuse, it is possible that the very high concentrations of cortisol which the child secretes in response to the dangers causes key parts of the brain not to grow properly (Dawson et al., 2000; Weniger et al., 2008). For example, on average, a woman who was sexually abused as a child has 5% less of the hippocampal region of the brain than one who was not; similar impacts have been shown on the amygdala (Teicher, 2002). Students of such cases hypothesise that it is the high cortisol resulting from abuse which causes the brain deficit. Looked at from the positive side, good-quality early experience has been shown to create stable, healthy cortisol secretion and growth of the relevant parts of the brain (Schore, 2001).

Overall, maltreated children who have been taken into institutional care and subsequently adopted are liable to have abnormal levels (Gunnar et al., 2006). Interestingly, the levels become most abnormal when in the company of adoptive parents, perhaps distressed by having to engage in personal relationships which may remind them of the risk of earlier abandonment or abuse (Wismer Fries et al., 2008). Studies of children who were placed in institutions following maltreatment and who were subsequently adopted into responsive, stable homes show that the abnormal cortisol levels often persist seven years after adoption (Gunnar et al., 2001).

Given all this, if day care is as distressing to under-threes as many researchers believe, it would not be surprising if it affected their cortisol levels: when distressed we usually secrete the hormone.

The initial key piece of evidence is that cortisol levels in toddlers are immediately affected after they are left by their mother in day care on the first and subsequent days. Ahnert et al. (2004) studied 70 15-month-old toddlers on three occasions: at home before starting child care, during the time the mother left the day care facility and after the mother had gone. Ahnert found that during the first hour after the mother had departed, cortisol levels almost doubled compared with the level when the toddler was measured at home before ever having experienced day care. This increase after the first hour was also found on the fifth and ninth days of going to day care. It is compelling evidence that in the short term, leaving a toddler in day care dramatically increases their cortisol levels in the hour after the mother departs.

But being left in a new situation and the disappearance of the mother might naturally make the toddler initially anxious. Perhaps the cortisol levels settle down once the toddler got used to the new place? Alas, no. When they were measured again after having attended day care for five months, although the amount of the increase in cortisol compared with the original level at home had decreased, it was still significantly higher (Ahnert et al., 2004).

The next piece of evidence is that meta-analysis of nine studies shows that day care causes increased cortisol during the course of the day compared with at home (Geoffroy et al., 2006; Vermeer et al., 2006). Cortisol in infants and toddlers decreases during the day at home, comparing mid-morning with teatime. When at day care, the level rises during the day. The most likely explanation is the stress of coping without mother and of being with so many other small children with more or less unfamiliar adults. The extent to which the levels are responses to the caring environment is suggested by the fact that they do not rise as much if the quality of the day care provision is good (Sims et al., 2005). However, even in the best-quality care provision, there is still a significant increase during the day in the day care setting compared with home (Wakamura et al., 2009). That day care and cortisol dysregulation have been so consistently shown to correlate strongly implies that there is something about day care which is stressful.

That cortisol levels are a direct response to quality of care is supported by two further studies showing that raised levels can be normalised if the care provided by parents becomes more sensitive. Mothers of high-risk children were taught how to care more sensitively and effectively, resulting in more normal cortisol (Brotman et al., 2007; Fisher et al., 2007).

In and of itself, these studies should be a cause for alarm about the impact of day care because there is abundant reason to suspect that dysregulation of cortisol is harmful to behaviour. Cortisol is known to dampen the immune system (Riechlin, 1993; Sapolsky, 2004) and this may partly explain the well-established fact that toddlers in day care suffer much more physical illness than those raised at home (Haskins, et al., 1986; of course, exposure to so many other children's infections is also a reason). But the worry becomes considerably greater when you learn that the impact of day care on cortisol levels continues long after early childhood. Measured at the age of 15, the longer a child was in day care when small, the more its cortisol levels were affected, statistically significantly so (Roisman et al., 2009). The other enduring factor was how sensitive the mother had been in the early years. These effects of early day care and sensitivity endured after controlling for other potentially key factors, like social class and the contemporary relationship of the 15-year-old with its mother.

It is important before we go any further to emphasise that it is not just day care which affects cortisol; other kinds of potentially distressing care does so too. If the child is cared for at home by an unresponsive parent it is just as big a problem. As mentioned at the outset, severely maltreated children who were subsequently taken into institutional care have cortisol dysregulation. But so do children of depressed mothers. This is a very important point: if a mother stays at home and cares for her child and becomes depressed, there is every bit as much risk that her child will be adversely affected as if she puts the child in day care. For example, a study measured how depressed mothers were and the cortisol levels of their children during the first 10 years (Gump et al., 2009). It showed that degree of depression and levels were related, as well as that there are enduring effects of the mother being depressed during the early years. There are many other studies indicating the same (Ashman et al., 2002; Ronsaville et al., 2006). Hence, while day care may be harmful to cortisol levels, a mother who is depressed and caring for her infant is equally likely to be so.

In terms of the implications for behaviour of the impact of day care on cortisol, the most well-established are aggression and disobedience. Several studies suggest that increased cortisol leads to greater aggression or fearfulness among children in day care. This has been shown among three- and four-year-olds (Tout et al., 1998; Dettling et al., 1999), as well as smaller children (Watamura et al., 2003). While the relationship between cortisol levels and aggression or other disturbances in older children may be complex, meta-analyses strongly suggest it exists (Alink et al., 2008). This brings us to the negative impact of day care about which all authorities are agreed: increased levels of aggression and oppositional, defiant conduct.

3. Day Care and Aggression

To recapitulate, there seems little doubt that day care raises cortisol levels. While disrupted cortisol levels may be associated with many problems, including depression and fearfulness, there is considerable evidence they also affect aggression and good conduct. If so, when children raised in day care are compared with ones raised at home, they should be more aggressive.

In a 2001 review, Belsky (2001) presented extensive evidence that this is so. Subsequent studies support his conclusion. For example, similar findings have been obtained in two large samples of English (Melhuish et al., 2001; Sammons et al., 2003) and Northern Irish (Melhuish et al., 2002) children. But most influential of all have been the results from the NICHD study which has followed 1,000 children from early childhood into teenage.

The study found that the more time a child spent in non-maternal care (most of it day care), the more disharmonious was its relationship with its mother when with her. This was equally true at six to 36 months (NICHD ECCRN, 1999) as at five years old (NICHD ECCRN, 2003a). The findings were similar for problem behaviours involving aggression and disobedience. The more time the child was in non-maternal care of any kind during its first five years, the greater their difficultness in three key respects (NICHD ECCRN, 2003):

⟨ Assertiveness: they talked too much, bragged or boasted and argued a lot
⟨ Disobedience: they talked out of turn, were disobedient at school, defiantly talked back at school staff and disrupted school discipline
⟨ Aggression: they got into many fights, were prone to cruelty, bullying or meanness, they physically attacked others and they destroyed their own possessions

These results were found whether the report about the child was being made by the teacher or the mother. In all, aged four and a half, 25% of children who had spent a lot of time in non-maternal care displayed these traits, compared with only 6% of those raised at home (NICHD ECCR, 2003, page 997). This is a huge difference and it was still the case when the children moved to kindergarten.

Of particular significance was the greater likelihood of these problems, as the quantity of time spent in non-maternal care increased. The percentages rise in direct relation to the hours spent in non-maternal care (0–9 hours a week, 6% (mother and substitute ratings combined); 10–29 hours, 15%; 30–34 hours, 16%; over 45 hours, 25%). Great care was taken to establish that the children really were worse behaved, rather than merely more independent and self-assertive as a result of having learnt to look after themselves young.

In all likelihood, they were angry and afraid. If so, that could explain why the aggression and misconduct ceased to show up in the sample after the age of eight (Belsky et al., 2007). At that age, they had bad work habits and poor social competence, although this ceased to be true at 11.

A very possible interpretation is that the anger and fear felt in early life started to express itself in a variety of ways, including being turned against the self – depression, shyness, social insecurity. This would have skewed the statistics, so that those who continued to express their rage through misconduct or aggression were fewer.

As we get older, we express ourselves through different means. If non-maternal care does disrupt cortisol levels and create an angry person, that can be expressed in many ways, including drug and alcohol abuse. It could explain why a different study of 585 American children found that non-maternal care was a highly significant predictor of substance abuse at age 18 (Dodge et al., 2009): substance abuse is strongly associated with aggression and depression.

Whatever the truth of this, a particularly telling study suggests a further possibility (Dmitreva et al., 2007). The United States has high rates of early day care, with over half of under-ones in non-maternal care full-time. By primary school, a majority of the pupils in most school classes have been exposed to day care. Given that such care increases aggression and misconduct, this could be contagious: children who were home-reared may be forced by the misbehaviour of the non-maternal cared children to begin misbehaving themselves. Dmitreva et al., (2007) confirmed this in a large sample (3,440) of children in 282 primary-school classes across America. She found that children who had been home-reared were significantly worse behaved, the greater the proportion of the peers in their class who had been in day care.

If replicated, this study could prove highly significant in influencing social policy. While it would take a brave politician to say so, the fact is that violence in the United States grew massively following the period in which increasing numbers of children were spending their early years in day care. There are many reasons for this, but it is at least plausible that one of them is that day care increased the proportion of the population that were angry, a key precursor to violence (James, 1995). Indeed, other studies suggest a connection between adult violence and non-maternal care: more children in non-maternal care eat sweets, early sweet-eaters are more likely to be violent in adulthood.

In a sample of 12,500 British children born after 2000, the ones whose mothers worked full-time were more likely to be consuming sweetened drinks, and snacking on sweets and crisps between meals (Hawkins et al., 2009). They were less likely to be eating three portions of fruit a day. The mothers' sheer lack of time was thought to be likely to be a major reason for this.

The connection between sweet-eating and violence was shown in a large nationally representative British sample followed from their births in 1970 (Moore et al., 2009). It found that men who had eaten confectionary daily when aged 10 were significantly more likely to be violent at age 34. The researchers showed that this was more than just a correlation.

It remained true after other key variables had been taken into account, like how the boys were cared for by their parents at age five (harsh physical punishment being the major cause of violence). In all, at age 34, 69% of the violent had been sweet-munchers when aged 10 compared with 42% of the non-violent. One hypothesised explanation was that sweets were being used by parents or carers in childhood as a short-term reward. This decreased the boy's ability to delay gratification, making him more impulsive and easily frustrated when thwarted. These characteristics are more common in people who use violence rather than words to express anger.

But there may also be a direct biological effect of the sweets. Additives in them have been shown to increase the risk of acting out – of putting thoughts into action rather than reflecting on the consequences or causes of the impulse. As children, this may have made them more violent, but this lasted into later life. Having acquired a taste for sweets, the violent men may have gone on eating them in adulthood, exposing them to the biological impact of additives on behaviour then.

Whatever the explanation, there is a link to having a working mother.

While debate exists about the extent of the effect of day care on aggression – how many children are affected, how much – nobody now disputes that this is a main effect of day care. Even if it only makes a small proportion, such as 10% of children, more aggressive, and even if the increase is simply at the level of defiance and disruptiveness rather than full-scale violence, this become enormously significant when the numbers of children involved are in the millions, over several generations. Unsurprisingly, very few researchers and no politicians at all are prepared to say it, but the huge rise in day care could be greatly increasing the levels of aggression, incivility and even violence in our society.

An immediate apparent contradiction to this claim is that the Scandinavian nations have used day care for the majority of their population for 50 years. If day care increases aggression, how come these are not the most aggressive, uncivil, violent societies? The answer may be that the adverse impact of day care on behaviour is not restricted to its effect on aggression. It could be that being stressed by day care does not necessarily express itself in that way if the care and the wider society channel the anxiety in different directions. As we saw earlier, day care raises cortisol levels and although fight is one of the ways this is expressed, it can also be expressed through flight, or a state of perpetual anxiety about which way to go: insecurity.

4. Insecure Attachment and Day Care

Thousands of scientific studies prove that we are made insecure if the care we receive between six months and three years of age is not responsive and reliable (Cassidy et al., 1999). The insecurity takes three main forms: clinging, avoidance or a confusing mixture of the two (known as 'disorganised').

Before anything is said about the possibility that day care increases insecurity, the fundamental causes need to be understood: rates of insecurity are easily highest among children cared for by unresponsive mothers. Some 60 studies suggest that 62% of children with such mothers are insecure (De Wolf et al., 1997). In many cases, the unresponsiveness is caused by depression. As we shall see, it is beyond doubt that the risk of insecurity is at least as great for a child cared for at home by an unresponsive mother than if the child has substitute care, including day care.

Overall, if insecure in early life, there is a much greater risk of being an insecure adult. One study measured responsiveness of maternal care at one, eight and 24 months (Beckwith et al., 1999). The degree of responsiveness at those ages independently predicted how insecure the person was 18 years later, over and above the many other events which might have influenced this in the intervening years. In about two-thirds of cases, people have the same pattern in adulthood as in early childhood (Weinfield et al., 2000; Waters et al., 2003). About 40% of adults are insecure (Bakersman-Kranenburg et al., 2009). While being insecure is not in itself a mental illness, studies of 10,500 adults show that the insecure are much more likely to suffer the commonest problems, such as depression (Bakersman-Kranenburg et al., 2009). In short, early care creates insecurity that often lasts into adult life, and such people are at greater risk of mental illness.

The insecure are more likely than the secure to have elevated or blunted cortisol levels (Gerhardt, 2004; Tarullo et al., 2006). If mothers are helped to provide security-inducing sensitive care, it improves cortisol levels (Bakermans-Kranenburg et al., 2008). Since children who have been in day care also have cortisol dysregulation, it would not be surprising if they were also more likely to be insecure.

A basic point is that when the security of children to their substitute carer is tested, it is considerably less than security to parents. A review of the security of 2,867 children investigated in 40 studies, mostly of the effects of day care, showed that only 42% of them were securely attached to the substitute, compared with 60% to their mother and 66% to their father (Ahnert et al., 2006). The larger the size of the group within which the children were cared for, and the higher the ratio of children to carers, the less the likelihood of secure attachment to the substitute. What was more, children were far more likely to be securely attached to a substitute if they were being cared for at home than at a day care centre – 59% versus 40%. Since so many children are insecurely attached to the substitutes who look after them in day care, it is plausible that this would decrease their security to their mothers.

When, in 1986, the distinguished American child psychologist Jay Belsky published a review of the evidence, overall 43% of children in non-maternal care for more than 20 hours a week were insecure (Belsky, 1986, 1988). By contrast, the proportion was 26% for children raised at home by mothers. Controversy subsequently raged in America for 10 years until the publication of the results of what was intended to be a definitive test of the matter, based on following 1,000 American infants from birth (NICHD ECCRN, 1997). It found that, in and of itself, non-maternal or day care did not cause insecurity. This single finding has led many commentators to cease regarding day care as a potential cause of insecurity.

However, that is to ignore the full findings of the study. If the mother was measured to be insensitive, then the combination of this with only 10 or more hours of non-maternal care a week during the first year did increase the risk of insecurity; the more hours, the greater the risk. This was true when insecurity was measured at six, 15 and 36 months. Insecurity was also increased if the childcare arrangements were changed several times or if the day care was low-quality (which is very common in the United States and Britain). In short, while insensitive mothering increased the risk of insecurity on its own, it did so more when combined with day care.

To dismiss altogether the studies suggesting that day care directly causes insecurity which Belsky reported in 1986 and 1988 on the basis of one study – however well designed – would be unusual. More common is to await replication of the finding. A British study of 1,000 children was indeed intended to supply a test of the NICHD finding (www.familieschildrenchildcare.org). For reasons that have never been explained, however, although some data were gathered on attachment security, they were never completed. The original authors having failed to analyse their data, they are now being studied by new researchers who may provide evidence which contradicts the NICHD finding. Since the NICHD study there have anyway been new studies which continue to strongly suggest that day care is a major cause of insecurity.

One study showed that 15-month-olds who had been secure before were at increased risk of becoming insecure three months after entering day care (Ahnert et al., 2004). This was significantly so, the longer the hours the mother worked and the more unreliable her work pattern. Conversely, the longer the mother stayed at the day care centre before leaving the child at the beginning of its time there, the less the risk of insecurity.

Another body of studies concerned day care in Israel (Oppenheim, 1998). For many years there it had been common practice not only for young children to spend the day in care but for them also to stay the night. Evidence accumulated that children who stayed overnight were much more at risk of insecurity than ones who only spent the day in care. This strongly suggests that extensive periods apart from parents increase the risk of insecurity and that this extreme form of day care independently causes it (indeed, overnight sleeping was subsequently discontinued in Israel).

Two further studies of Israeli children provided a direct challenge to the NICHD findings. The first, with a large sample of 758 infants, contradicted the NICHD finding in that insecurity was independently caused by day care, after allowing for other factors (Sagi et al., 2002). The most likely to be secure were infants raised at home by a relative other than mother, the most insecure were the ones in day care. The day care provided was mostly of very poor quality, with large numbers of infants per carer – the day care centre with the best ratio was 6 infants for 1 carer and the average was 8:1, whereas a 3:1 ratio is recommended by UNICEF for under-twos (UNICEF, 2008). It was also the case that the most likely to be insecure were infants whose mothers were insensitive. Nonetheless, the fact that day care alone did cause insecurity – irrespective of the mother's sensitivity or other factors – is grounds for questioning the NICHD claim that this is not the case.

The second study looked more closely at a subsample of 151 infants from the first. Its conclusion repays quotation (Koren-Karie et al., 2005, page 122) : 'Can exposure to early and extensive center care be viewed as risk factors that might contribute to insecure infant-mother attachment relationships? According to the NICHD Early Child Care Research Network study (1997) conducted in the United States, the answer is no at the main effect level … According to the Haifa Study of Early Child Care (Sagi et al., 2002) the answer is yes. In this study, center care infants were insecurely attached to their mothers at a higher rate than infants who were either in maternal care, individual nonmaternal care, or family day care. Therefore, contrary to the NICHD Early Child Care Research Network (1997) conclusion, the Israeli study suggests that center care in and of itself does increase the likelihood of insecurity attachment relationships between infants and their mothers.'

It has been objected that these findings do not necessarily have wider implications since they refer to low-quality day care. However, as noted above, there is good evidence that only 9% of American day care facilities are high-quality. Given that 91% of American (and British) day care is more or less of low quality, the Israeli findings are surely of considerable importance. As also noted, there is a strong tendency for interested parties to gloss over the uncomfortable evidence that most care is not of high quality.

There is another highly significant fact that recent studies have uncovered which is also rarely given much attention: the kind of mother who leaves her child in day care is more likely to be insecure herself and those who see returning to work as beneficial to their child are more likely to be insensitive in relating to their baby. These facts must be handled with care, of course, because they can run the risk of stigmatising working mothers. But they surely must be faced up to and considered when attempting serious analysis of what is in the best interests of under-threes, for they are highly significant in explaining both the decision to use day care and its effects.

The NICHD study found that when mothers said they believed it was beneficial for their child if they worked, their infants were more likely to be insecure (NICHD ECCRN, 1997, page 875). For example, such mothers strongly agreed with the statement 'children whose mothers work are more independent and able to do things for themselves'. Mothers with these views were less sensitive or responsive. They were more likely to have their children in poorer-quality care, at earlier ages, for more hours per week and they were more likely to move their child rather than sticking with one arrangement. There is likely to be a large overlap between such mothers and Raphael-Leff's (2005) Regulator (my Organiser).

A number of linked findings need to be added to these, also demonstrating that the sort of mother who prefers day care is different from one who does not. Generally, mothers who return to work while their child is under one are more likely than average to be better educated, have higher incomes and a higher professional status (Melhuish et al., 1991; Dench, 2010). They also have less belief in the idea that exclusive maternal care is important for young infants (Melhuish et al., 1991; NICHD ECCRN, 1997). Those mothers who say they prefer day care as an option shortly after birth report a stronger career identity (Hock et al., 1988). Working mothers who choose day care express more negative attitudes to the role of motherhood than stay-at-home mothers (Melhuish et al., 1991). In these respects, they overlap with Raphael-Leff's (2005) Regulator (my Organiser).

A key additional finding is that mothers who prefer day care also are more likely to be insecure themselves (Koren-Karie, 2001). Seventy-one middle-class mothers of under-ones had their security measured. Half of them subsequently sent their infants to day care, the other half cared for them at home. Whereas only 17% of the at-home mothers were insecure, 39% of the working ones were. This finding is important because it is well established that insecure parents are less sensitive than secure ones (George et al., 1999). Insensitive and negative-intrusive parenting is also commoner in mothers who have very high and very low cortisol levels (Mills-Koonce et al., 2001). Mothers who are anxious or depressed before birth or after it are more prone to insensitive mothering and to have children with elevated cortisol (Grant et al., 2009). This chain of findings link together maternal working, maternal insecurity, insensitivity and dysregulated cortisol in both mother and child.

Taken together, it seems clear that there is a particular sort of woman who favours day care over other kinds. She is more likely to be insecure and insensitive. She is more likely to believe that her work is beneficial to her child, and to leave the child for longer, in lower-quality day care, changing the arrangements more frequently, all of which increase the risk of insecurity and cortisol dysregulation (and aggression) in the child. Given all this, it would hardly be surprising if studies found that the combination of such mothers with the potential stress of day care would mean a higher percentage of their children were insecure than ones cared for by their mothers at home.

5. Day Care and Other Potential Problems

It should be clear by now that it seems very likely that day care, in and of itself, increases the risk of three problems for children: cortisol dysregulation, aggression and insecurity. There are also a number of other problems which it might cause that have not been directly assessed.

For example, there is considerable evidence that extremely neglectful care causes children to develop 'indiscriminate friendliness', in which the child acts with equal niceness to strangers and people it knows, possibly in an attempt to attract love and attention, and because it has not learnt the most basic elements of intimacy. For example, Romanian orphan toddlers who had spent more than eight months in an orphanage displayed significantly more indiscriminate friendliness than ones who had been adopted or who had always been with their birth parents (Chisholm, 1998). There were similar findings in fostered children who had suffered severe prior maltreatment (Albus et al., 1999; see also Wolf et al., 1999). Adopted children are at considerable risk of dysregulated cortisol (Gunnar et al., 2001, 2006; Wismer Fries et al., 2008). If the study were done, it would not be surprising if children in low- or medium-quality day care (91% of American children in day care) for long hours exhibited some elements of indiscriminate friendliness.

Likewise, it would be unsurprising if a greater vulnerability to depression in adult life were found among children who had been in low- or medium-quality day care for long hours. Prolonged separation from parents has been shown to have caused long-term depression and insecurity in large samples of adults who were evacuated during the Second World War when measured decades later. In one sample, there was a higher likelihood of adult depression if the evacuation occurred aged four to six years old rather than at age 13 (Rusby et al., 2009). In another, depression was nearly twice as common in evacuees compared with children not separated, or ones with their mothers but not with fathers, absent due to military work (Pesonen et al., 2007). In a final study, those evacuated between the ages of four and six years showed much higher likelihood of insecure attachment (54%), compared to those not evacuated (32%), the younger the age of evacuation, the greater the insecurity (Rusby et al., 2008). Other findings indicate that extended or repeated separation from the mother in itself causes long-term emotional problems in adulthood, in particular, borderline personality disorder. This was so even after other factors were controlled, and the longer and earlier the separation, the greater the risk of developing this problem (Crawford et al., 2009). Again, as with indiscriminate friendliness and adoption, these are extremes. But day care entails repeated and more or less prolonged separation from mother. It would not be surprising if it has similar, albeit less severe, long-term effects.

Taken with the established adverse effects of day care, these observations provide a basis for speculating about the impact of differing national caregiving practices. In the case of Scandinavia, for example, despite decades of nationalised day care, there has not been one single study evaluating its emotional consequences. As a leading Dane told me, such research would not be commissioned in case it demonstrated problems that were felt to be ideologically incompatible with the high number of working mothers of under-threes (James, 2007, page 239). Yet such research seems urgently required because, despite having much higher-quality care than in the United States or Britain, there might still be significant adverse effects (James, 2007, pages 230–45). As discussed earlier, overt aggression is unlikely to be one of these –

Scandinavian nations do not have high rates of assault or other violence perhaps because, as also pointed out, there is a strong cultural pressure to be friendly and cooperative, particularly emphasised in the nursery system. However, it could be that anger and fear generated by day care do exist and are simply channelled in other ways, including internalising disorders and indiscriminate friendliness. It is also possible that they show up in the extremely elevated rates of teenage alcohol abuse, although this also has other causes as well (James, 2007). Of particular interest would be studies measuring security of attachment, comparing home-reared versus day care. If the NICHD study is right, there should be no difference, but as noted, other studies have different findings. Equally interesting would be measurement of basic levels of attachment security among the adult Scandinavian population – are they elevated compared with nations in which most of the population are reared at home when under-three, such as Austria?

Cross-national comparison of rates of attachment security correlated with prevalence of day care, including measures of quality of care, should be revealing. It would seem highly probable that the adult population of Israel have high rates of insecurity, given the high proportions who have experienced extensive day care from early childhood and the well-established high rates which result from it (Sagi et al., 2002; Koren-Karie et al., 2005). Another intriguing comparison is between adults reared in early childhood before 1989 in East rather than West Germany. When the Berlin Wall came down in 1989, 56% of East German under-threes were in day care (23% of under-ones and 89% of two- to three-year-olds), often for very long days, with after-school care added on to enable mothers to work longer hours (Ahnert et al., 2001). This is a far higher proportion than was the case in West Germany then, or today (UNICEF, 2008). Trained to do so by the state, the carers in East Germany strongly emphasised social competence and conformity, rather than individuality, in the children. This training was radically altered after reunification, with much greater emphasis on emotional needs and individual requirements of the child, and a reframing of the carer role from teacher to companion (Ahnert et al., 2001). When attachment security of infants was measured in East Germany before and after reunification, the proportion of insecure children was twice as large beforehand, a whopping 80% (Ahnert et al., 2001, page 1850). That it was still 61% after reunification is remarkable. The samples were small (40 and 64) but if these figures were duplicated nationally, it would predict huge differences in security between middle-aged East and West German populations as a whole.

Such large-scale comparisons may produce worrying evidence regarding the consequences of British government policies during the last 13 years, in which the Sure Start programme has greatly increased the number of children from low-income families in day care and in which considerable financial inducements have been offered to all families to use it (Inter-Departmental Review, 2002).

The key comparisons would concern cortisol dysregulation, aggression and disobedience, and insecurity of children who had been in day care while under three, compared with those cared for by mother at home. Based on the evidence of this review, I would predict an overall effect of day care: increasing the risk of cortisol dysregulation, aggression, disobedience and insecurity. The effects should be largest for the combination of low-quality day care and maternal insensitivity.

6. Conclusions

This review of the evidence regarding the effects of day care leads to two uncomfortable conclusions which, taken together, make for a particularly worrying story:

⟨ The younger and longer an under-three spends in day care, and the lower the quality of the care, the greater the risk that the child will have dysregulated cortisol (elevated or blunted) levels, be aggressive and disobedient, and suffer insecurity

⟨ Mothers who regard their work as beneficial to their under-three, or who favour day care over other substitute care, are more insensitive in relating to their children and are more likely to leave their child in lower-quality day care for longer, from younger ages, chopping and changing the care

This suggests that, on its own, day care considerably increases the risk of important problems for children. But it also shows that day care is at its most harmful when it is low-quality and when mothers are insensitive. The tragedy would appear to be that the very infants who are most at risk of being adversely affected by day care – ones with insensitive mothers – are the very ones who are most liable to be placed in it. Since low-income mothers are more liable to be insensitive (NICHD ECCRN, 1997), it might suggest that British government policy has been peculiarly ill-conceived in the last 13 years, or at least, since little day care is high-quality, ill-executed.

This is a highly contentious matter. Less so is a simple fact: a middle-class parent who chooses even high-quality day care as substitute care for their child should not expect it to gain, cognitively, and it will run unnecessary increased risk of cortisol dysregulation, aggression and disobedience, and insecurity. That is always assuming the parent can find a high-quality day care setting.

While it must also be said that the majority of children in day care do not suffer any adverse consequences, judged by the measures currently used, these measures are limited. If factors like indiscriminate friendliness and depression were measured, and if the long-term effects in adulthood were measured, the proportion suffering adverse effects may actually be much higher.

The Mommy Wars: Time for a Peace Treaty

During the 1990s a savage war broke out in the United States between working and non-working mothers, fuelled by newspapers and pop psychologists. Since then, something similar has occurred in Britain. The titles of two books encapsulate the issues, with that extreme bluntness in which authors of American self-help manuals so excel. Against working mothers was *Parenthood by Proxy: Don't have them if you won't raise them* (Schlessinger, 2000; the absence of an exclamation mark after that subtitle showed surprising restraint). The case for the working mothers' defence was called *When Mothers Work: loving our children without sacrificing ourselves* (Peters, 1997).

Even without these shrill combatants, there is built into the culture of most developed nations a vicious predicament for mothers. Whether they work or not they are in the wrong: damned if they do, damned if they don't. This is nicely illustrated by a study of articles about mothering in women's magazines which identified several cruelly contradictory positions into which mothers are coerced (Johnstone et al., 2004). In particular, mothers of all kinds are served a series of unreturnable, head-whanging aces:

WORKING MOTHERS

The culture tells you that babies need unconditional and omnipresent loving care

BUT

you are compelled by financial need, or pressure to 'have it all', to get a paid job when your children are small and in most cases, you cannot afford substitute care which will come up to the unconditional, omnipresent care standard.

On the one hand, working mothers feel exhorted to provide a quality of service for their infant that has almost certainly never been achieved anywhere. The baby or toddler must be loved with an unconditional adoration. It must have someone providing this at all times.

On the other hand, the wider culture strongly pressurises mothers to return to work while their baby is small. This is partly practical, so that a great many mothers find themselves with the choice between near penury if they do not work, or giving their baby over to substitute care which in many cases is very far from ideal – hardly any day care nurseries, for example, provide anything like the kind of care that would meet the magazine ideal. Pressures are arguably every bit as great for more affluent mothers – except the very richest – who are in a highly competitive consumer society with massive mortgages, huge outgoings if they buy children's education and tremendous demands to consume cars, services and fashions that keep up with Joneses, as well as to keep on paying the health insurance. In the United States these pressures are even greater and as a result, fully half of American under-threes have a mother who works full-time (however, interestingly, only 1% of magazine content is concerned with mixed feelings mothers might have about returning to work – the mags are miles away from addressing the real issues for many American mums (Johnstone et al., 2004)).

AT-HOME MOTHERS

The culture also tells you that only you are the natural person to supply the necessary care and you must trust your instincts

BUT

you must also listen carefully to expert advice and constantly worry whether you are doing it 'right' because media of all kinds constantly imply that you are inept and incapable carers in all sorts of ways, and anyway, only paid work is estimable.

On the one hand, the magazines tend to present the ideal mother as the biological one, at-home full-time, middle-class, Caucasian and entirely and completely fulfilled by her domestic role.

On the other hand, a torrent of magazine articles, books and television programmes question whether mothers are caring for their children in the 'right' way. Mothers who are at-homers by definition are not going to be writing in these media or presenting or producing broadcast programmes, nor are they going to be famous. Indeed, there is strong evidence that the pro-work, 'the baby must adapt to the mother' views of some middle-class mothers get a very disproportionate amount of attention (Dench, 2010). The total absence of famous at-home role models is conspicuous in a society where only paid work is esteemed. The implicit message is that only losers looked after their children full-time, like drug-addicted single mothers or 'trailer trash' who were too stupid or mad to get a job.

Given these mind-spinning contradictions, unsurprisingly, two-thirds of both at-home and full-time working mothers feel they live in a culture that is hostile to them (Johnstone et al., 2004). Both groups tend to stereotype the other – the 'mommy wars' – to help themselves feel better about their decisions. The research of Johnstone et al. (2004) established the following:

⟨ The at-homers often characterise the full-timers as denying their 'natural' tendencies, as secretly wishing they could be at-home too. At-homers also say to themselves 'full-timers are neglectful mothers, whereas I am not'. They regard full-timers as cold, efficient machines

⟨ While less directly critical of the at-homers, full-timers see themselves as victims of widespread criticism. They feel portrayed as bad, heartless mothers

⟨ Part-timers tend to side with the at-homers, to some degree, feeling that the national culture is on the side of the full-timers. However, they believe that the society is gradually shifting towards greater support of at-homers

In short, whatever sort of mother you are, the tendency is to feel that the culture is against you. Mother is pitted against mother and all feel badly stigmatised by a hostile cultural environment.

'Worker' Versus 'Mother' Identities: Mummy Mental Gymnastics

For most of history mothers just did the done thing of their society – 'it is the way of our people'. Whether living in Victorian England, medieval Russia or ancient Egypt, most mums had neither time nor money to debate the pros and cons of breastfeeding or 'naughty steps', and even if they did, there was little room for challenging the *status quo* (De Mause, 1974). Your own mother or a mother-in-law would be breathing down your neck and whether deciding to become an Earth mother or returning to your job as a brain surgeon (not that women had such jobs in those days), breaking with convention was inadvisable because you could end up being booted out of the home or even murdered. It was not, however, very likely to occur to you to buck the trend because such individualism was completely alien.

By contrast, today most mothers have to make up their own mind about the best way. While about half draw heavily on the way their own mother did it and many of the remaining half are conscious of reacting against what their mother did, in most cases the main source of day-to-day emotional support and advice is their peers, not their mother (Johnstone et al., 2008). But the wider society still has a big influence on basic ideas about what a good mother is.

Immediately after the Second World War most mothers followed the teachings of a very strict disciplinarian health reformer called Sir

Frederic Truby King. Then, in the1950s, along came Dr Benjamin Spock, putting the needs of the baby ahead of everything. To this day, his ideas inform most mothers' basic feeling about what a good mother should supply, although there is wide variation in how to do it.

In general, few mothers doubt that both babies and toddlers require intensive, moment-to-moment attention to physical and emotional needs, and considerable educational guidance and nurture (Johnstone et al., 2004). While experts stress that you can only hope to be good enough rather than perfect, nonetheless, the closer you approximate to delivering this intensive-care silver service, the more you are a 'good mother'.

The trouble is, alongside their good mother identity, most modern women have another one: worker. Although this takes many forms, prior to getting pregnant nearly all women relied heavily on their worker identity for their notion of who they are (Hakim, 2000). All shapes and sizes are found but there is nearly always a significant conflict between worker and mother.

At least one third of women are from low-income homes and most of them have never regarded themselves as having a career; their work is a job (Dench, 2010). Only 7% of unskilled adult women work full-time, compared to 68% with professional and managerial jobs (Hakim, 2000, page 103). While making money is an important component and though the work may not in itself be regarded as especially satisfying or stimulating (supermarket checkout operative, call-centre worker), the social life at the workplace and surrounding it (socialising in the evening or at weekends with workmates) have been central parts of their life (Odone, 2009) – 40% of people now meet their spouse at work. The desire to maintain the enjoyable social life and independent income they had as a worker can feel at odds with the desire to be a good mother.

Although a university degree is increasingly common among women from families in the top two-thirds of earners, there are still many women from relatively affluent homes who do not have further education. Most of them also do not look on their work as a career but as a job. Many work in offices where they may be given considerable responsibility, perhaps as personal assistants to senior managers or as office managers. Their role may give them status and the satisfaction of knowing they make a significant contribution to the success of the business. The money they earn is vital for affording both basics and luxuries. And on becoming a mother, their desire to be a good one can seem seriously at odds with the person they were at work.

Far more than is often openly admitted, those women who do attend university do not see a degree as a stepping stone to a career (Hakim, 2000). These women may never have been especially concerned with doing well at exams or fired up by scholarship or the acquisition of qualifications, although they may have succeeded in both respects. They regarded university primarily as an opportunity for an enjoyable social life. Such women may always have regarded motherhood as their ultimate goal, expecting either to give up work altogether or to work only part-time, when they have children. The knowledge obtained through degrees can be described as an intellectual dowry that they bring to their marriage, which might sound insulting – except it is a perfectly reasonable way of thinking about things from their viewpoint. They want a partner who is an interesting man with good prospects, and they want to be able to communicate with him on an equal footing and to have his respect, and getting a degree is a rational way of achieving those goals. They do not necessarily see themselves as unintelligent or less capable than more career-minded women or than their partners, but they see motherhood as their long-term ambition. However, having spent many years in the workplace after university, their work identity remains something they value for the independence money brings, as well as for the social element. Completely giving these up may conflict with their desire to be a good mother.

Then there is the professional woman, such as a highly educated GP or lawyer, who has identified herself, usually from teenage years onwards, as more or less ambitious in aspiring to become an established figure within a respected career hierarchy (consultant, firm partner). Often diligent, studious and authoritative, they get used to commanding respect for their profession both at work and in their social lives. They have worked hard to get where they are, whether they intend to become a leading figure in their field or are satisfied with middle or lesser ranking. Studies show (Hakim, 2000, page 110) that women who made clear plans for their careers in their teens are much more likely in later life than those who did not, to work longer hours, have larger salaries and rise to more senior positions. Relinquishing their rosy job prospects and large salaries (compared with most of the population) may seem very unattractive, especially if they have a partner who is not so high-earning. Yet they also want to be a good mother. Can they have it all? If they continue with their career, inevitably, they are liable to feel criti-cised for not being a good mother however nurturant when they are at home and however assiduous in organising first-rate substitute care.

The same applies to successful businesswomen, who are increas-ingly likely also to have been to university. Whether working in a corporation or as an entrepreneur with her own small business, this woman has often aspired to a particular career trajectory from a young age, whether success be measured in salary, share ownership or hier-archical ascent. Like her professional sister, she has worked jolly hard to get where she is. At the point when she becomes pregnant, whether she has titanic ambitions to become a mistress of the universe (for example, a top City hedge fund manager earning zillions) or to have part ownership of a medium-sized small business, being a good mother may seem emotionally hard to square with being a whiz kid. Again, if they continue with their career the pressure to feel guilty – however good the substitute mothering arrangements they put in place – is considerable.

Finally, in marked contrast to all of the above, there is a proportion of women for whom motherhood is the be-all and end-all (Hakim, 2000; Odone, 2009; Dench, 2010). This ranges from those for whom it has been true since early on, as in mothers who will say 'I wanted only to be a mother from when I was a little girl', to those who discover it much later in life – 'I would never have guessed I would feel like this when I was working, before I had my baby'. However, even for these women there is a problem. They have no conflict between worker and mother identities since they truly place nil value on the worker bit. But they live in a society which does the opposite: it is the mother role that has a status somewhat less than that of street-sweeper; only paid work is valued. While some may genuinely not care, a considerable proportion naturally feel aggrieved that their mothering identity is so looked down upon (if you do not believe me try this for yourself: next time you meet a stranger who asks what you do say 'I work for the council sweeping the streets' or 'I look after the kids at home'; the street sweeper may be taken much more seriously).

Mental Acrobatics in Justifying Your Mummy–Worker Decisions

Nearly all mothers feel some conflict between their mummy identity and their worker one. Like everyone else, they have to find a way to rationalise the contradictions.

Four main mental wheezes have been identified for doing so (described in Johnston et al., 2007). Unfortunately, none of them is terribly effective overall. While they may help you to keep going day-to-day, the evidence suggests it is best to move heaven and earth to create a solution which as much as possible really reflects your true desires: telling yourself stories ultimately leads to a more or less positive patina that covers a life of quiet desperation.

BLANKING

You buy wholly into either work or motherhood and deny altogether that the other exists as an aspect of your life or as even a possibility for you. This is commonest as a mental routine among at-home mothers.

Many at-homers totally disregard any option that they might have to work, saying 'it would be completely out of the question, I never even think about it'. Three-quarters of at-homers say it is essential for the well-being of their child. They convey an absolute certainty and confidence that any paid work is out of the question, regarding it as a moral duty to provide intensive, omnipresent care.

Alternatively, one quarter of at-homers disregard work more because they never felt a very strong worker identity. It seems an easy and obvious decision to give it up – preferably forever – as work was always dull and unfulfilling to them. For some there is no financial pressure to work but even for those who have little money coming into the home, not working and being poor is preferable.

Whether disregarding work because it bored them or because it seemed their bounden duty, of all categories of mothers, at-homers who use this tactic for dealing with the work–mummy clash feel least divided. However, nearly half of them acknowledge that they do have days when they wish they had a part-time job. They do not miss career achievements or even the camaraderie of the office, but at such times they report feeling excluded from the world of adults and relegated to a world of kids. The lack of an adult identity is being mourned more than that of a worker.

Much more troubled are mothers who feel a strong commitment both to work and to intensive mothering but who try to blank out their working identity; 28% of at-home mothers fit into this category. They justify being at home as vital for their child, particularly stressing how vulnerable and needy the children are. They also bolster their decision by contrasting themselves favourably with employed mothers, stereotyping them as failing to meet their children's needs. The difficulty is that they secretly also long to fulfil a wholly suppressed worker identity, creating a nagging resentment.

Some 28% of part-time employed mothers also play down their work identity to such a degree that it amounts to blanking. They talk with the same passion of the importance of the needs of the child and of how mothering is 'the whole of my life', even though they may spend 20 or 30 hours a week at work. Again, it is an uneasy position because the truth of their actual life keeps challenging it.

Only a small minority of full-time working mothers use blanking of their mothering identity to solve the work–mummy problem. This is easiest for women with enough money to pay others to do most of the mothering. In such cases they may be very open about it. In one case, on the only day that she takes her son for extra football coaching, when she meets other mothers she will say, only semi-jokingly, 'I am impersonating a mother. I'm not really one at all.' Indeed, she and her husband leave the care of their children to a nanny and are sometimes travelling in connection with his work for months on end, only speaking to the children on the telephone.

SEPARATE LIVES IN DIFFERENT BOXES

A tactic for some working mothers is to try to forget about one identity when occupying the other; 17% of full-timers do this. They evade a sense of contradiction between mother and worker by completely forgetting about one while being the other. Phone calls about home when at work are avoided as much as possible, and vice versa. The office desk or wallet contain no pictures of children and partners. If there is an office at home, it is a no-go area for children.

Unfortunately, bits of both identities have a way of getting out of their box, with the two lives inevitably colliding from time to time. Children get ill. Minders do too. It is extremely hard to seal off a work life from children, and for women with senior jobs, their work has a way of chasing them on to the beach, even if they have turned off the BlackBerry (their PA has got their partner's mobile number).

BLENDING

Because 'separate lives' is not a very efficient manoeuvre, some full-time employed mothers try to do the opposite: find a way to make mummy-person and worker-person coexist at home and work. In a few cases, this might entail taking the child to work, like the newsagent with the toddler out the back. More common would be to work from home, relatively easy to arrange for computer-based jobs. However, in most cases it does not work very well at all. Work spills into home, home spills into work. Most mothers adopting this tactic report feeling they are not doing either mothering or work as well as they would like. Nor do they feel very fulfilled, reporting they are missing out on time with friends, leisure pursuits (getting to the gym or the book group) and time to care for themselves, mentally and physically.

Of full-time employed mothers, 53% report feeling constant conflict between mummy and worker identities. Just as at-home mums offer the essential needs of the child as an 'unanswerable' basis for their choice, some full-timers offer the need to earn money. The necessity for it is presented as self-evident and unquestionable, exactly as a baby's need for its mother is supposed to be according to at-homers. Interestingly, however, the extent to which full-timers used money as the reason for their choice is unrelated to how much they earned: a salary of £65,000 or £20,000 does not predict which mothers say they need the money. Hence there are women on £65,000 who say it is essential, yet there are others on less than £20,000 who never mention needing money as their reason for work.

There are plenty of full-timers who do not mention money, or for that matter job satisfaction or some kind of contribution to the wider society, as their goal. At least as common as money is the enjoyment gained from being part of the social world in their workplace. Interestingly, having a baby rarely alters how full-timers perceived their career or job goals. Whether it's becoming CEO, making masses of money, enjoying the company of peers or not wasting their hard-earned training, it remains the same motivation when asked before the birth and a year later.

Despite feeling a strong imperative to work, full-timers nearly always subscribe to the importance of intensive mothering. However, compared with part-timers or at-homers, they subtly redefine what a baby requires. They tend to emphasise the importance of meeting physical needs, such as cleanliness and regular nourishment, and of safety. They regard the child as in need of education and stimulation in order for it to get on with other children and do well. They emphasise the need for cuddling and physical affection less than part-timers or at-homers. Interestingly, they tend to perceive child development as a series of Big Bangs, of firsts, like 'the first step' or 'the first poo in the loo'. Part-timers and at-homers see it as more gradual, small increments rather than great leaps forward.

Overall, Blending rarely satisfies as a way of making sense of the mummy–worker conflict. Usually it results in a state of perpetual disequilibrium, with the woman ricocheting between identities, never feeling either is being well-executed.

REFRAMING

Whereas blenders try to mix up worker and mummy as if they are indistinguishable, reframers accept that they are quite distinct but present each identity as beneficial to the other. Their mantra is that doing work makes them a better mother and that being a mother makes them better able to appreciate work: it's win-win in their version.

At first it often appears that what they have really done is to compromise on the intensive mothering bit, pretending to themselves that they are fulfilling this goal but not carrying it out in reality. However, closer scrutiny reveals that they have subtly reframed what is meant by intensive mothering, compared with at-homers. The crucial shift is that, although they still maintain that a baby and toddler requires intensive nurture and attention at all times, *the person providing this does not have to be the biological mother*. Part-timers are especially likely to use this tactic. While differentiating themselves from at-homers by saying others can meet the child's needs, they also discriminate from full-timers: they are 'missing out' on raising their children by working so hard.

Almost three-quarters (72%) of part-timers repeatedly claim that they have successfully and satisfyingly integrated mummy and worker, with win-win reframing as their method. While half of them say they have a strong worker identity, they are much less likely than full-timers to emphasise money as their goal and instead name personally fulfilling elements. While 31% of part-timers do nonetheless stress money as an important factor, they qualify it by mentioning the fulfilment component too.

Just under one in three (30%) of full-timers also reframe, in their case by separating out altogether the caregiving and mothering elements in intensive mothering. So long as they give high-quality mothering when they are there, all that matters is that the substitute meets the child's basic need. More than the part-timers, they reframe the benefit for the child as being its social development – making friends, learning to cooperate – and the benefit for them and the family of the extra money from working longer hours.

REVIEW 7 (R7)

The Perils of Geneticism

Beware of 'The Little Devil' Attribution

Assuming that your child's attributes are an unchangeable, genetically determined destiny tends to be accompanied by the feeling that you have little control in the relationship. Mothers who attribute a lot of power to their children are at greater risk of maltreating them.

Two studies (Bugenthal, 1989, 2004) show that parents with low perception of control of their babies are more likely to attribute blame for negative interactions or behaviour to the child. This leads to greater harshness and more likelihood of physical abuse, as well as correlating with higher rates of depression in such mothers. Rather than seeing themselves as having greater power than their under-ones, such parents saw themselves as victims of the child, at its mercy. They believed they could do little to prevent negative outcomes, whereas the baby could do so. If the baby was independently measured as being born with a relatively difficult temperament (for example fussy or irritable), abuse was more likely from parents with low perceived control (Bugenthal, 2004). However, the studies were able to demonstrate that the way the parent perceived the baby was not to do with what the baby was actually like: extent of perceived control was measured before the birth and did not change according to independently measured temperament after the birth. Indeed, there is good evidence that how mothers perceive their babies is strongly linked to their own early childhood experiences (Grusec et al., 1995; Belsky et al., 2005).

A further literature, discussed below, indicates that perceiving children as wilful and intentionally bad, the 'oh they can be little devils' way of thinking, is associated with abusive parenting and adverse outcomes. Such thinking tends to presume genetic causality for the badness. Conversely, there is also evidence (Himmelstein et al., 1991) that parents are more likely to attribute positive attributes, like doing well in tests, to their nurture rather than nature.

One study (Guzell et al., 2004) showed that parents who have low perceived control also tend towards 'categorical' thinking about their child's psychology, labelling them as having traits which are unchangeable, possibly because genetically caused. In a sample of 66 parents with one-year-olds, the mothers with low perceived control were more likely to be directive if they perceived their child to be difficult. They were more prone to urge, remind, restrain, question and correct their child during a play situation, reflecting adult-centred rather than child-centred ways of relating. Such directive mothers were also less sensitive to their children's needs.

Another study (Chavira et al., 2000) illustrated this. It examined 149 three- to 19-year-old mentally retarded children and showed that most of their mothers did not view problematic behaviour by their children as the child's fault. However, the more that parents did so, attributing wilfulness to them, the greater the likelihood of the mother reporting anger and frustration, and responding with aggressive or harsh reactions.

Another study (Kiang et al., 2004) shows how maternal assumptions feed into a lack of empathy with toddlers and subsequent lack of curiosity. It investigated maternal preconceptions of mothering before birth and about a child's temperament at six months, and then measured her sensitivity to the child at 12–15 months and the inquisitiveness of the child at 21–24 months in a sample of 175 mother–child dyads. Mothers with pre-natal negative preconceptions (measured as low perceived control, unrealistic expectations about being a mother, low expected empathy level with child and high expected use of physical punishment) were more likely to report a difficult temperament in their six-month-old. Such mothers were less sensitive to their toddlers at 12–15 months and had less inquisitive children at 21–24 months. Conversely, mothers who were sensitive at 12–15 months had more inquisitive children at the later age.

A final study (Maniadaki et al., 2005) of 634 parents showed that attributing deliberate wilfulness to behaviour increased harsh, abusive parenting. The parents were given a hypothetical story to read about a child who displayed many of the symptoms of attention deficit and hyperactivity disorder (ADHD). Half were given a version of the story in which the child was a boy, half given the story about a girl. Those told about the boy were much more likely to label the problem ADHD but most importantly, having done so, they were more likely to assume the boy's difficult behaviour was expressing his intentions, was wilful. If so, these parents advocated harsh responses: attributing wilfulness increased the likelihood of authoritarian parenting.

This body of evidence provides strong grounds for parents to avoid assuming their child has a genetically caused trait that cannot be changed. Further, it suggests it is best not to assume that your baby or toddler is deliberately, wilfully, intentionally seeking to behave badly (based on this unchangeable trait) because you are more likely to react angrily and with frustration if you think they are trying to wind you up, and you are at greater risk of responding with harsh, aggressive and even abusive parenting behaviour. As countless studies have proven (James, 2002), it is that kind of parenting (and not genes) which actually causes children to become aggressive, hostile, violent and to have attention deficits.

Encouraging Your Child to See Themselves as Malleable – Not Fixed by Their Genes – Can Improve Their Abilities

Believe it or not, a crucial determinant of how your child performs at school is whether they themselves think their intelligence is fixed (whether by genes or background) or changeable. Indeed, it has now been shown that just four lessons devoted to cultivating a malleable, 'I am what I choose' mindset (not to be confused with that overrated 'science', positive psychology), significantly improves performance.

A 1990 study (Henderson et al., 1990) showed that first-year secondary pupils who took a malleable view of their abilities got significantly higher grades than ones who believed they were fixed. This was true after allowing for the predictive power of prior academic performance.

Tipped off by this finding, two studies (of teens and undergraduates) put it into practice (Good et al., 2003). They taught samples to think of themselves as being malleable rather than fixed. Compared with groups given no such tuition, the malleable got significantly better grades as a result of the tuition, regardless of their prior SAT scores.

What was needed was more detail of how this works: are kids who see themselves as changeable made optimistic by this belief, or are they already cleverer tryers? And would it work with all kinds of children, even that notorious thicko at the back of the class? Cue two studies putting theoretical flesh on the bones (Blackwell et al., 2007).

The first looked at 373 children aged 13, following them over a two-year period. To measure the malleability/fixity of their beliefs, they were asked how much they agreed or disagreed with statements such as 'You have a certain amount of intelligence, and you really can't do much to change it' or 'You can always greatly change how intelligent you are'. Then they were tested as to motivations: attitude to learning ('I do school work best when it makes me think hard'), confidence that effort brings results ('If you're not good at a subject, working hard won't make you good at it'), and when faced with failure, tendencies towards helpless or positive reactions.

Sure enough, during the two years of study, children who subscribed to malleable beliefs steadily improved in their maths performance. The malleable were more successful than the fixed because they liked being made to think, redoubled efforts if not succeeding and did not feel helpless. But which came first, the try-hard motive or the malleable belief?

This time, 91 13-year-olds, mostly from low-income homes and doing badly at maths, were followed over a year. Half of them were given four lessons in malleability, the others were taught about other matters during those hours.

As before, the intervention group became more likely to subscribe to malleable beliefs as a result of the teaching and the average maths score of that group rose, whereas the control group continued to do badly. The greatest improvement over the year was found in the children who had started with a fixed view of their abilities and had been taught to think of it as malleable: fixity is bad for performance. But above all, the sequence was clear: change the belief, you change the motivation, and that improves the grades.

The implications seem considerable: set aside four lessons for teaching the malleability of talents! But more than this, it is important that both teacher and pupils' parents also develop a malleable view.

Studies of teachers with fixed views show that they are more likely to let their expectations for pupils' performance bias how they treat them (Lee, 1996). Regarding parents, an impressive recent study showed clearly that mothers need to avoid fixed ideas (Pomerantz et al., 2006). If they had a negative view of the child's capacities, a year later such offspring were the most likely to have done badly. True, offspring of fixed parents with high expectations did well, but if the child faltered, there could be big trouble.

The Danger of Perceiving Mental Illness in Yourself or Your Children as Caused by Genes

Whether it's you, your child or a professional, if genes are believed to be the cause of a mental illness there are worse outcomes in a number of respects. Parents with this belief react less helpfully if their child is diagnosed with schizophrenia. Patients who believe it is genetic do worse and professionals subscribing to that belief are also less effective.

A key factor identified in parents of schizophrenics is whether they relate to their child with what is known as high 'expressed emotion' (EE – controlling, angry, condemnatory reactions). Parents who do so are more likely to explain their child's problem as being an illness (Read et al., 2004, page 263) – encouraged by the medical profession, they absorb the story that schizophrenia should be seen as a purely mechanical defect, one no different in kind from a broken arm. Labelling the problem as an illness increases the likelihood of having a biogenetic view of causation. Held by parents, the biogenetic view is associated with much more negative attitudes and behaviour. The patient behaves less well and the parent develops a lower opinion of their behaviour, becoming increasingly pessimistic about recovery (Read et al., 2004, pages 138–9).

Professional staff with a biogenetic view are more likely to interpret the patient as disturbed and to involve the patient less in the planning of treatment. By contrast, if staff or patients have a psychosocial view of causality, both are more likely to make a greater effort to achieve a recovery. The less the patient believes they can change, the greater their risk of alcoholism and depression, and the more passive they become about their management, leaving it to the experts.

Thankfully, the majority of populations in most developed nations tend to assume that extreme mental illness, like schizophrenia, is caused by such entities as 'trauma' or 'childhood abuse' (Read et al., 2006). However, the efforts of the drug companies and their pharmacists, the psychiatric establishment, are constantly seeking to persuade the public of a genetic model. It should never be underestimated how much the drug companies drive matters in this field. A worrying example is that studies of the efficacy of psychotropic drugs show that the proportion of them sponsored by drug companies rose from 25% in 1992 to 57% in 2002 (Kelly et al., 2006). Worrying, because there is good reason to suspect bias: 78% of drug company-sponsored studies report positive outcomes compared with only 48% doing so where there is no such sponsorship.

On a wider scale, people living in traditional societies in the developing world are both much less likely to develop schizophrenia and, if they do so, are much more likely to recover. Part of the reason for this may be that many fewer families react to a child having that illness with what is known as high EE. Only 8% do so, compared with 54% in families of developed nations (Read et al., 2004, page 255).

Another interesting fact is that people living in east Asian nations are much less likely than those in the developed Western countries to attribute personality and emotional dispositions to fixed, non-malleable traits. In eastern Asia, they are more likely to explain what someone is like by reference to their social context, including their family background. It is also true that the amount of mental illness in east Asian countries is much lower than in Western ones. There are many reasons for this (as discussed in Chapter 3, James, 2007, and James, 2008, Chapter 1; see also Chiao et al., 2009). But it is possible that lesser adherence to biogeneticism is one of the them.

The Causes of Maternal Depression

Three factors are critical in deciding which mothers get depressed. The first is the extent of vulnerability created by their own childhood history, as explained in *They F*** You Up* and well demonstrated by a study of 800 mothers by Bifulco et al. (1998). The second is their contemporary social situation, including low income and lack of social support (see Brown et al., 1978). The third is what is known as role strain, which I shall briefly outline as it has been a major element in this book.

In 1979 Gove listed six reasons why the social role of modern women should make them more depressed than men (Gove et al., 1979).

First, full-time housewives have only one potential arena for gratification – the home – compared with men who have their job as well. If a man is unhappy in one arena, he can turn to the other as an alternative source of gratification. This is not an option for a housewife.

Second, for most full-time housewives their primary focus is childcare and homemaking but these activities do not require a great deal of skill and are of low status. Women with high educational qualifications and intellectual abilities would find such unprestigious and undemanding work frustrating.

Third, the lack of structure and invisibility of the housewife role makes it easy to let things slide into a brooding, ruminative state which then feeds on itself. There is no workplace to distract the mother from her problems and the work is held to be inherently depressing.

Fourth, for those women who do work, it is usually ill paid and of low status, seen as secondary to that of the man. Coupled with the arduous childcare and housework, these mothers end up working longer hours than their man and yet are accorded less reward than he is.

Fifth, the female role is unclear and contingent compared to that of males. It leaves women feeling uncertain and lacking in control.

Sixth, in the past families were larger and women were responsible for childcare for most of their adult lives. Housework required considerably more skill and the houswife was seen as being an integral part of a family enterprise. With the advent of small families, modern equipment and industrial employment, the homemaking role lost respect.

Gove concluded with the following prediction: 'If this analysis is correct much of the presumed stress on women is a relatively recent phenomenon ... given the present changes that are occurring in the role of women, their roles will become more commensurate with the roles of men and the two sexes will (again) experience similar amounts of stress, with the consequence that their rates of mental illness will become relatively similar.' Alas, as we have seen throughout this book, this turned out to be a somewhat overly optimistic conclusion.

How Many Mothers Get Depressed?

Just having a baby greatly increases the risk of a woman becoming depressed. Five weeks after birth, women are three times more likely to be clinically depressed than beforehand (Cox et al., 1993). A review of 59 studies showed that about 13% of mothers suffer (Gibson et al., 2009). Less severe, between half and two-thirds get the baby blues, a transitory state of weepiness, around the third or fourth day. This usually entails despondency, feelings of being overwhelmed, and loss of concentration and memory (O'Hara et al., 1996; Nicolson, 1998, page 31).

In fact, caring for an infant in the earliest months produces dysphoria, a state of low-grade, depressed mood allied to total exhaustion, in the vast majority of mothers – it is exceptional for this not to be the case. Hence, in a 2002 survey of 1,000 British mothers, over half said their exhaustion left them in 'a state of despair' and highly irritated by their babies, four hours' sleep a night being the average for those with small ones (*Mother & Baby Magazine*, 2002). Four-fifths of mothers of under-twos said the infant had placed their relationship with partners or husbands under 'immense strain', with rows commonplace and two-thirds of the women having been 'completely put off sex'. While at times they doubtless also feel an unprecedented sense of fulfilment and achievement, until the infant has settled into stable patterns of sleeping and eating, on a daily (and especially, nightly) basis they will be liable to terrifying feelings of loss of control, periodically violent impulses towards their baby and chronic desperation.

Basic Causes of Post-Natal Depression

At the most basic level, one of the strongest predictors of post-natal depression is having been depressed before (Henshaw, 2003). To summarise the many other factors, I shall begin by reproducing my observations in James (2002, pages 223–4), before getting into the details of the evidence of the effect of working versus not working, and of the different approaches to mothering (Hugger versus Organiser versus Flexi).

Most people imagine that post-natal depression is a largely or purely biological misfortune, the flipping of a hormonal switch, but there is no evidence whatever that it has a primarily physical cause. While all women's hormonal levels alter during pregnancy and for a few weeks after the birth, a difference has never been demonstrated between the hormones of the ones who become depressed and those who do not (Nicolson, 1998). By contrast, it is possible to predict with a fair degree of accuracy which mothers are most likely to become post-natally depressed by asking them about their psychological histories during pregnancy: the kind of childhood they had and their current circumstances, not hormones or genes, predict post-natal depression (O'Hara et al., 1996). In most cases, it is the combination of these with the sheer hell of trying to meet the needs of the infant which tips them into depression. The fundamental problem is the total dependence of the baby, 24 hours a day, resulting in an equally total loss of autonomy in the mother. The great majority of mothers do not have someone else there at all times to help them out when the grinding relentlessness of meeting the infant's needs becomes too much. Whereas in the societies that existed before the industrial revolution, people lived in extended families and there would always be sisters, mothers and other relatives on hand (Hess, 1995, pages 122–5), all too often when the exhausted modern mother of a tiny infant is at the end of her tether, there is no one to give her a break.

Having money certainly reduces the risk of depression because it buys mechanical (cars, washing machines) and human (maternity nurses, nannies) support. In the definitive study of the subject, whereas nearly one third of the mothers from poor homes with an under-six-year-old suffered from full-scale depression, only 4% of middle-class ones did (Brown et al., 1978, pages 151–2). But it is not only a matter of money. Women who breastfeed are at greater risk, since they get less sleep and producing the milk is tiring (Nicolson, 1998; Alder et al., 1983; Alder et al., 1986); likewise, women who lack strong intimate relationships, putting divorcees and single mothers in particular danger (Brown et al., 1997; Bifulco et al., 1998, pages 145–50). So are those whose own mother died when they were young (Brown et al., 1978; Harris et al., 1987) and if their own mother is still alive, the risk is greater for those having a bad current relationship with her or who did so when small (and are insecurely attached adults as a result; Brown et al., 1994). The sheer number of children is also a factor. Having three or more under 14, especially if one of them is under six, increases the risk: even if you have survived the firstborn, trying to cope with a second or third newborn offspring is nightmarish with little support (Brown et al., 1978). The increased risk of having more than one child to care for is neatly illustrated by the simple fact that significantly more mothers who have twins, rather than singletons, are depressed (Thorpe et al., 1991).

All these factors, mostly predictable from before birth and many of them preventable if our society were better organised, affect whether the mother becomes depressed. However, it is also true that how difficult the baby is when it is born also affects whether the mother becomes depressed, if she is already vulnerable. Hence, about one-fifth of babies are colicky and this increases the risk; likewise if the baby is floppy (Murray et al., 1993).

Risks of Depression Associated with Different Mothering Approaches

The definitive study examined 205 English mothers before the birth and six to eight weeks afterwards (Sharp et al., 1995, 2004). Of the Organisers, 30% were depressed post-natally, compared with 14% of the Huggers and 11% of the Flexis. Measured in pregnancy, the Organiser approach predicted more than three times greater risk of being post-natally depressed and of the depression developing soon after birth rather than later. Hence, only 37% of Organisers said they enjoyed mothering the baby when it was newborn, whereas by the time the baby was three months old 60% said they were enjoying it. During pregnancy, the Organisers were liable to see themselves as trapped by the role of new mother, more so than other types. They were waiting to get back to normal life rather than enjoying the new way of life required by pregnancy. Despite having these ideas, they did not become more likely than other types to get depressed until after the birth – measured ante-natally, they were not significantly more depressed. A key depression predictor for all the mothers was the extent to which their expectations were disappointed with regard to what the birth and subsequent mothering would be like. For Organisers, depression was increased by having a low income, which would make it harder to pay substitutes. For Organisers, depression risk was increased if they were single or felt they had an unsupportive partner. It was also more likely if their own mother had been very controlling when they were young.

Another study, of 403 women, examined them during pregnancy and again at eight to 12 and 20–25 weeks after the birth (Bussel et al., 2008). It found that Organisers were more prone to anxiety and depression than Huggers, both during the pregnancy and afterwards. However, Huggers were more likely to be irrationally anxious about being separated from their babies than Organisers, at 20–25 weeks. This evidence supports the idea that Organisers find babies more distressing than Huggers. But it also suggests that Huggers sometimes find it hard to tolerate the growing independence of their baby as it gets older.

Does Working Increase or Decrease the Risk of Depression in Mothers of Under-Threes?

Annoyingly, to the best of my knowledge, no study has directly addressed this question, so we can only approximate the answer.

Overall, just as with men, employed women are less likely to be depressed than unemployed ones (for nine studies reporting this, see footnote 9, Schwartz, 1991). But this does not take into account whether the women have children or young ones. Broadly speaking, the more children and the younger the children, the greater the depression risk (Brown et al., 1978). Most at risk are lone or separated mothers (Mirowsky, 1989). But the crucial issue concerns employment and children.

Overall, the evidence suggests that mothers working full-time are most at risk of depression, part-timers least, and at-homers are in between. Alas, this evidence does not take into account the age of the children when the mother is working. Brown et al. (1990) identified

354 low-income mothers with at least one child under 18 still living at home. None of the mothers was depressed at the time of first interview and they were interviewed again a year later. The most depressed were the full-timers and at-homers. A sample of 200 mothers (Bifulco et al., 1998, page 173) reports the same. Owen et al. (1988) also reports several studies showing full-time mothers to be more dissatisfied than part-timers. But none of these specifies if the children are under three, or even under five, and since the earliest years are the most likely to engender depression, this is a disgraceful lack in the literature.

There is good evidence that the amount of dissatisfaction with the balance between work and home is a crucial factor among those who do work. Hence, a review of the evidence cites many studies showing that feeling a strong conflict between work and family predicts depression, alcohol abuse and cigarette smoking (Allen et al., 2000, page 300). In a sample of 36,000 Canadians, Wang (2006) found that only 3.6% were depressed if satisfied with their work–home balance compared with 21% who felt they had never been balanced in the last month. In the same vein, Melchior et al. (2007) followed 11,000 middle-aged French people for nine years, checking their sickness records. Women (many of whom will have been mothers) with high work stress levels and more than four dependents were five times more likely to have been mentally ill, twice as likely for men. Hoppman et al. (2006) puts some flesh on these bones. She measured cortisol levels in a sample of 53 dual-earner couples, both of whom were working more than 20 hours a week and who had at least one pre-school-aged child. They were higher at moments in which the parents were engaged in activities, whether at work or home, which hindered highly desired goals. Since this was associated with negative mood, it suggested that not doing things you want to do and having to do other things which get in their way plays a significant role in making us anxious and depressed, especially in parents.

A crucial factor is how satisfied both partners in a relationship are with the work–family balance. The single most impressive study of this was done by Mirowsky (1991), who identified four different kinds of marriage in a sample of 680 couples.

In the first type, the wife does not have a job, she and her husband believe her place is in the home and she does all the housework and childcare. The wife was more likely to be depressed than the husband in this kind of marriage but less likely to be depressed than in the second type.

The second type is the same as the first except that the wife has a job – even though both partners disapprove of her doing so. This is bad for both parties. The wife is more depressed than in any other condition and *the husband is actually considerably more likely than the wife to be depressed*: the opposite of the usual ratio.

In the third type of marriage, the wife also has a job but both partners approve of it and the wife does all the homemaking. Here, the man is contented but the wife is about as depressed as in the first type: while her husband approves of her job, she ends up having to run the home and feels this is neither sensible nor fair.

Finally, in the fourth type both spouses approve of the wife's employment and share the running of the home. The wife is still considerably more prone to depression than the husband but this is the least depressing for both sexes and the ratio between them is (only by a small margin) the smallest.

This study suggests that role strain is extremely important for whether a woman (and a man) feels depressed and the size of the sex difference ratio. As noted above, there are many studies showing that on the whole, employed wives are less depressed than unemployed ones but the significance of this difference is not simply a matter of 'women like working and find homemaking depressing'. The more that there is tension about the woman's employment – from the woman as well as the man – the worse it is, and there are many other studies showing the centrality of this role strain: the importance of both partners' attitude to the principle of a mother working and of how much the husband helps out with childcare and housework if she does work (see footnotes 1 and 19–27 in Schwartz, 1991).

Notes

Introduction

2   **a little known fact that nicotine is a potent antidepressant:** Gilbert, (1995); Anda et al. (1999); Gilbert et al. (2002, pages 142–52).

2   **if no one much tunes into you and is responsive when you are an infant, you build up less of a sense of self:** Ogawa et al. (1997); Lyons-Ruth (2003).

2–3   **you are prone to emotional insecurity in relationships:** James (1995); Cassidy et al. (1999).

3   **the evidence for the role of genes has been greatly exaggerated:**
Many naturally incline to the cosy answer that 'it's a bit of both' nature and nurture but the evidence I presented eight years ago in *They F*** You Up* (Chapter 1) already showed that, even if you accepted the validity of studies of identical twins (which I do not) on which nearly all claims about the role of genes were based, they did not support this idea. For the vast majority of common traits, like sociability, memory or creativity, heritability was closer to a quarter.

     Then came the findings of the Human Genome Project, in 2001. To the horror of geneticists, Craig Venter, one of the main researchers, pointed out that the fact that we only have about 25,000 genes meant psychological differences between individuals could not be much determined by them – 'our environments are critical', he concluded.

     Initially, geneticists disputed this, but the last decade has seen an increasingly rapid retreat. After many millions of pounds and thousands of studies, attempts to identify genes that have much effect on our psychology have failed. The most distinguished researchers now admit that it is extremely unlikely that there are single genes for major mental illnesses, like schizophrenia. After decades of hearing from such people that there would be 'a gene for' almost everything, I admit to having felt a twinge of smugness.

Their fallback position is that it's lots of different genes interacting together that matter. But that very much remains to be seen and recently came the first sign that the geneticists may eventually have to admit defeat.

An editorial of the Journal of Child Psychology and Psychiatry was entitled 'It's the environment, stupid!'. The author, Edmund Sonaga-Burke (2010) confesses that 'serious science is now more than ever focused on the power of the environment ... all but the most dogged of genetic determinists have revised their view of the primacy of genetic factors'.

In Sonaga-Burke's own field, ADHD, he states that 'even the most comprehensive genome-wide scans available, with thousands of patients using hundreds of thousand of genetic markers ... appear to account for a relatively small proportion of disorder expression'. In plain English, genes hardly explain at all why some kids have ADHD and not others.

Another fallback is to claim that genes create vulnerabilities which environments may or may not cause to be expressed. This position took a massive blow at the end of 2009. Some studies had shown that people with a particular gene variant were more likely to become depressed if they were maltreated as children: the variant created a vulnerability. This was all but disproved.

An analysis of the 14,250 people whose DNA had been mapped in 14 different studies showed that those with the variant were not at greater risk of depression than those without it (Risch et al., 2009). Nor were they more likely to be depressed when the variant was combined with childhood maltreatment. Another recent study bears this out equally strongly. It showed that the nations with the lowest rates of depression are the ones most likely to have the variant that is supposed to cause depression (Chiao, J.Y. et al., 2009).

In Darwinian terms it has always made much more sense that we should be born plastic. Obviously genes confer fundamentals, like the capacity for humour or anger, but how much and how we express these is in response to our particular family situation, for which we need flexibility, not predetermination.

If genes play little part in how our children turn out, that is incredibly good, not bad news, for us as parents and as a society. Unlike our DNA, we can do something about them.

3   **the prism through which you experience your world**: Graham et al. (1999); Perry (2002); Gerhardt (2004).

5   **British psychoanalyst and psychologist called Joan Raphael-Leff**: Raphael-Leff (2005).

5   **About a quarter of British mums have this approach**: the proportions for the three approaches are in Raphael-Leff (2005).

5   **They are the ones who are most likely to have a full-time paid job**: the proportions of different kinds of mothers who work are discussed by Hakim (2000, page 6). Strictly speaking, this is an estimate because the categories Hakim has developed do not precisely overlap in all respects with those of Raphael-Leff. However, I believe they are sufficiently similar for it to be safe to assume that they are comparable. Hakim's categories are Home-Centred (my Hugger, Raphael-Leff's Facilitator), Work-Centred (my Organiser, Raphael-Leff's Regulator) and Adaptive (my Fleximum, Raphael-Leff's Reciprocator). Hakim argues that the total proportion of women who fit into the adaptive category varies between 40 and 80%, depending on the society. I have estimated it is half of current British mothers but this has not been properly tested; it could be more or less.

8   **are more at risk of emotional problems**: Melhuish et al. (2001).

9   **the other half do something different**: Johnston et al. (2008).

9   **you are liable to provide the same to your children**: Belsky et al. (2005).

9   **Studies of monkeys show the same**: Suomi (1997, pages 182–97); Cassidy et al. (1999).

10   **conflict between two cornerstones of their identity**: Johnston et al. (2007).

11   **rising to 7% at 12 months**: Leach (2009, page 49).

Chapter 1

17   **THE NEEDS OF BABIES**: much of the language used in this section was provided to me by Lucy Astor (2009, personal communication).

19   **picking up a pillow to do something, anything, to restore silence**: Fairbrother et al. (2008).

19   **About 15% of newborns**: Carey et al. (1995); Turecki (1995).

19   **made difficult by the pregnancy or birth: irritable or floppy or fussy**: in the vast majority of cases, this is not due to genes but to experiences during the pregnancy and the birth: Vaughan et al. (1999).

19   **slow to adapt to change and easily distracted**: Weiss et al. (2004).

19   **During the second month, as many as one fifth develop colic, often lasting several months**: Gormally et al. (1997).

19   **Undoubtedly, this increases the risk of the mother becoming depressed, depending on her vulnerability**: Murray (1993).

20   **it turns out all right in the end, with happy, secure babies and toddlers**: Vaughan et al. (1999).

20   **in which mother tunes into baby and gets the message**: Jaffee et al. (2001); Sander (2002); James (2002, chapter 5); Bakermans-Kranenburg et al. (2003); Gerhardt (2004); Jaffee (2007); Mcgowan (2008); Beebie et al. (2010).

20   **as vital to a baby's emotional health as vitamins for its physical survival**: Bowlby (1953, page 50).

20   **Having responsive care is equally vital for toddlers**: James (2002, chapter 4); Bakermans-Kranenburg et al. (2003); Gerhardt (2004); Mcgowan (2008).

20   **that being separate from mummy is enjoyable**: the most sophisticated account of this problem for both infant and toddler of getting to grips with the difference between 'me' and 'not-me', albeit quite a demanding read, is Winnicott (1972).

21   **they 'need' other children to play with at this age**: although there is no doubt that children can interact with others from early infancy (Hay et al. 2004), it is only during the third year that sustained interactions gradually become possible. As one authority puts it, 'Interactive skills enabling the generation of extended sequences of social interaction on a common cooperative theme progress rapidly during the third year of life', (Eckerman et al., 1988). Four out of five 18-month-olds will grab at toys, doing so an average of four times in a 45-minute period (Hay et al., 2000, page 45). Although the amount of such grabbing decreases as the child grows, a year later, the average number of grabs per 45 minutes is still two and a half, (Hay et al., 2000). Since such grabbing is still so common then, there needs to be close adult supervision of under-threes when in the company of peers. There is clear evidence that a toddler's risk of physical injury is increased if parental supervision is lax

(Morrongiello et al., 2008). When alone with mother, her sensitivity is critical in determining whether any potential for aggressive behaviour is expressed (Van Aken et al., 2007). If this is the case when alone with mother, given the limited capacity of toddlers to communicate and understand another child's viewpoint (Hay et al., 2004), it is all the more necessary for close adult supervision for under-threes when not with her. While developmental psychologists tend to stress the fact that both infants and toddlers have ever-growing capacities for social related-ness, despite providing evidence clearly proving that these are very limited, they tend to underplay this fact in reviewing the evidence, (e.g. Hay et al., 2004).

21   **Myth Two**: see Review 3.

22   **Myth Three**: a key point here is the difference between mainland Europe, where formal education rarely starts before age seven, and Britain. The Europeans have strong grounds for concentrating more on free play and nurture than teaching: Heckman (2006); UNICEF (2008). For an account of how early pressure to work hard for external rewards (praise, high exam marks) risks emotional damage, see James (2008, pages 85–108).

23   **those who have been coerced through fear**: James (2008, pages 85–108).

PART ONE

Chapter 2

27   **THE ESSENTIAL ORGANISER**: this section draws heavily on Raphael-Leff (2005, see esp. pages U84–107).

29–30 **An au pair or nanny is already in place in three-quarters of cases of Organisers who can afford it**: Raphael-Leff (1985).

30   **As Joan Raphael-Leff puts it**: Raphael-Leff (2005, page 357).

31   **it [...] becomes unresponsive, confirming your feeling**: Main (1989); Fonagy et al. (1991); James (1995, chapter 2).

33   **rises to 60% once the baby is older**: Sharp (1995).

33   **30% are, compared with 14% of Huggers and 11% of Fleximums**: Sharp et al. (2004).

34   **looking for a paid job and unable to find one**: see Review 8.

34   especially with a first-born male: Raphael-Leff (2005, page 334).

36–7 between half and three-quarters have at least a few days of baby
      blues: O'Hara et al. (1996, page 31); Nicolson (1998).

39   found their work dull, or disliked being in an office: Johnston et al.
      (2007).

39   it is absolutely essential for their child's well-being: Johnston et al.
      (2007, pages 447–59). See R5 and R6.

39   working mothers of under-threes: Leach et al. (2006); Leach (2009);
      Odone (2009); Dench (2010).

39   less likely to see it as important than poorer ones: Johnston et al.
      (2007).

41   subtly different from stimulation: James (2002, chapter 5);
      Bakermans-Kranenburg et al. (2003); Gerhardt (2004); McGowan
      (2008); Beebie et al (2010).

41   but not at such a young age: Heckman (2006); UNICEF (2008);
      James (2008, pages 85–108).

41   Organisers struggle to be on the same wavelength as a baby:
      NICHD ECCRN (1997, page 875); see also R3, pages 296–7.

43   the venom is at its most plentiful and poisonous: Smith et al. (2007).

45   often affect its future behaviour: Fonagy et al. (1991); Broussard et al.
      (2010, pages 159–72).

Chapter 3

52   what life is like for many high-achieving women: Berger (2000), a
      fascinating study of the psychology involved. This passage is extracted
      from James (2007).

53   the theory has been modified: Byrne (1999).

53   against the opposing efforts of other things or other persons:
      Feideman (1974).

53   in many senior managers or leaders: Board et al. (2005).

53   more are men than women: Sorensen et al. (1987).

53   critical of co-workers than non-Type As: Vroege et al. (1994).

53   work even longer hours than male Type As: Sorensen et al. (1987,
      pages 323–36).

53   less likely to place a high value on family life: Vroege et al. (1994).

53   tend to report having felt unloved as children: Matteson et al. (1987).

53–4 had parents who set high standards: Houston et al. (1991).

54 feelings of failure by attributing them to their offspring: Kliewer et al. (1987).

54 greater risk of depression than other women: Forgays et al. (2001).

54 As mothers: Haralson et al. (1992).

54 they are more controlling: Copeland (1990).

54 what is called psychodynamic therapy: the strongest evidence for the superiority of psychodynamic therapy over CBT is Knekt et al. (2008). For a meta-analysis of 23 studies revealing the effectiveness of psychodynamic therapy see Leichsenring et al. (2008). See also Shedler (2010).

54 instead of a real solution to the fundamental causes: for a critique of the effectiveness of CBT, see Westen et al. (2004).

56 tuned into their needs at one, eight and 24 months: Beckwith et al. (1999).

57 same pattern in adulthood as in early childhood: Waters et al. (2003); Weinfield et al. (2000).

57 About 40% of adults are insecure: Bakersman-Kranenburg et al. (2009).

57 commonest problems, like depression: Bakersman-Kranenburg et al. (2009).

Chapter 4

67 good scientific evidence that he would quickly calm down: Van Den Boom (1994); Vaughan et al. (1999); Jaffee (2007), Beebie et al. (2010).

Chapter 5

69 the other half react against it: Johnston et al. (2008).

72 self-critical by an over-controlling mother: James (2002, pages 68–71); James (2007, pages 182–9): detailed accounts of this pattern between mothers and daughters, resulting in pathological perfectionism.

72 Perfectionists can be healthy: Zhang et al. (2007, pages 1529–40).

73 punitive, authoritarian or over-controlling families: see pages 68–71, James (2002, pages 68–71); James (2007, pages 182–9).

74   boys show greater distress at the time: Coleman et al. (2009, page 89).
75   relationship with each parent and her age at the break-up: Rodgers
      et al. (1998).

Chapter 6

80   relatively unscathed by public commentary: Johnston et al. (2004).
81   trying to speed up its development at this stage: Heckman (2006);
      UNICEF (2008); James (2008, pages 85–108).
82   cases of autism: Dawson et al. (1997).
82   better outcomes (within the parameters of the disability): Dawson
      et al. (1997); Tully et al. (2004); Jacobsen et al. (2004); Brotman et
      al. (2007); Fisher et al. (2007).
88   evidence that you need to take on board: O'Connor et al. (2005).
89–90 these methods really do work: Mental Health Foundation (2009).
90   their partner is not pulling his weight: Sharp et al. (1995, 2004).
90   turn to neighbours, friends and family: Raphael-Leff (2005, page 357).
92   genes do not play a big part in causing it: Risch et al. (2009).
93   as people given the real thing: Healy (1997); Parker (2009).
93   Regarding the talking cures: Cooper et al. (2003).
93   confirmed Freud's basic ideas: James (2002, pages 88–90).
94   short-term treatments was published in 2008: Knekt et al. (2008).
94   23 other studies had similar findings: Leichsenring et al. (2008).
      See also Shedler (2010).
94   more important than their orientation: Roth et al. (1996).
96   Parent–infant psychotherapy: Bakermans-Kranenburg et al. (2005);
      Juffer et al. (2005); Lieberman et al. (2008).
98   with rejection by rejecting: Main (1989); Fonagy et al. (1991);
      James (1995, chapter 2).
101   help mothers to bond with their babies: Flacking et al. (2007);
      Zhang et al. (2008).
101   breastfed babies sleep better than bottle-fed ones: Doan et al.
      (2007).
101–2 There is also reason to suppose they are more secure: Montgomery
      et al. (2006).
103   do not lead to so-called contented babies: for not sleeping
      through the night as a result of going to babies when they wake up,

or if co-sleeping, see Johnson et al. (2008; see pages 765–6 for further studies supporting this). For greater insecurity as a result of strict sleep routines, see Higley et al (2009; see page 348 for three further studies showing insecurity and sleep problems go together). For evidence of greater irritability and fussiness as a result of routines, see St James-Roberts et al. (2006).

103   satisfied children and productive schoolchildren: Beckwith et al. (1999); Weinfield et al. (2000); Waters et al. (2003); Jaffee (2007); Bakersman-Kranenburg et al. (2009).

103   punitive patterns of punishment are harmful: James (2002, pages 106–9).

104   a depressed mother are insecure: for this statistic and the succeeding ones in this paragraph, see Belsky et al. (2000).

104   by substitutes, the greater the risk: NICHD ECCR (2003, page 997).

105   higher than the original ones at home: Ahnert et al. (2004).

105   nine different studies of under-threes in day care: Geoffroy et al. (2006); Vermeer et al. (2006).

105   time they spent in day care when under-three: Roisman et al. (2009).

105   greater risk than ones with no day care: Wakamura et al. (2009).

105   possible to normalise levels through better care: Brotman et al. (2007); Fisher et al. (2007).

106   There is overwhelming evidence: Hakim et al. (2008).

106   closer the substitute care is to a one-to-one ratio, the better: NICHD ECCRN (2000).

106   as likely to be as secure as those cared for at home by their mother: Ahnert et al. (2006).

107   au pair or sitter, and 10% were in day care: Leach (2009, page 49).

107   takes longer over settling a child into substitute care: NICHD ECCRN (2000).

108   getting on hunky-dory; as surveys show: James (2002, page 223).

109   it will be good for the child to be with its gran: Fergusson et al. (2008).

110   do not return to work for the money: Hakim et al. (2004); Leach et al. (2006); Leach (2009).

112   fixated on day care as a policy: Sinclair (2009, page 44).

PART TWO

Chapter 7

124 **THE ESSENTIAL HUGGER**: this section draws heavily on Raphael-Leff (2005).

124 **monkeys duplicate the amount that they were loved**: Suomi (1997, pages 182–97); Cassidy et al. (1999).

124 **intergenerationally, for human mothers**: Grusec et al. (1995); Johnston et al. (2008).

124 **faults seem like reasons for adoration**: Tallis (2005).

128 **of post-natal depression is having been depressed before**: Henshaw (2003).

129 **rather than being dangerous, it is natural**: McKenna et al. (2007).

130 **that the earlier the experience (good or bad), the greater its subsequent impact**: James (2002, pages 153–9).

130 **the kind of care provided is critical**: Vaughan et al. (1999).

133 **to demand attention during the night**: St James-Roberts et al. (2006).

133 **the child may feel more secure**: Johnson et al. (2008); Beebie et al. (2010).

133 **and sleep easier in later life**: Higley et al. (2009).

Chapter 8

136 **getting married and looking after their children**: Hakim (2000, page 6).

137 **when this advice is given it promotes successful breastfeeding outcomes**: Renfrew et al. (2010).

138 **The definitive study**: Van den Boom (1994); see also Jaffee (2007).

138 **likely if the mother is warm and supportive in early life**: Tully et al. (2004).

138 **if the mother is emotionally sensitive and mentally stimulating**: Jacobson et al. (2004).

139 **having overcome their initial impairment**: Jaffee (2007).

139 **with only half of infants not given this kind of care**: Scher et al. (2001, pages 325–33).

139 **but they have been done with monkeys**: Cassidy et al. (1999, pages 192–3).

141 **get depressed during the early months**: Sharp et al. (2004).

141 never letting them be themselves: Sharp et al. (2004).

141 concerned about their baby's welfare in inappropriate situations: Scher et al. (2000).

141 are at greatly increased risk of depression: Scher et al. (2000); Sharp et al. (2004).

142 having to work or having an unsupportive partner: Sharp (1995).

142 part-timers are least at risk: Brown et al. (1990).

145 who is completely tuned into them: Jaffee et al. (2001); Sander (2002); Mcgowan (2008).

146 if the parents go to them and offer nurture: Johnson et al. (2008, see pages 765–6 for further studies supporting this).

146 they are more likely to be insecure at age one: Higley et al. (2009, pages 347–63; see page 348 for three further studies showing insecurity and sleep problems go together).

146 are less irritable and fussy at three months: St James-Roberts et al. (2006, pages 146–55).

146 depression when they get to the age of three, four and five: James (2002, see pages 153–161, especially page 156); Jaffee (2007).

146 in later life related to lack of early responsiveness: Ogawa et al. (1997); Weinfield et al. (2000); Lyons-Ruth et al. (2003); Waters et al. (2003); Bakermans- Kranenburg et al. (2009); Broussard et al. (2010).

147 factors (like maltreatment) are taken into account: O'Connor et al. (2005).

Chapter 9

152 they do not return to paid work primarily for the money: Leach et al. (2006); Johnston et al. (2007); Hakim et al. (2009); Odone (2009); Dench (2010).

152 sharing life with peers in the workplace: Hakim (2000, page 101).

155 60% lower incomes than ones with two: Offer (2006, page 254).

161 want to be a breadwinner: Hakim (2000, page 71).

Chapter 10

164 very early levels of attunement to the baby have a big effect: Jaffee et al. (2001); Sander (2002); James (2002, chapter 5); Bakermans-

NOTES

Kranenburg et al. (2003); Gerhardt (2004); Jaffee (2007); Mcgowan (2008); Beebie et al. (2010).

165 **mothers and babies supports Charlotte's theory**: Jaffee et al. (2001); Sander (2002); Mcgowan (2008); Beebie et al. (2010).

167 **who did provide some love**: Egeland et al. (2003).

170 **passion can make adults suicidal**: Tallis (2005).

170 **imagining dangers, becoming oversolicitious**: Scher et al. (2000).

170 **may sense its mother's distress**: Jaffee et al. (2001).

170 **Hugger babies are less likely to suck thumbs**: Scher et al. (2000).

Chapter 11

173 **a calm, satiable, fulfilled adult**: Ogawa et al. (1997); Weinfield et al. (2000); Lyons-Ruth et al. (2003); Waters et al. (2003); Bakermans-Kranenburg et al. (2009).

173 **genes probably play a negligible role**: James (2002, chapter 1).

173 **the well-being of babies**: Jaffee et al. (2001); Sander (2002); St James-Roberts et al. (2006); Mcgowan (2008); Higley et al. (2009); Beebie et al. (2010).

174 **mothers with other approaches**: Johnston et al. (2007).

176 **a big difference to their level of functioning**: Dawson et al. (1997).

176 **if your child is born with a severe limitation to its cognitive potential**: Tully et al. (2004); Jacobson et al. (2004).

176 **the early weeks and three months old**: Gormally et al. (1997).

176 **neonates born floppy, irritable or fussy**: Carey et al. (1995).

176 **resulting from the pregnancy and birth**: Vaughan et al. (1999).

177 **a beneficial approach**: McKenna et al. (2007).

180 **regular habit, as is suggested by the evidence**: Gershoff et al. (2007, pages 231–72).

179 **half of mothers have done so**: Fairbrother et al. (2008).

180 **punitive currency becomes devalued**: Patterson (1982).

181 **perfectionist control freak themselves**: Zhang et al. (2007); see also refs for Perfectionism in the indices of *They F*** You Up* and *Affluenza*.

184 **as studies of this method have demonstrated**: Weich et al. (2006, pages 3–12).

193 **anything other than look after their children**: Hakim (2000, page 6).

PART THREE

Chapter 12

199 **THE ESSENTIAL FLEXIMUM:** This section draws on Raphael-Leff's (2005) account of the Reciprocator orientation to motherhood. However it deviates from her account in some important respects. Raphael-Leff's Reciprocator category does not include a pathological variant, so she does not believe there is an Extreme Reciprocator (Raphael-Leff uses Extreme to describe some Huggers and Organisers indicating potential pathology). Whereas she regards both Hugging and Organising as sometimes defence mechanisms that mothers use when the vulnerability of their infant reminds them of their own infancy, she does not see the Reciprocator approach as a defence. Nor do we altogether agree about the implications for children of this approach. So although the concept of the Fleximum is originally derived from that of the Reciprocator, there are important differences between our formulations.

201 **strong positions in the Mommy Wars:** Johnston et al. (2004).

202 **harm will come to them, like accidents:** Scher et al. (2000).

Chapter 13

215 **not only their mother who can meet their needs:** Johnston et al. (2007).

215 **stressing personally fulfilling elements instead:** Johnston et al. (2007).

Chapter 14

222 **an hour after the mother has left:** Ahnert et al. (2004).

223 **known as avoidant attachment:** James (2002, pages 176–8).

Chapter 15

232 **indeed, it may be the secret for everyone:** James (2008, pages 108–117).

Chapter 16

237   peddled by the likes of Paul McKenna: James (2007, chapter 3).

Chapter 17

249   the mother uses the baby to comfort herself: Jaffee et al. (2001).

249–50 children significantly more than Organisers, for example: Haimov (1995).

250   something which will produce an insecure child: Scher et al. (2001).

250   actually produces irritable, fussy three-month-olds: St James-Roberts et al. (2006).

250   badly upset the baby and toddler: NICHD ECCRN (1997, page 875).

250   who have a weak sense of self: Jaffee et al. (2001); Sander (2002); Mcgowan (2008).

250   leaves them feeling empty and sad: Ogawa et al. (1997); Weinfield et al. (2000); Lyons-Ruth et al.(2003); Waters et al. (2003); Bakermans-Kranenburg et al. (2009).

251   45%, versus 8% extreme Huggers: Scher et al. (2001).

252–3 significantly elevated five months after starting day care: Ahnert et al. (2004).

255   win-win 'reframing' as their method: Johnstone et al. (2007).

256   worker are successfully integrated: Johnstone et al. (2007).

257   culture constantly encourages them to be more selfish: Twenge (2007).

258   32% of 16–24-year-olds) … McManus et al. (2009).

Bibliography

Administration on Children, Youth and Families, 2002, *Making a difference in the lives of Infants, Toddlers and Their Families,* Washington D.C.: Dept Health and ——Human Services.

Ahnert, L. et al., 2001, 'The East German child care system: associations with caretaking and caretaking beliefs, and early attachment and adjustment', *American Behavioural Scientist,* 44, 1843–63.

Ahnert L. et al., 2004, 'Transition to child care: Association with infant-mother attachment, infant negative emotion and cortisol elevations', *Child Development,* 75, 639–50.

Ahnert, L. et al., 2006, 'Security of children's relationships with nonparental care providers: a meta-analysis', *Child Development,* 77, 664–79.

Albus, K.E. et al., 1999, 'Indiscriminate friendliness and terror of strangers in infancy', *Infant Mental Health Journal,* 20, 30–41.

Alder, E. and Cox, J.L., 1983, 'Breast feeding and postnatal depression', *J. of Psychosomatic Research,* 272, 139–44.

Alder, E. and Bancroft, J. 1986, 'The relationship between breast feeding persistence, sexuality and mood in postpartum women', *Psychological Medicine,* 18, 389–96.

Alink, L.R.A. et al., 2008, 'Cortisol and externalizing behavior in children and adolescents: mixed meta-analytic evidence for the inverse relation of basal cortisol and cortisol reactivity with externalizing behavior', *Developmental Psychobiology,* 50, 427–50.

Allen, TD et al., 2000, 'Consequences associated with work-to-family conflict', *J of Occupational Health Psychology,* 5, 278–308.

Anda, R/F/ et al., 1999, 'Adverse childhood experiences and smoking during adolescence', *JAMA,* 282, 1652–8.

Ashman, S.B. et al., 2002, 'Stress hormone levels of children of depressed mothers', *Development and Psychopathology*, 14, 333–439.

Bakermans–Kranenburg, M.J. et al., 2003, 'Less is more: Meta-analyses of sensitivity and attachment interventions in early childhood', *Psychological Bulletin*, 129, 195–215.

Bakermans–Kranenburg, M.J. et al., 2005, 'Disorganized infant attachment and preventive interventions: a review and meta-analysis', *Infant Mental Health*, 26, 191–216.

Bakermans–Kranenburg, M.J. et al., 2008, 'Effects of an attachment–based intervention on daily cortisol moderated by dopamine receptor D4', *Development and Psychopathology*, 20, 805–820.

Bakersman–Kranenburg, M.J. et al., 2009, 'The first 10,000 Adult Attachment Interviews: distribution of adult attachment representations in clinical and non-clinical groups', *Attachment & Human Development*, 11, 223–63.

Beckwith. L. et al., 1999, 'Maternal sensitivity during infancy and subsequent life events relate to attachment representations at early adulthood', *Developmental Psychology*, 33, 693–700.

Beebe, B. et al., 2010, 'The origins of 12-month attachment: A microanalysis of 4-month mother-infant interaction', *Attachment & Human Development*, 12: 1, 3–141.

Belsky, J. et al., 2000, 'Attachment: theory and evidence', in Rutter, M. et al., *Developmental Principles and Clinical Issues in Psychology and Psychiatry*, Oxford: Blackwell.

Belsky, J. et al., 2005, 'Intergenerational transmission of warm-sensitive-stimulating parenting: A prospective study of mothers and fathers of 3-year-olds', *Child Development*, 76, 384–96.

Belsky, J. et al., 2006, 'Effects of Sure Start Local Programmes on children and families', *British Medical Journal*, 332 (7556): 1476.

Belsky, J., 1986, 'Infant day care: a cause for concern', *Zero To Three*, September, 1–7.

Belsky, J., 1988, 'The 'effects' of day care reconsidered', *Early Childhood Quarterly*, 2, 333–73.

Berger, B., 2000, 'Prisoners of liberation: a psychoanalytic perspective on disenchantment and burnout among career women lawyers', *J of Clinical Psychology*, 56, 665–73.

Berger, L.M. et al., 2005, 'Maternity leave, early maternal employment and child health and development in the US', *The Economic Journal*, 115, F29–F45.

Bifulco, A. et al., 1998, *Wednesday's Child*, London; Routledge.

Blackwell, L.S. et al., 2007, 'Implicit theories of intelligence predict intelligence', *Child Development*, 78, 246–63.

Board, B.J. et al., 2005, 'Disordered personalities at work', *Psychology, Crime and Law*, 11, 17–32.

Bowlby, J., 1953, *Child Care and the Growth of Love*, London: Penguin.

Brotman, L.M. et al., 2007, 'Effects of a psychosocial family-based preventive intervention on cortisol responses to a social challenge in preschoolers at high risk for antisocial behavior', *Archives of General Psychiatry*, 64, 1172–79.

Brown, G.W. and Moran, P., 1994, 'Clinical and psychosocial origins of chronic depressive episodes I: a community survey', *British J. of Psychiatry*, 165, 447–56.

Brown, G.W. and Moran, P., 1997, 'Single mothers, poverty and depression', *Psychological Medicine*, 27, 21–33.

Brown, G.W. et al., 1990, 'Motherhood, employment and the development of depression', *British J of Psychiatry*, 156, 169–79.

Brown, G.W., and Harris, T., 1978, *Social Origins of Depression*, London: Tavistock.

Bugenthal, D.B. et al., 1989, 'Perceived control over caregiving outcomes: implications for child abuse', *Developmental Psychology*, 25, 532–9.

Bugenthal, D.B. et al., 2004, 'Predicting infant maltreatment in low-income families', *Developmental Psychology*, 40, 234–43.

Bussel, J.H. et al., 2008, 'Anxiety in pregnant and postpartum women. An exploratory study of the role of maternal orientations', *Journal of Affective Disorders*, 114, 232–242.

Byrne, D.G., 1999, 'Type A behavior, anxiety and neuroticism: reconceptualizing the pathophysiological pathos and boundaries of coronary-prone behaviour', *Stress and Medicine*, 12, 227–38.

Carey, W.B. et al., 1995, *Coping with Children's Temperament*, New York: Basic Books.

Cassidy, J. et al., 1999, *Handbook of Attachment*, New York: Guilford.

Chavira, V. et al., 2000, 'Latina mothers' attributions, emotions and reactions to the problem behaviours of their children with developmental disabilities', *Child Development*, 41, 245–52.

Chiao, J.Y. et al., 2009, 'Culture–gene coevolution of individualism–collectivism and the serotonin transporter gene', *Proceedings of the Royal Society B*, February 22, 2010, 277, 529–537.

Chisholm, K., 1998, 'A three year follow–up of attachment and indiscriminate friendliness in children adopted from Romanian orhphanages', *Child Development*, 69, 1092–1106.

Coleman, L. et al., 2009, *When Couples Part*, London: One Plus One.

Cooper, P.J. et al., 2003, 'Controlled trial of the short- and long-term effect of psychological treatment of post–partum depression', *British J of Psychiatry*, 182, 412–9.

Copeland, A.P., 1990, 'Behavioral differences in the interactions between Type A and Type B mothers and their children', *Behavioral Medicine*, 15 (Fall), 111–8.

Cox, J.L. et al., 1993, 'A controlled study of onset, duration and prevalence of postnatal depression', *British Journal of Psychiatry*, 184, 34–40.

Crawford, T.N et al., 2009, 'Early maternal separation and the trajectory of borderline personality disorder symptoms', *Development and Psychopathology*, 21, 1013–30.

Dawson, G. et al., 1997, 'Early intervention in autism', in Guralnick, M.J., *The Effectiveness of Early Interventions*, 307–26, Baltimore MD: Brookes.

Dawson, G. et al., 2000, 'The role of early experience in shaping behavioural and brain development and its implications for social policy', *Development and Psychopathology*, 12, 695–712.

Daycare Trust, 2009, *Quality Costs*, London: Daycare Trust.

De Mause, L., 1974, *The History of Childhood*, London: Souvenir Press.

De Wolf, M.S. et al., 1997, 'Sensitivity and attachment', *Child Development*, 68, 571–91.

Dench, G., 2010, *What Women Want: Evidence from British Social Attitudes*, London: Hera Trust.

Dettling, A.C. et al., 1999, 'Cortisol levels of young children in full-day child-care centers: relations with age and temperament', *Psychoneuroendocrinology*, 24, 519–36.

Dex, S. et al., 2007, *Parental Care and Employment in Early Childhood*, London: Institute of Education.

Dmitrieva, J. et al., 2007, 'Child care history, classroom composition and children's functioning in kindergarden', *Psychological Science*, 18, 1032–9.

Doan, T.R.N. et al., 2007, *Journal of Perinatal & Neonatal Nursing*, 21(3), 200–206.

Eckerman, C.O. et al., 1988, 'Lessons drawn from observing young peers together', *Acta Paediatrica Scandinavica Supplement*, 344, 55–70.

Egeland, B. et al., 2003, 'Resilience as process', *Development and Psychopathology*, 5, 517–28.

Ermisch, J. et al., 2000, *The Effect of Parents' Employment and Children On Children's Educational Attainment*, IZA: Discussion Paper No 215.

Ermisch, J. et al., 2001, *The effect of parents' employment on children's lives*, York: Joseph Rowntree Trust.

Fairbrother, N. et al., 2008, 'New mothers' thoughts of harm related to the newborn', *Archives of Women's Mental Health*, 11, 221–9.

Feideman, M. 1974, *Type A Behavior and Your Heart*, New York: Knopf.

Feinstein, L., 2003, 'Inequality in the early cognitive development of British children in the 1970 cohort', *Economica*, 70, 73–97.

Fergusson, E. et al., 2008, 'Which children receive grandparental care and what effect does it have?', *J of Child Psychology and Psychiatry*, 49, 161–9.

Fielding, H., 1997, *Bridget Jones's Diary*, London; Picador.

Fisher, P.A. et al., 2007, 'Effects of a therapeutic intervention for foster preschoolers on diurnal cortisol activity', *Psychoneuroenocrinology*, 32, 892–905.

Flacking, R. et al., 2007, ' "I wanted to do a good job": Experiences of 'becoming a mother' and breastfeeding in mothers of very preterm infants after discharge from a neonatal unit', *Social Science and Medicine* 64 (12), 2405–2416.

Fonagy, P. et al., 1991, 'Maternal representation of attachment during pregnancy predict the organization of infant-other attachment at one year of age', *Child Development*, 62, 891–905.

Forgays, D.K. et al., 2001, 'Parenting stress in employed and at-home mothers in Italy', *J of Family and Economic Issues*, 22, 327–51.

Geoffroy, M.C. et al., 2006, 'Daycare attendance, stress and mental health', *Canadian Journal of Psychiatry*, 51, 607–15.

George, C. et al., 1999, 'Attachment and caregiving', in *Handbook of Attachment*, Cassidy, J. et al., London: Guilford Press.

Gerhardt, S., 2004, *Why Love Matters*, Hove: Brunner–Routledge.

Gershoff, E.T. et al., 2007, 'The case against corporal punishment of children', *Psychology, Public Policy and Law*, 13, 231–72.

Gibson, J et al., 2009, 'A systematic review of studies validating the Edinburgh Postnatal Depression Scale in Antepartum and Postpartum women', *Acta Psychiatrica Scandinavica*, 119, 350–64.

Gilbert, D.G., 1995, *Smoking: Individual Differences Psychopathology and Emotion*, London: Taylor and Francis.

Gilbert, D.G. et al., 2002, 'Mood disturbance fails to resolve across 31 days of cigarette abstinences in women', *J of Consulting and Clinical Psychology*, 70, 142–52.

Good, C. et al., 2003, 'Improving adolescents' standardized test performance: An intervention to reduce the effects of stereotype threat', *J of Applied Developmental Psychology*, 24, 645–62.

Gormally, S. et al., 1997, 'Of clinical pies and clinical clues', *Ambulatory Child Health*, 3, 137–53.

Gove, W.R. et al., 1979, 'Sex differences in the epidemiology of mental disorder: evidence and explanations', in Gomberg, E.S. et al., *Gender and Disordered Behaviour*, New York: Brunner/Mazel.

Graham, Y. et al., 1999, 'The effects of neonatal stress on brain development', *Development and Psychopathology*, 11, 545–65.

Grant, K.-A. et al., 2009, 'Maternal prenatal anxiety, postnatal caregiving and infants' cortisol response to the still-face procedure', *Developmental Psychobiology*, 51, 625–37.

Grusec, J.E. et al., 1995, 'Features and sources of parents' attributions about themselves and their children', in Eisenberg, N., *Social Development, Review of Personality and Social Psychology*, 15, 49–73, Thousand Oaks, CA: Sage.

Gump, B.B. et al., 2009, 'Trajectories of maternal depressive symptoms over her child's life span: relation to adrenocortical, cardiovascular and emotional function in children', *Development and Psychopathology*, 21, 207–225.

Gunnar, M.R. et al., 2001, 'Salivary cortisol levels in children adopted from Romanian orphanages', *Development and Psychopathology*, 13, 611–28.

Gunnar, M.R. et al., 2006, 'Bringing basic research on early experience and stress neurobiology to bear on preventive interventions for neglected and maltreated children', *Development and Psychopathology*, 18, 651–77.

Guzell, J.R. et al., 2004, 'Parental perceived control over caregiving and its relationship to parent-infant interaction', *Child Development*, 75, 134–46.

Haimov, Y., 1995, 'Maternal didactic and social behaviour in free play at ages one, two and three years', Thesis for MA Degree, Haifa: University of Haifa.

Hakim, C. et al., 2008, *Little Britons*, London: Policy Exchange.

Hakim, C., 2000, *Work-Lifestyle Choices in the 21st Century: Preference Theory*, Oxford: OUP.

Haralson, T.L. et al., 1992, 'The relationship of parenting styles and social competency to Type A behavior in children', *J of Psychosomatic Research*, 36, 625–34.

Harris, T.O. et al., 1987, 'Loss of parent in childhood and adult psychiatric disorder: the role of social class position and premarital pregnancy', *Psychological Medicine*, 17, 163–83.

Haskins, R. et al., 1986, 'Daycare and illness', *Pediatrics*, 77, 951–82.

Hawkins, S.S. et al., 2009, 'Examining the relationship between maternal employment and health behaviour in 5-year-old British children', *J of Epidemiological Community Health*, O, 1–6.

Hay, D.F. et al., 2000, 'Toddlers' use of force against familiar peers: a precursor of serious aggression?', *Child Development*, 71, 457–67.

Hay, D.F. et al., 2004, 'Peer relations in childhood', *J of Child Psychology and Psychiatry*, 45, 84–108.

Healy, D., 1997, *The Antidepressant Era*, Cambridge: Harvard University Press.

Heckman, J.J., 2006, *Investing in Disadvantaged Young Children is an Economically Efficient Policy*, presented at the Committee for Economic Development/ The Pew Charitable Trusts/PNC Financial Services Group Forum on 'Building the Economic Case for Investments in Preschool', New York, January 10, 2006.

Henderson, V.L. et al., 1990, in Feldman, S. et al., *At The Threshold: The Developing Adolescent*, MA: Harvard University Press.

Henshaw, C., 2003, 'Mood disturbance in the early puerperium: a review', *Archives of Women's Mental Health*, 6, s.33–s.42.

Hess, L.E., 1995, 'Changing family patterns in Western Europe', in Rutter, M. and Smith, D.J., *Psychosocial Disorders in Young People*, Chichester: Wiley.

Higley, E. et al., 2009, 'Nightime maternal responsiveness and infant attachment at one year', *Attachment and Human Behaviour*, 11, 347–63.

Hill, J.L. et al., 2005, 'Maternal emploment and child development', *Developmental Psychology*, 41, 833–50.

Himmelstein, S. et al., 1991, 'An attributional analysis of maternal beliefs about the importance of child-rearing practices', *Child Development*, 62, 301–10.

Hock, E. et al., 1988, 'Maternal separation anxiety' in *Maternal Employment and Children's Development*, Gottfied, A. et al., Plenum: New York.

Hoppman, C. et al., 2006, 'Daily goal pursuits predict cortisol secretion and mood states in employed parents with preschool children', *Psychosomatic Medicine*, 68, 887–94.

Houston, B.K. et al., 1991, 'Cynical hostility; developmental factors, psychosocial correlates and health behaviors', *Health Psychology*, 10, 9–17.

Inter-Departmental Childcare Review, 2002, *Delivering for Children and Families*, London: ONS.

Jacobson, S.W. et al., 2004, 'Maternal age, alcohol abuse history, and quality of parenting as moderators of the effects of prenatal alcohol exposure on 7.5 year intellectual functioning', *Alcoholism: Clinical and Experimental Research*, 28,1732–45.

Jaffee, J. et al., 2001, 'Rhythms of dialogue in infancy: coordinated timing in development', *Monographs of the Society for Research in Child Development*, 66.

Jaffee, S.R., 2007, 'Sensitive, stimulating caregiving predicts cognitive and behavioural resilience in neurodevelopmentally at-risk infants', *Development and Psychopathology*, 19, 631–47.

James, O.W., 1995, *Juvenile Violence in a Winner-Loser Culture*, London: Free Association Books.

James, O.W., 2002, *They F*** You Up*, London: Bloomsbury.

James, O.W., 2007, *Affluenza*, London: Vermilion.

James, O.W., 2008, *The Selfish Capitalist*, London: Vermilion.

James, O.W., 2010, *Britain on the Couch*, London: Vermilion.

Johnson, J.G. et al., 1997, 'Childhood maltreatment increases risk for personality disorders during early adulthood', *Neuroscience and Biochemical Review*, 16, 115–30.

Johnson, N. et al., 2008, 'Preschoolers' sleep behaviour', *J of Child Psychology and Psychiatry*, 49, 765–73.

Johnston, D.D. et al., 2004, 'Mom hating moms: the internalization of Mother War rhetoric', *Sex Roles*, 51, 497–509.

Johnston, D.D. et al., 2007, 'Cognitive acrobatics in the construction of the worker–mother identity', *Sex Roles*, 57, 447–59.

Johnston, D.D. et al., 2008, 'Mother's work history in the construction of adult daughter's worker-mother discursive strategies', *Sociological Focus*, 41, 159–176.

Juffer, F. et al., 2005, Chapter 11, 'Enhancing children's socioemotional development a review of intervention studies', in The *Handbook of Research Methods in Developmental Science*, Teti, D.M., Oxford: Blackwell.

Kelly, R.E. et al., 2006, 'Relationship between drug company funding and outcomes of clinical psychiatric research', *Psychological Medicine*, 36, 1647–56.

Kiang, L. et al., 2004, 'Maternal preconceptions about parenting predict child temperament, maternal sensitivity and children's empathy', *Developmental Psychology*, 40, 1081–92.

Kliewer, W. et al., 1987, 'Type A behavior and aspirations: a study of parents' and children's goal setting', *Developmental Psychology*, 23, 204–9.

Knekt, P et al., 2008, 'Randomized trial on the effectiveness of long- and short-term psychodynamic psychotherapy and solution-focused therapy on psychiatric symptoms during a 3-year follow-up', *Psychological Medicine*, 38, 689–703.

Koren–Karie, N., 2001, 'Mothers' attachment representations and choice of infant care: center care vs. home', *Infant and Child Development*, 10, 117–27.

Koren–Karie, N. et al., 2005, 'The emotional quality of childcare centers in Israel', *Infant Mental Health Journal*, 26, 110–26.

Leach, P. et al., 2006, 'Child Care Before 6 months of Age', *Infant and Child Development*, 15, 471–502.

Leach, P., 1994, *Children First*, London: Michael Joseph.

Leach, P., 2009, *Child Care Today*, Cambridge: Polity Press.

Lee, K., 1996, 'A Study of Teacher Responses Based on Their Conceptions of Intelligence', *J of Classroom Interactions*, 31, 1–12.

Leichsenring, F. et al., 2008, 'Effectiveness of long-term psychodynamic psychotherapy: a meta-analysis', *JAMA*, 300, 13, 1551–65.

Lieberman, A.F. et al., 2008, *Psychotherapy with infants and young children: Repairing the effects of stress and trauma on early attachment*, London: Guilford Press.

Love, J.M et al., 2001, *Building Their Futures*, Washington D.C.: Dept. Health and Human Services.

Love, J.M. et al., 2005, 'The effectiveness of early head start for 3-year-old children and their parents: lessons for policy and programs', *Developmental Psychology*, 41, 885–901.

Lyons-Ruth, K., 2003, 'Dissociation and the parent–infant dialogue', *J American Psychoanalytic Association*, 51, 883–912.

Main, M., 1989, 'Parental careism to infant-initiated contact is correlated with the parents' own rejection during childhood', in Brazelton, T.B. et al., *Touch*, New York: IUP.

Mandiaki, K. et al., 2005, 'Parents' causal attributions about attention deficit/hyperactivity disorder: the effect of child and parent sex', *Child Care Health and Development*, 31, 331–40.

Matteson, M.T. et al., 1987, 'A test of cognitive social-learning model of Type A behavior', *J of Human Stress*, 13, 23–31.

McGowan, J., 2008, 'The microanalytic precursors of secure versus insecure attachment: A brief report', *Graduate Student J of Psychology*, 10, 46–51.

McKenna, J.J. et al., 2007, 'Mother–infant cosleeping, breastfeeding and sudden infant death syndrome', *American J of Physical Anthropology*, 134, 133–61.

McLaughlin, A.E. et al., 2007, 'Depressive symptoms in young adults: the influences of the early home environment and early educational child care', *Child Development*, 78, 746–56.

McManus, S. et al, 2009, *Adult Psychiatric Morbidity in England, 2007*, London: Office of National Statistics.

Melchior A. et al., 2007, 'The mental health effects of multiple work and family demands', *Social Psychiatry and Psychiatric Epidemiology*, 42, 573–82.

Melhuish, E. et al., 2001, 'Cognitive and social/behavioural development at 3-4 years in relation to family background', Technical Paper 7, *The Effective Provision of Pre-school Education Project*, London: Institute of Education/DFES.

Melhuish, E. et al., 2002, *Pre-school experience and social/behavioural development at the start of Primary school*, Belfast, N.I.: Stranmills Univ Press.

Melhuish, E.C. et al., 1991, 'How similar are day care groups before the start of day care?', *J of Applied Developmental Psychology*, 12, 331-46.

Mental Health Foundation, 2009, *Mindfulness Q&As*, London: MHF.

Mills-Koonce, R. et al., 2009, 'Psychophysiological correlates of parenting behaviour in mothers of young children', *Developmental Psychobiology*, 51, 650-61.

Mirowsky, J. et al., 1989, *Social Causes of Psychological Distress*, New York: Aldine De Gruyter.

Montgomery, S.M. et al., 2006, 'Breast feeding and resilience against psychosocial stress', *Archives of Disease in Childhood*, 91, 990-994.

Moore, S.C. et al., 2009, 'Confectionery consumption in children and adult violence', *British Journal of Psychiatry*, 195, 366-7.

Morrongiello, B.A. et al., 2008, 'Interactions between child behaviour patterns and parent support', *Child Development*, 79, 3, 627-38.

Mother and Baby Magazine, 'Mother and Baby Sleep Survey', 2002, April.

Murray, L., 1993, 'The role of infant irritability in postnatal depression in a Cambridge (UK) community population', in Brazelton, T.B. and Lester, B.M., *The Cultural Context of Infancy, Vol. 3*, New Jersey: Ablex.

NICHD-ECCRN, 1997, 'The effects of infant child care on infant–mother security', *Child Development*, 68, 860-79.

NICHD-ECCRN, 2000, 'Characteristics and quality of child care for toddlers and preschoolers', *Applied Developmental Science*, 4, 116-135.

NICHD-ECCRN, 2003, 'Does amount of time in child care predict socioemotional adjustment during the transition to kindergarden', *Child Development*, 74, 976-1005.

NICHD-ECCRN, 2003a, 'Early child care and mother–child interaction from 35 months through First Grade,' *Infant Behavior and Development*, 26, 345-70.

Nicolson, P., 1998, *Post-Natal Depression: Psychology, Science and the Transition to Motherhood*, London: Routledge.

O'Connor, T.G. et al., 2005, 'Prenatal anxiety predicts individual differences in cortisol in pre-adolescent children', *Biological Psychiatry*, 58, 211-7.

Odone, C., 2009, *What Women Want*, London: Centre for Policy Studies.

Offer, A., 2006, *The Challenge of Affluence*, Oxford: OUP.

Ogawa, J. et al., 1997, 'Development and the fragmented self: longitudinal study of dissociative symptomatology in a nonclinical sample', *Development and Psychopathology*, 9, 855–79.

O'Hara, M.W. et al., 1996, 'Rates and risk of postpartum depression – a meta-analysis', *International Review of Psychiatry*, 8, 37–54.

ONS, 2010 (personal communication to the author on request for this statistic).

Oppenheim, D., 1998, 'Perspectives on infant mental health from Israel: the case of changes in collective sleeping on the Kibbutz', *Infant Mental Health Journal*, 19, 76–86.

Owen, M.T. et al., 1988, 'Maternal employment and the transition to parenthood', in Gottfried, A.E. et al., *Maternal Employment and Children's Development*, New York: Plenum Press.

Parker, G., 2009, 'Antidepressants on trial: how valid is the evidence?', *British J of Psychiatry*, 194, 1–3.

Patterson, G.R, 1982, *Coercive Family Processes*, Eugene, OR: Castalia Publishing.

Peisner–Feinberg, E, et al., 1997, 'Relations between preschool children's care experiences and concurrent development', *Merril–Palmer Quarterly*, 43, 451–77.

Perry, B., 2002, 'Childhood experience and the expression of genetic potential: what childhood neglect tells us about nature and nurture', *Brain and Mind*, 3, 79–100.

Pesonen, A-K. et al., 2007, 'Depressive symptoms in adults separated from their parents as children', *American J of Epidemiology*, 166, 1126–33.

Peters, J., 1997, *When Mothers Work: loving our children without sacrificing ourselves*, Reading, MA: Perseus Books.

Pomerantz, E. M. et al., 2006, 'The effects of mothers' perceptions of children's competence: The moderating role of mothers' theories of competence', *Developmental Psychology*, 42, 950–961.

Ramey, S.L., 2005, 'Commentary', in NICHD-ECCRN, *Child Care and Child Development*, New York: Guilford Press.

Raphael-Leff, J., 1985, 'Facilitators and Regulators: vulnerability to postnatal disturbance', *J of Psychosomatic Obstetrics and Gynaecology*, 4, 151–68.

Raphael–Leff, J., 2005, *Psychological Processes of Childbearing*, London: The Anna Freud Centre.

Read, J. et al., 2004, *Models of Madness*, Hove: Brunner–Routledge.

Read, J. et al., 2006, 'Prejudice and schizophrenia: a review of the 'mental illness is an illness like any other' approach', *Acta Psychiatrica Scandinavica*, 113, 1–16.

Renfrew, M.J. et al., 2010, 'Breastfeeding promotion for infants in neonatal units: a systematic review', *Child: Care, Health and Development*, 36, 165–78.

Riechlin, S., 1993, 'Neuroendocrine-immune interactions', *New England Journal of Medicine*, 329, 1246–53.

Risch, N. et al., 2009, 'Interaction between the serotonin transporter gene (5-HTTLPR), stressful life events and risk of depression: a meta-analysis', *JAMA*, 301, 2462–71.

Rodgers, B. et al., 1998, *Divorce and Separation*, York: Joseph Rowntree Foundation.

Roisman, G.I. et al., 2009, 'Early family and child care antecedents of awakening cortisol levels in adolescence', *Child Development*, 80, 907–20.

Ronsaville, D.S. et al., 2006, 'Maternal and environmental factors influence the hypothalamic-pituitary-adrenal axis response to corticotropin-releasing hormone infusion in offspring of mothers with or without mood disorders', *Development and Psychopathology*, 18, 173–194.

Roth, A. et al., 1996, *What Works For Whom*, London: Guilford.

Rusby, J.S.M. et al., 2008, 'Childhood temporary separation', *Attachment & Human Development*, 10, 207–21.

Rusby, J.S.M. et al., 2009, 'Long-term effects of the British evacuation of children during World War 2 on their adult mental health', *Aging and Mental Health*, 13, 391–404.

Sagi, A. et al., 2002, 'Shedding further light on the effects of various types and quality of early child care on infant-mother attachment relationship', *Child Development*, 73, 1166–86.

Sammons, P. et al., 2003, 'Measuring the impact on children's social behavioural development over the pre–school years', *The Effective Provision of Pre-school Education Project*, London: Institute of Education/DfES.

Sander, L.W., 2002, 'Thinking differently: principles of process in living systems and the specificity of being known', *Psychoanalytic Dialogues*, 12(1), 11–42.

Sapolsky, R. M., 2004, *Why zebras don't get ulcers* (3rd ed.), New York: Henry Holt.

Scher, A. et al., 2000, 'Night waking among one year olds: a study of maternal separation anxiety', *Child: Care, Health and Development*, 26, 323–34.

Scher, A. et al. 2001, 'Facilitators and regulators: maternal orientation as an antecedent of attachment security', *J of Reproductive and Infant Psychology*, 19, 325–33.

Schlessinger, L., 2000, *Parenthood by Proxy: Don't have them if you won't raise them*, New York: Harper Collins.

Schore, A.N., 2001, 'Effects of a secure attachment relationship on right brain development, affect regulation, and infant mental health', *Infant Mental Health Journal*, 22, 7–66.

Schwartz, S, 1991, 'Women and depression: a Durkheimian perspective', *Social Science and Medicine*, 32, 127–40.

Sharp, H.M. 1995, 'Women's expectations of childbirth and early motherhood: their relation to preferred mothering orientation, subsequent experiences, satisfaction and postpartum depression', Doctoral thesis, University of Leicester.

Sharp, H.M. et al., 2004, 'An empirical evaluation of a psychoanalytic theory of mothering orientation: implications for the antenatal prediction of depression', *J of Reproductive and Infant Psychology*, 22, 71–89.

Shedler, J., 2010, 'The efficacy of psychodynamic psychotherapy', *American Psychologist*, 65, 98-109.

Sims, M. et al., 2005 'Children's cortisol levels and quality of child care provision', *Child: Care, Health and Development*, 32, 453–66.

Sinclair, A., 2009, *0–5: How Small Children Make a Big Difference*, Provocation Series, 3, No. 1, London: The Work Foundation.

Smith, RH et al., 2007, 'Comprehending envy', *Psychological Bulletin*, 133, 46–64.

Sonaga-Burke, E., 2010, 'Editorial: It's the Environment, Stupid', *J of Child Psychology and Psychiatry*, 51, 113–5.

Sorensen, G. et al., 1987, 'Relationships among Type A behavior, employment experiences and gender', *J of Behavioral Medicine*, 10, 323–36.

St. James-Roberts, I. et al., 2006, 'Infant crying London, Copenhagen and when parents adopt a "proximal" form of caring', *Pediatrics*, 117(6), e1146-55.

Suomi, S.J., 1997, 'Early determinants of behaviour: evidence from primate studies', *British Medical Bulletin*, 53, 170–84.

Sylva, K. et al., 2007, 'Family and child factors related the use of non-maternal infant care', *Early Childhood Research Quarterly*, 22, 118–36.

Tallis, F., 2005, *Love Sick*, London: Century.

Tarullo, A.R. et al., 2006, 'Child maltreatment and the developing HPA axis', *Hormones and Behavior*, 50, 632–9.

Teicher, M.H., 2002, 'The neurobiology of child abuse', *Scientific American*, March, 54–61.

Thorpe, K. et al., 1991, 'Comparison of prevalence of depression in mothers of twins and mothers of singletons', *British Medical J*. 302, 875–8.

Tout, K. et al., 1998, 'Social behaviour correlates of cortisol activity in child care', *Child Development*, 69, 1247–62.

Tully, L.A. et al., 2004, 'Does maternal warmth moderate the effects of birth weight on twins' attention-deficit/hyperactivity disorder (ADHD) symptoms and low IQ?', *J of Consulting and Clinical Psychology*, 72, 218–226.

Turecki, S., 1995, 'Temperamentally difficult children', in Parker, S. et al., *Behavioural and Developmental Paediatrics*, Boston; Little Brown.

Twenge, J., 2007, *Generation Me: Why Today's Young Americans Are More Confident, Assertive, Entitled – And More Miserable Than Ever Before*, London: Free Press.

UNICEF, 2008, The Child Care Transition, *Innocenti Report Card 8*, UNICEF, Innocenti Research Centre, Florence.

Van Aken, C. et al., 2007, 'The interactive effects of temperament and maternal parenting on toddlers' externalizing behaviours', *Infant and Child Development*, 16, 553–72.

Van den Boom, D., 1994, 'The influence of temperament and mother on attachment and exploration', *Child Development*, 65, 1457–77.

Vaughan, B.E. et al., 1999, 'Attachment and temperament', in Cassidy, J. et al., *Handbook of Attachment*, New York: Guilford.

Vermeer, H.J. et al., 2006, 'Children's elevated cortisol levels at daycare: a review and meta-analysis', *Early Childhood Research Quarterly*, 21, 390–401.

Vroege, J.A. et al., 1994, 'Type A behaviour and social support among employed women', *Behavioral Medicine*, 19, 169–73.

Wang, J.L., 2006, 'Perceived work stress, imbalance between work and family/personal lives, and mental disorders', *Social Psychiatry and Psychiatric Epidemiology*, 41, 541–8.

Watamura, S.E. et al., 2003, 'Morning to afternoon increases in cortisol concentrations for infants and toddlers at childcare', *Child Development*, 74, 1006–20.

Watamura, S.E. et al., 2009, 'Cortisol patterns at home and childcare', *J of Applied Developmental Psychology*, 30, 475–85.

Waters, E. et al., 2003, 'Attachment security and early adulthood: a twenty year longitudinal study', *Child Development*, 71, 684–9.

Weich, M.G. et al., 2006, 'Outcomes of prolonged parent-child embrace therapy among 102 children with behavioural disorders', *Complementary Therapies in Clinical Practice*, 12, 3–12.

Weinfield, N.S. et al., 2000, 'Attachment from infancy to early adulthood in a high–risk sample', *Child Development*, 71, 695–702.

Weiss, S.J. et al., 2004, 'The temperament of pre-term, low birth weight infants and its potential biological substrates', *Research In Nursing and Health*, 27, 392–402.

Weniger, G. et al., 2008, 'Amygdala and hippocampal volumes and cognition in adult survivors of childhood abuse with dissociative disorders', *Acta Psychiatrica Scandinavica*, 118, 181–90.

Westen, D. et al., 2004, 'The empirical status of empirically supported psychotherapies', *Psychological Bulletin*, 130, 631–63.

Winnicott, D.W., 1972, *Playing and Reality*, London: Penguin.

Wismer Fries, A.B., et al., 2008, 'Neuroendocrine dysregulation following early social deprivation in children', *Developmental Psychobiology*, 50, 588–99.

Wolf, P.H. et al., 1999, 'The orphans of Eritrea', *J of Child Psychology and Psychiatry*, 40, 1231–7.

Zhang, X. et al., 2008, 'Effects of prolonged and exclusive breastfeeding on child behavior and maternal adjustment: evidence from a large, randomised trial', *Pediatrics*, 121, e435–e440.

Zhang, Y et al., 2007, 'Perfectionism, academic burnout and engagement among Chinese college students', *Personality and Individual Differences*, 1529–40.

Acknowledgements

First and foremost, heartfelt thanks to all the mothers who let me interview them. Since their execution of the role of mother receives less status and recognition in our society than that of a street sweeper, they must be the first to be acknowledged. As I try to explain in the conclusion, I am dazzled by their devotion and endurance in the face of enormous difficulties. I can only dimly realise how tired and overstretched they often feel, and therefore, how kind it was of them to make time for me to speak about their very intimate relationships with their babies and toddlers.

Clare, my wife, very much ends up holding our babies during the considerable disruption that writing books causes. But in this case, she has played a decisive role in the end product, helpfully suggesting some major cuts and also proposing a crucial reorganisation of the ordering of the Parts of the book. In addition, I have learnt a great deal from watching her caring for our children. So I am more than usually indebted. Thank you Clare, for making such a big difference to the content of the book, both by your mothering and your editorial skills.

I am hugely in debt to Joan Raphael-Leff. Her theories and evidence, set out in her book *Psychological Processes of Childbearing*, have hugely influenced me. I am most grateful to her for taking the time to speak to me in detail, explaining the ideas and studies more fully. It is my earnest hope that her work reaches a wider audience as a result of this book.

Special thanks to my Cognitive Hypnotherapist friend Lucy Astor (see www.lucyastor.com). Her words of wisdom regarding Huggers and the needs of under-threes are quoted extensively (sometimes for sentences on end), unacknowledged. I am extremely grateful for the inspiration they provided at a critical moment in the writing of the text.

Thanks, too, to my sisters Jessica, Mary and Lucy, all of whose mothering has been a lesson to me over the years, and for their useful comments on the manuscript.

Particular gratitude to Francesca Quercy. Her aid was invaluable.

Thanks to Jemima Biddulph, always a rock-solid, reliable editor and sounding post. If I am heading in the wrong direction, be that content or tone, she can be trusted to let me know the truth.

Thanks also to Catherine Hakim for having stuck at her researches so doggedly, on which I have been drawing now for 13 years.

Thanks to Jill Kirby and Cristina Odone at the Centre for Policy Studies for barking up the right tree in this area, too.

For their useful commentaries on the text, thanks to Emma Festing and Judy Cummins, neither of whom have much time to be reading. The development of their babies and children are far more important than manuscripts about such matters.

Thanks to Clare Alexander and Gillon Aitken, as ever, at my literary agent, Aitken Alexander Associates.

At Vermilion, special thanks to my editor Julia Kellaway for her patient forbearance in the latter stages of the project. Thanks also to Jenny Rowley for her support, as well as to Cindy Chan. Thanks to Caroline Newbury and Sarah Bennie, who have the usual thankless task of publicising my work. Thanks, too, to the woman who is the boss of all of these women at Vermilion – Fiona MacIntyre – without whose backing there would be no book.

Thanks to Faber and Faber and to the Larkin Estate for permission to reproduce 'This Be The Verse'. Thanks also to Ian Hislop, *Private Eye* and Pressdram for permission to reproduce the Polly Filla extract.

Many thanks to James and Margaret Sainsbury for putting up with the proof stage and to James for his helpful suggestions regarding *This Be Another Verse*.

Thanks to Adrian Mitchell and Penny Garner for their inspiration for *This be Another Verse*.

Index

About the author

Oliver James trained and practised as a clinical child psychologist and, since 1988, has worked as a writer, journalist, broadcaster and television documentary producer and presenter. He lives in Oxfordshire with his wife and two small children. His books include the bestselling *They F*** You Up*, *Affluenza* and *Contented Dementia*.

Also available from Vermilion by Oliver James:

Affluenza

An epidemic of 'affluenza' is sweeping through the English-speaking world; an obsessive, envious, keeping-up-with-the-Joneses, that makes us twice as prone to depression, anxiety and addictions than people in developed nations. And now we are infecting the rest of the world with this virulent virus.

In this eloquent account, James reveals how issues like consumerism, property fever and the battle of the sexes vary across societies with different values, beliefs and traditions. And leads us to an unavoidable and potentially life-changing conclusion: that to ensure our mental health we can and must pursue our needs rather than our wants.

£8.99
ISBN 9780091900113

Order this title direct from www.rbooks.co.uk/oliverjames

Also available from Vermilion by Oliver James:

Britain on the Couch

In the bestselling *Affluenza*, Oliver James toured the globe for an answer to the question: Is it possible to be successful and stay sane? In *Britain on the Couch* James brings the focus back to Britain.

Between the 1950s and the end of the 1970s depression mushroomed, especially among the poor and young women. Yet this was a time when all of us got richer. In the case of both women and the poor, they had unprecedented access to education, new freedoms and wealth. In his seminal work, James shows that what depressed them and the rest of us was a rampant keeping-up-with-the-Joneses and a Gender Rancour between the sexes that may be the worst the world has ever seen.

£8.99
ISBN 9780091929848

Order this title direct from www.rbooks.co.uk/oliverjames